D0641015

The Authentic Teacher

SENSITIVITY AND AWARENESS IN THE CLASSROOM

Clark Moustakas

THE MERRILL-PALMER INSTITUTE
DETROIT, MICHIGAN

HOWARD A. DOYLE PUBLISHING COMPANY
Cambridge, Massachusetts 02139

THE AUTHENTIC TEACHER

Copyright © 1966 by Clark Moustakas. Printed in the United States of America. All rights reserved. This book, or parts thereof, may not be reproduced in any form without permission of the publishers.

Library of Congress Catalog Card Number 66-27546

Second Printing, 1967

HOWARD A. DOYLE PRINTING COMPANY
CAMBRIDGE, MASSACHUSETTS 02139

371.3
M93t
1966

86641

For
MELVYN J. BAER
AND
MELVIN SUHD

Teachers who generate excitement
and new life in the classroom

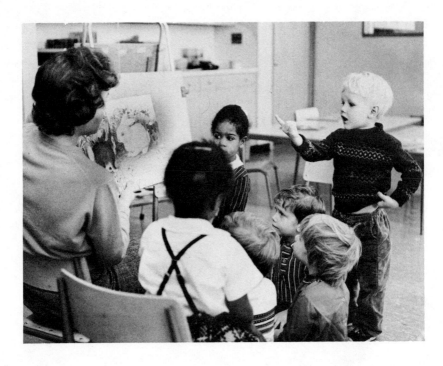

Photo by Merrill-Palmer

Preface

This book is a thoroughly revised edition of *The Teacher and the Child,* originally published in 1956. The impetus for reintroducing and revitalizing the book has come from many sources: teachers who found it a useful guide in facilitating emotional expression in the classroom and releasing damaging tensions and repressed feelings in children's experiences; parents who felt their children were becoming remote and distant or antagonistic and who were looking for ways to establish more meaningful relationships; educators who were conducting institutes, workshops and seminars aimed at fostering teacher sensitivity and awareness to the personal factors in learning and teaching; and counselors in elementary and secondary schools who were interested in developing mental health principles and practices in their work with children, teachers, and administrators.

In the ten years since the publication of *The Teacher and the Child,* in my experiences with teachers and children from kindergarten through high school, illustrations of significant interpersonal relations in the classroom have multiplied many times. However, since the original illustrations still offer sound examples of mental health in the school, for the most part they have been kept intact.

In the present volume, the illustrations are perceived differently, and the meaning of the personal relationship is viewed from a new set of principles, concepts, and values. *The Authentic Teacher* is an expanded search into the sources of health in the individual and in the home and school that contribute to the evolution of genuine selfhood and authentic relatedness. Freedom, choice and the capacity to choose, and responsibility are among the new concepts explored. Three ways are presented in which the teacher contributes to healthy development of the self: first, through confirming the child as a being of non-comparable and non-measurable worth, in his individual ways and as a whole person; second, by being authentically present and open to honest encounters with children and by being a resource for learning and enrichment; and third, by making other resources available—colors, shapes, forms, audio-visual materials, and reference books, which can be encountered, explored, and tested in exercising capacities, in expanding awarenesses, and in developing skills. Authentic resources are based on the child's own interests, wishes, directions and patterns of expression, enabling the actualization of unique potentials and the expansion of reality by furthering interest, meaning, and relatedness.

The sources of sickness in the home and school are also considered. The nature of betrayal, its widespread impact on teacher and child in destroying universal values and self-values; ways in which parents and teachers contribute to the process; and the relationship of betrayal to distortion, duplicity, dehumanization, and alienation are examined and discussed.

The Authentic Teacher attempts to provide a basis for more genuine commitment to the interpersonal process; it suggests ways in which the teacher can bring his own unique self to the classroom, facilitate actualization of potentialities in himself and in children, and evolve the kind of relationship with children that leads to significant learning; it suggests ways in which creative capacities and hidden potentials may be released through sensitive and open interaction between teacher and child.

This book is not meant as a prescription for the ideal relationship but rather is an opportunity for the individual teacher to experience something in his own right through the personal interactions of other teachers and of children. It presents a point of view regarding the individual experience of reality and principles of individual psychology with special reference to education and learning. It attempts to show in detail how the perceptions of teachers are expanded and enriched as they explore in the classroom the essence of their relationships with individual children and with groups.

The basic premise throughout is that every teacher wants to meet the child on a significant level; every teacher wants to feel that what he does in his contacts with children makes an important difference, brings about significant events and experiences. Emphasis is upon understanding the child in his own terms, values, and meanings rather than in terms of external procedures of diagnosis and evaluation. When authenticity and love are combined with freedom to make choices, and be responsible for them, real life emerges and the teacher relates with children, whether in conflict or harmony, on a meaningful, human basis.

ACKNOWLEDGMENTS*

I wish to thank all the teachers, counselors, and principals enrolled in my Seminar In Human Relations, from 1949 to the present date; each of these persons has contributed to my own growth in perception and understanding of interpersonal relations in the classroom. More specifically, I would like to mention the following teachers whose careful, detailed notes and records helped me to re-create to some extent the personal interactions between teacher and child.

From the Birmingham Public Schools, Birmingham, Michigan: Grant W. Barber, Mabel Dickey, Dorothy L. Haven, Edwin K. Crandell, Carolyn Lochran, Johanna E. Leonard, Margaret McArdle, Harriet Merritt, Carolyn Pacheco, Jacqueline Schouten, Susan Sutfin, Marjorie Tate, Minnie Wilkinson, Jo Anne Wellman, Joan F. Winston, and Carolyn Wright.

From the Berkley Public Schools, Berkley, Michigan: Ethel Bauer, Vivien Hapke, Mary M. Josie, Anita Peterson, and Betty Van Wagnen.

From the Highland Park Public Schools, Highland Park, Michigan: Pansy Eliot, Marion Greene, Madeline Henzie, Lillian Kuttnauer, Nell Rossow, and Nancy Strohm.

From the Ferndale Public Schools, Ferndale, Michigan: Robert Blume and Minnie Berson; also Mr. Leo Dolenga, a parent, who took some of the photographs.

I want to thank the following administrators who in various

* Titles and locations are no longer accurate for many of the individuals listed in the acknowledgments.

ways facilitated the development of the study: Paul Carter, Assistant Superintendent, Birmingham Public Schools; Mary M. Josie, Director of Home and Family Living, Berkley Public Schools; Al Perrilli, Curriculum Consultant, and Roy Robinson, Superintendent, Ferndale Public Schools; Marjorie Cosgrove, Director of Family Living, and George Halloch, Director of Pupil Personnel, Highland Park Public Schools; Eugene Alexander, School Psychologist, Mildred Field, Principal, and Russell Isbister, Superintendent, Plymouth Public Schools; Maude Price, Assistant Superintendent, Royal Oak Public Schools; and Walter Gibson, Principal, and Everett Winslow, Superintendent, Lincoln Park Public Schools.

Several other people have helped to expand my awareness of the value of personal being in human interaction. In this respect I am especially grateful to Dorothy Lee and David Smillie. I wish also to thank Pauline Park Wilson Knapp, President of The Merrill-Palmer Institute, without whose encouragement and sponsorship my work with teachers and counselors would not have been possible. I thank Donna Harris, who photographed most of the teachers and children and then rushed processing and delivery; Mavis Wolfe, for her patience and welcoming spirit at each deadline; and Mel Suhd, who insisted that the book be redone and infused fresh life into it. I express my special appreciation to my wife Betty for her encouragement and support throughout and especially in the final moments.

Detroit, Michigan
June, 1966

CLARK MOUSTAKAS

Contents

ix

Contents

CHAPTER 1

Authenticity or Betrayal?

One of the most devastating evils in modern living is betrayal; devastating because it spreads quickly and quietly and has become so commonplace it is considered normal; devastating because it turns men into machines—a transformation which seems natural enough in a technological society; devastating because in one sharp turnabout friendship and love become exploitation and hypocrisy and professionalism becomes another name for manipulation and control; devastating because what appears to be an enduring trust between persons is suddenly broken; devastating because it breeds new evils—suspicion, fear, dehumanization, fragmentation, and ultimately alienation of men from themselves and from each other. The whole process is often without any awareness that the mask, the role and the status symbol are killing the real sources of life in the self and in the community.

Betrayal is an everyday occurrence in the home and in the school, unrecognized and hidden, often unseen in its destructive forms, but nevertheless when effectively executed it initiates a dehumanizing process which results in the moral and psychic decay of human relationships. In some instances the meaning of betrayal is so twisted that we are more afraid of the truth than the lie, and more shocked by sensitivity and kindness than by violence and brutality.

In this chapter, I shall outline some of the forms of betrayal which destroy the individual in his search for himself and his efforts to live authentically in the world. I shall point out how

1

betrayal flourishes in the modern classroom and discuss the anti-
dote to its destructive powers in the form of sources of health in
the individual, and authentic teachers who live by truth and
value and love and not by the textbook and by the clock.

Betrayal of Universal Values

Universal values are the values which collectively represent
health and life, the values which have remained essential
throughout human history, giving the individual and human
life as a whole a meaning. Ultimately universal values represent the good. In terms of human relationships, some values
which differentiate meaning and depth from superficiality and
trivia are freedom, love, beauty, justice, and truth. If there is
love and honesty in the individual and in his relationships, then
the person is genuinely present and present in such a way that
his freedom is used responsibly; growth of his self is rooted
in genuine existence, in justice and in truth.

Every act of failure to stay with universal values is a form
of betrayal. Some common violations are: failure to keep alive
the good in the face of evil, not speaking out when justice is
being violated, invading the privacy of individuals and breaking confidence and trust, knowing the truth but permitting the
lie to spread, listening to gossip, backbiting and slander and
participating in the destruction of a man's dignity, seeing brutality and violence and not responding humanly, making no
effort to prevent further destruction, and failing to bring meaning and love to bear in the presence of feelings of hatred, rejection and inferiority. Jules Henry in his study of attitude
organization in elementary schools, summarizes some violations of human values. Here is his description of the *witch-hunt
syndrome* (8) which he believes is present in both organized
and unorganized states in many classrooms.

In this witch's brew *destructive criticism* of others is the toad's
horns; *docility* the body of the worm; *feelings of vulnerability* the

chicken heart; *fear of internal (intragroup) hostility* the snake's fang; *confession of evil deeds* the locust's leg; and *boredom and emptiness* the dead man's eye.

Recently, I visited a second-grade classroom during a reading lesson. When the children saw the principal and me enter the room, they were eager to read to us. The teacher asked for volunteers. A child, with a smiling face and shining eyes, sitting next to me, is called to read. She sighs with joy as she begins, "Casey Joins the Circus." Apparently, she has learned that a good reader varies her tone of voice, reads loud enough for others to hear and reads fluently. Wanting to make an impression, wanting to get the praise of her teacher and classmates, she hurries through the paragraph assigned to her. But something is wrong. Mrs. Bell interrupts the child. She pushes the book away from the child's face and says in a slow deliberate voice, hovering over the child, "You are reading carelessly. That's not showing respect for what is printed on the page. It's not showing respect for our visitors or the other boys and girls. You are making sense but you simply are not reading the words in the book. I've told you about this before, Betsy. Now you go back and read what's printed there so we can all follow you." The child returns to the beginning of the paragraph but something has happened. She has no direct, open way of responding. The staring, judging faces of the other children frighten her. She reads in a reluctant manner, pronounces words haltingly. There is a weak, muffled quality in her voice. She has been hurt. She is no longer certain. She completes the reading and slumps wearily into her chair.

The real tragedy is not in the critical words of the teacher or in the subdued, minimized child, but in the fact that no relationship exists. There is the teacher as law-giver and statement-maker, as the one in authority. There is the adult voice, belittling, shaming, minimizing, humiliating the child into exact reading. The teacher uses the visitors, the other children, herself, to prove her point and impress the child. She does not keep the issue between herself and the child, where it belongs. And it is all done matter-of-factly, as professional duty. It is all so impersonal and feelingless.

No individual is perfect. We all make mistakes. But to commit a wrong, to lower the dignity of a child and not be aware that that dignity has been impaired, is much more serious than the child's skipping of words during oral reading. The real tragedy is the teacher's lack of sensitivity and awareness, her failure to recognize the child as a person.

When the adult loses sight of the child as a human being, when the adult fails to gather in the child's presence as a person, there is no reality between them, there is no relationship. There is no mutuality.

And this is what happens in many situations where potential growth and love exist between persons. The persons are lost. The discrepancy or issue becomes all that matters. And the loudest voice, the strongest figure, the person in authority carries out his office of command. Gradually the child is forced into a process of desensitization where feelings and senses are muffled and subdued until eventually he is no longer aware that he is not experiencing from within. When people reject, humiliate, hurt, belittle, control, dominate, and brutalize others, without any awareness of what they are doing, when there is no concern on the part of others for what is being done to them, there is extreme danger that man will cease to be man, that whatever is distinctly human will be impaired or so significantly reduced that the life of man will be as automatic as a self-moving machine and as mechanical as counting beads on an abacus.

Betrayal of Self-Values

The self-values are the values and resources which exist within the regions of the self. They are the interests, meanings, and desires that get their initial impetus from the uniqueness of the individual, from the movements of his body, from his growing awareness of life, from his wish to explore life on his own terms, from his knowing of what is personally satisfying and meaningful and what is not. Self-values are in jeopardy in any climate where freedom and choice are denied, in any

situation where the individual rejects his own senses and substitutes for his own perceptions the standards and expectations
of others. Self-betrayal means that the person does not use his
own faculties in determining which experiences contribute to
self-realization and which are irrelevant or impeding; the person
no longer uses his own powers and organs to create reality
and venture into new life. He forces himself to fit into another
person's plans and to do work that has no meaning or value.
Thus he does not trust his own immediate experience and he
is neither open to himself nor to the world. Betrayal of self-
values occurs initially through rejection; the rejection may be
direct and hostile or it may be devious and duplicitous. The
rejection of the individual often begins when ambitious parents
(and later teachers) set up goals and communicate expectations, either directly or deceptively, so that what they really
want and expect from the child registers at subliminal levels
regardless of what they say. Sometimes adults program the
child's life with incentives and rewards so that he progresses
step-by-step toward their definitions, toward their goals, toward
their expected achievements. In the process the unique child
as a growing person is cancelled out and what remains is a
definition, a role, a mechanical man, that takes its direction
from external judgments and cues. In other words, the self of
the child is eliminated from daily existence. A young woman in
examining her own experience describes the process (9):

How is it possible to lose a self? The treachery, unknown and un-
thinkable, begins with our secret psychic death in childhood—if and
when we are not loved and are cut off from our spontaneous wishes.
(Think: What is left?) But wait—it is not just this simple murder of a
psyche. That might be written off, the tiny victim might even "out-
grow" it—but it is a perfect double crime in which he himself also
gradually and unwittingly takes part. He has not been accepted for
himself, as he is.

Or, they "love" him, but they want him or force him or expect him
to be different! Therefore he must be unacceptable. He himself learns
to believe it and at last even takes it for granted. He has truly given
himself up. No matter now whether he obeys them, whether he clings,
rebels or withdraws—his behavior, his performance is all that matters.
His center of gravity is in "them," not in himself—yet if he so much as

noticed it he'd think it natural enough. And the whole thing is entirely plausible; all invisible, automatic, and anonymous!

When betrayal of self-values occurs through duplicity, the individual is caught up in a double-bind. The message communicated by parents and teachers is two-fold and contradictory. Outwardly these adults say they respect the child's own perceptions, interests and preferences but at the same time another message is conveyed; namely, that they prefer and expect the child to conform to their own wishes and standards. Outwardly the words sound affirmative and accepting but inwardly there is a range of bodily tensions and meanings which also registers in the child's world. Duplicity enters the situation and is a form of betrayal when parents and teachers do not say what they mean—that is they say one thing but mean another—or when words and feelings are in opposition in the same person or when any double, contradictory series of messages are being communicated from adult to child.

The ultimate consequence of betrayal of self-values is alienation and inauthenticity. The young person searching for identity and self-affirmation, lacking recognition, and threatened by the withdrawal of love, launches himself into an alien life. He substitutes the spontaneous, genuine self for a controlled, calculating self-system dominated by the rules and "shoulds" of the adult world. The original self-awareness becomes self-deception and the individual no longer realizes he has abnegated his real self in favor of a substitute, that alienation has replaced authentic development of the self. Thus alienated individuals wear masks that bear no resemblance to the faces that wear them, carry out functions and roles that have no personal significance or meaning, and, in general, engage in daily pretenses that are far removed from authentic life.

Alienation which often begins in the home is reinforced and extended in the school where the focus is on group standards and norms, grades, adjustment, and the rules of convention and propriety.

The student in the school becomes alienated in the same way that any worker can become alienated from his work. He develops an estranged attitude toward his school work; he is outside of it, he is bored and engages in school work under coercion and compulsion, either from the threat of punishment by the teacher or parent or from the restrictive demands and directives of his own "should" system. In the school he is labeled—gifted, average, retarded; and, he is classified—fast, average, slow. In many ways he is stereotyped and fixed and expected to play the role defined by professional nomenclature, abstract goals, and unseen faces. He is expected to become a replica of the stereotype and give up his own fresh, spontaneous contact and response to life. He is prodded; he is motivated; he is directed; he is rewarded and he is punished. He is assigned lessons from a teacher's manual which dictates what he should read, how much, and in what manner. And, he moves from one subject to another by virtue of invisible authorities whom he does not know, would not recognize, and does not ever meet. His education is detached, impersonal, fragmentary, and guided by anonymous hands. No wonder school is a burden and work is a chore. No wonder, more and more, he becomes numb and deadened in the process of moving from grade to grade. No wonder there is no excitement or joy in learning and no involvement. He is denied as a self; *he* does not exist except as the generalized other; his creative energy is restrained, stifled, and almost totally ignored.

Life comes from life and the teacher is the living agent in the school. The teacher must not abdicate the human dimensions which he can communicate to the child—respect for his individuality, recognition of his particular interests, needs, and directions, encouragement of honest expression of feelings and growth in self-identity. Within the context of personal human attributes, the teacher can engender real life and significant learning can occur.

Betrayal of Unity and Wholeness

Perhaps in modern society no aspect of human life is more frequently violated than that of the unity or wholeness of the self. The shattering of unity or wholeness is taken for granted in a compartmentalized world. No societal force contributes more to fragmentation than societal fixation on intelligence and intellectual values. The emphasis is so extreme that spontaneity, spirit, feeling, wonder, and other aesthetic and moral dimensions of the self are repressed or harnessed and controlled in order to accumulate more and more facts and more and more money. Knowledge and academic credentials often are used to enhance the individual's marketing of himself and to enable him to exploit, compete, and win economic, status and prestige rewards.

In the school the teacher hangs on to intellectual values in the form of scores, achievement, and facts that justify the curriculum and prove that the battle to defeat imagination, creative thought and activity, and spontaneous expression of feeling is worth it; in the end, the scores are higher, and the number of months of upgrading in the subject areas can be pointed to with pride. What happens in the process? The child is further alienated from himself. The activities he engages in have nothing to do with his own integrity and response to life. To succeed he must fragment himself and act as if only facts and knowledge are important to him. He must pretend (and sometimes he almost believes it) that knowledge is more important than his own unified impulse to find excitement, meaning, and vitality in life; he must act as if he would rather memorize facts and follow the dictates of a textbook than the strivings of his own heart and mind. In other words he must exaggerate and distort his own involvement and interest; he must compartmentalize his world into a series of unrelated, and usually irrelevant, subjects and topics which are better suited for specialized machines that produce parts of a whole object and operate on a schedule than human beings who can become so totally absorbed and so fully committed to an interest or activity that all surrounding life ceases to exist for a while. Genuine learning requires a sense of mutuality, an encounter with life involving one's entire being. The encounter in learning stems from a unity of one's self in experience followed by labor, exertion and hours of searching and struggling. The more burning the curiosity and meaning, the deeper the perplexity, the less apt is the child to seek for narrow explanations and discrete, isolated facts, or for isolated subjects to examine. When he is concerned with his own questions, or issues and problems, he explores whatever resources are available to him, as a whole person.

Intellectuality, convention, the system is out of focus today; it is overstressed and overused and in exaggerated forms stifles creativity and spontaneity. When intelligence is used to establish rigid systems and hierarchies, when it becomes a substitute for human concern and human involvement, when intellectual values are more important than self-values, they then become destructive, violating individual integrity and human decency. The system—any system which chooses intelligence over morality—is rooted in mechanics and laws which, basically, are no more than the values of authoritarian individuals who prefer death to life, submission to courage, routines and habits to inventiveness and ingenuity, and, on the whole, anything that passes for order, efficiency, and organization.

CONDITIONS FOR AUTHENTIC GROWTH
IN THE INDIVIDUAL

The sources of health in the individual, in addition to the potentialities, talents and resources which are present at birth, are his freedom of being, his capacity to make choices and determine which experiences are positive and which are negative for his own growth, and his sense of responsibility for being true to his own self.

Freedom To Be

The first condition for creative emergence and expansion of self is already present at birth.

Freedom to be is an original gift of life, the natural way for a newly formed being to make contact with the world. The infant meets reality and relates to his surroundings with whatever resources and possibilities exist at the moment. Through freedom of being new patterns of expression emerge and new directions evolve. From the start, there is a free flow of life out into the world, and a return. Day by day, the infant's world, originally made up of fleeting movements, awarenesses and perceptions, becomes more distinct and varied; he relates to it in different ways. Having gotten over the shock and stress of the birth experience, he begins to take active note of the world, begins to be more and more aware of his surroundings—his eyes span broader horizons; his ears pick up distant sounds; his body turns, touches, explores, experiments, savors and avoids. Human nature, as directly observed, is no matter of intellect or viscera alone but is life reaching out to explore the possibility of surfaces, lines, colors, and tones and, later on, the symphonies, mountains, and stars (16).

The young child trusts his own senses to confirm or deny, to lead to harmony and fit; he cries out in protest against the thwarting, alienating, unfitting dimensions of the environment. By his perceptual and sensual contacts and freedom of movement, he participates in life, choosing the fitting and rejecting that which is not in harmony, that which does not create a sense of well-being, continuity, and fulfillment. From the beginning, there is "Yes" and "No" in the individual's response to life. Rogers (18, p. 222) postulates the following as characteristics of the human infant: (1) His *experience* of reality is his reality; (2) He has a greater potential awareness of what reality is for him than does anyone else in his environment; (3) His relationship to reality is based on his basic actualizing tendency; (4) In the interaction between infant and world, the infant expresses himself as an organized whole; (5) He engages in an organismic valuing process, positively valuing experiences which are enhancing and negatively reacting to those which are not.

What begins as contact with the environment eventually becomes collaboration. The young child engages in mutual enrichment of self-environment. The environment is transformed by the presence of the individual just as the individual is creating and expanding with life. Dimensions of the environment call the child into action. The process is a kind of laboring together like that of the farmer who initiates a change in the soil through cultivating, caring, and introducing nutrients, which eventually not only enrich the soil but yield an abundant, healthy crop. Thus, the farmer serves the environment and is served by it.

It is this condition, freedom to be, which teachers must recognize as important in the school. Through valuing the child's freedom of being, making room for his own spontaneous self-expressions and desire to explore life on the basis of his own interests and desires, the teacher contributes to the enhancement of the child's individuality and makes possible authentic relatedness to him. To be at all, the child must experience a freedom to be; the teacher can create an atmosphere in which the experience of freedom is facilitated and encouraged.

Choice and the Capacity to Choose

The individual, being free to be, makes choices and decisions affected by willing, feeling, thinking, and intending. Through self-awareness, the person enters situations already pointed or set in certain directions. Later the experience of the individual in making choices is often based on conscious, self-determined thought and feeling. The making of choices, as a free being, which can be confirmed or denied in experience, is a preliminary step in the creation of values. Choices which confirm being and lead to enriching and expanding self-awareness, choices which deepen experience and lead to new experience, choices which challenge uniqueness and talent and lead to actualizations, enable the person to establish further his own identity. Ultimately those choices which confirm life and enable the individual to become what he can be are chosen as values. As long as the flow of real life is affirmed, then further life is facilitated. Increasingly, through a process which includes freedom, will, intention, desire, choice, confirmation and responsibility, the individual is growing and expanding in authentic ways; the individual is creating new awarenesses and values; the individual is coming to be what he can be in the light of opportunities and resources outside and potentialities and challenges inside.

In the classroom, freedom of being and freedom in choosing

make the difference between spontaneous, alert, genuine connections with the flow of life, and controlled, mechanical projections; between continual building and expanding of self, and the static still-born repetitions and fixations; the difference between new forms and directions constantly emerging, and routines and habits fixed by teachers' manuals and lesson plans; between variety and diversity of expression, and the rigid patterns of behavior that can be conditioned through skillful manipulation of environment and strategic use of reward and punishment.

Responsibility and Self-Confirmation

A third value inherent in life is self-confirmation, the early form of responsibility. Through trusting one's own organismic connection with life, through trusting one's own senses in confirming or denying, the individual is owning himself and taking charge of his life. In actualizing himself as a free being, the individual is fulfilling a basic or primary responsibility, to be who he is at any moment, to place himself authentically in the universe, and in this connection to accept the happenings and consequences. Therefore, teachers and parents should respect the child's own verdict on his experience and allow his judgment to stand until his own senses tell him otherwise. Wrong choices are made along the way of life which hold the person stationary for awhile but as he lives with error, as a free agent, the individual learns from it and moves on. Difficulties are experienced in the process of self-emergence but they will not stunt growth as long as the individual can live with them and learn from them and continue on to new forms of development and creation. Only when error is magnified and exaggerated can it have paralyzing effects which stifle potential discovery.

Thus in the early development of the self, self-confirmation precedes the confirmation of others. Affirming the value of one's own experience comes first in the process; recognition and valuing of others come later. However, to continue to appreciate and respect one's self, the individual, to some extent, is dependent upon the response of others.

Conditions for Authentic Growth
In the Environment

Variety and diversity in the environment provide the best opportunity for stimulation and challenge of interest and desire and offer the basis for inviting the individual to joint activity in self-realizing values. The free exploration and experimentation with resources which confront and engage the individual in commitment and activity enable the whole person to emerge, vivacious, alive, authentic, with new attitudes, awarenesses, skills, knowledge. Then genuine meaning exists between the person and the world, meaning emerges which forms a bridge between self and other, between subject and object, between the known and the knower; then there is mutuality; there is genuine connection with life.

The home and the school may contribute to the development of creative individuality and genuine relatedness in three essential ways. First, parents and teachers may confirm the child as a unique being, thus encouraging further development of the self. Second, when adults are authentically present, they become sources of life and can stimulate and challenge children and enable them to further establish and clarify self-identity and deepen and extend relations with others. Third, parents and teachers may provide opportunities and resources which children need to actualize their potentialities and gain new perceptions and insights of man, nature, and the universe.

The Confirmation of Others

From the beginning the individual is *of* the world, as well as *in* the world. The confirmation of others has a significant impact on the growing person. Affirmation of the individual strengthens him and enables him to continue to realize himself as a unique being related to life. The individual gains a sense of well-being, a feeling of delight and wonder in the universe, and the joy of being one's self. By cherishing and holding the child in absolute esteem, the teacher is establishing an environmental climate that facilitates growth and becoming. Confirming the child means trusting in the process of his own creative development, valuing his presence as an enriching factor in life, and accepting his own pacing and timing. Basically it means an assertion of "Yes" to the child's own ways of being in the world. Thus confirmation includes trust in a process of growth; love of this unique, unfolding life; and affirmation of the particularity of the child and his own patterns of expression. To be able to confirm the being of another, one must of course be present as a being, alert, open, receptive and real. Confirmation of others enables two processes to continue to exist: the individual is recognized and encouraged in his developing autonomy and relatedness, and the individual continues to live in a real, enthusiastic, and zestful way. Growth of the self and vitality in living are both enhanced.

Authentic Presence of Adults

The second way in which other persons serve the growing individual is through genuine presence, by being sources of life itself. In relation, in genuine encounters with others, the individual grows in awareness and widens his world of sensitivity and perception. To the extent that the teacher is a resource for the growing child, the child is enabled to develop new feelings, learn new patterns, discover different ways of considering and relating to life, and emerge with new awarenesses which lead to differentiation and actualization. In genuine encounter, the center of one person resonates with the center of another and new perspectives and meanings are formed. Then there is mutuality, a sense of joint participation in life. It is very much like the joint creation of a poem, or painting or symphony. Each person affects the other in the creation. If the collaboration between the adult and the child is a true and healthy one, individuality is enhanced and patterns of mutuality emerge which have value. Obviously this does not occur through manipulation. No genuine form arises out of manipulation. The significant adult must exist for the growing individual as someone there, to be met, related to and affected by, as a real person whose very presence helps to evolve awareness and beauty, stimulates and challenges potentialities, and provides an opportunity for expansion of self in the aesthetic and spiritual realm, as well as in intellectual pursuits. The adult can be present as an alive, genuine person. To the extent that this presence fits it will have a bearing on the emerging feelings and values of the child. Thus the individual, in a healthy climate of growth and development, will learn from others, beyond the social amenities and routines, certain values of the self—sensitivity, gentleness, kindness, respect and ways of genuine participation and joint effort.

The significance of authentic presence, involving a six year old boy and his father, is beautifully illustrated in Agee's *A Death In The Family* (1). A meeting is portrayed in which a relatively restricted and restrained relationship between father and son suddenly opens and expands to new depths and awarenesses, moments of mutuality and encounter in which new vistas of meaning and value evolve, moments of silence and solitude where self and other merge and each person grows in self-perception and understanding. Each person recognizes the power and impact of love when there is freedom of being, exploratory ranging of the senses, and bonds of interdependency, mutuality and respect. Rufus and his father share an evening walk, quietly, slowly, anticipating the event, savoring it and finding a strange tranquility in it; they sit on a rock, each experiencing a kind of contentment unlike any other he has known. Rufus does not experience the inner quietude in words or ideas; it is simply something he feels and knows; and he knows that his father feels it too, and that in this mutuality of experience there is contentment. During their quiet moments together on the rock, Rufus becomes aware that a part of his sense of complete contentment lays in the feeling that he and his father are reconciled; in other places they are divided; and a feeling of estrangement settles between them; but on the rock there is a sense of unity, firm and assured. Rufus in this quiet place suddenly understands his father; he realizes that although his father loves their home and all of them he is more lonely than this family love can help; the love of his family increases his loneliness and makes it hard for him not to be lonely; but on the rock he feels completely himself and is on good terms with his loneliness. An important part of this feeling of love and communion between Rufus and his father comes from their being together away from home, sharing together moments of solitude and meditation, very quietly, in the dark, listening to the leaves and looking at the stars. Rufus knows that each of them knows of the other's well-being, that each depends on the other, that each means more to the other than anyone or anything else in the world; and that the best of this well-being lays in this mutual knowledge, which is *neither concealed nor revealed*. Rufus knows these perceptions and sensations very distinctly but not in words, or even ideas or clearly formed emotions.

Providing Opportunities and Resources

The third way in which adults can constructively participate in the development and evolution of the self of the child is by providing opportunities and resources which are relevant to the child's own tendencies, preferences, or patterns of expression. By taking cues from the child, by being sensitive to the child's own enthusiasm and direction, the adult can make available resources—colors, shapes, forms, materials, which can be tested, explored, and used in expanding perception, in exercising capacities, and in developing skills. The environment can be enriched by providing raw materials that can be chosen or not, fashioned or discarded, as they fit the inner life of the young organism in its searchings and stretchings to encounter new life. Sometimes, all that is required to activate a potential source of growth is to point to it. This is a way for the young individual to see what has not been seen before, to have an aspect of the world come to light within his own perceptions and then to confirm or deny its relevance as the situation demands. If he chooses it then it becomes part of reality for him; it challenges further expression and self-actualization.

In terms of genuine evolution of selfhood, there is a basic difference between the arranging of conditions and resources in the environment in order to direct and change and arranging conditions because they have meaning in themselves, to the person who creates the situation. There is a difference between setting up objectives and goals aimed at altering the behavior of others in the direction of specific outcomes, and making available materials and resources based on the preferences, interests, and wishes of the person, without any intention of manipulating or changing. When conditions are arranged as a means of changing the individual, the intention is definitely to modify the behavior of the other but when the arrangement itself has value, it is simply the way in which one self is authentically expressed in the presence of another self. In the one case, the adult has the desire to change others, and he plans and organizes his world with this in mind; in the other case the arrangement is merely an invitation, an opportunity for encounter—but it may be chosen or not. The adult who arranges a situation as an invitation, accepts as reality that it may not actually serve the other person, it may not be a way to self-realization for the other person, and he respects and appreciates the person's own choices.

Concluding Comments

Being open to the inherent life in the classroom means first of all being open to one's own inner life as a person; it means centering oneself in evolving perceptions and potentialities which come to fulfillment in living itself; it means being aware of human values as well as intellectual and social values; it means being open to the unfolding process in learning and to values and meanings which include but transcend facts or techniques; it means letting each person be himself, encouraging and valuing individuality and letting it shine forth. It means recognizing the child as a valuable being in his own autonomy and independence and understanding the child through listening, communion and genuine presence. It means being open to all experiences and participating in each experience as a new venture. It means respecting and affirming the validity of the child's perceptions and accepting as fact the reality of those perceptions for the child.

The authentic teacher recognizes the uniqueness of the learner and confirms him as an individual self; makes the classroom a place for open, genuine human relations; presents material which is vital to his own growing self and in the process initiates new experience, awareness and sensitivity, for himself and for the child; encounters the child in meaningful activity whether in conflict or harmony; and perceives the classroom as a human relations laboratory where authentic life emerges through respect for differences, cherishing of the child as a person, and permitting opportunities for honest expression of feelings and expansion of the self through meaningful, self-chosen interests and activities.

REFERENCES

1. Agee, James. *A Death in the Family*. New York: Avon Books, 1959.
2. Andrews, Michael F. *Creativity and Psychological Health*. Syracuse University Press, 1961.
3. Bateson, Gregory; Jackson, Don D.; Haley, J.; and Weakland, John. Toward A Theory of Schizophrenia. *Behavioral Science*, 1956, 1, 251–264.
4. Bugental, J. F. T. *The Search For Authenticity*. New York: Holt, Rinehart, and Winston, Inc., 1965.
5. Frank, Lawrence K. The Teacher As Communicator. *Wheelock Alumnae Quarterly*, Vol. 34, No. 4, Fall 1963.
6. Frankl, Viktor E. *Man's Search for Meaning*. New York: Washington Square Press, Inc., 1963.
7. Hartman, Robert S. *The Individual in Management*. Lecture presented to The Nationwide Management Center, Columbus, Ohio, November 7, 1962.
8. Henry, Jules. Attitude Organization in Elementary School Classrooms. *Amer. J. Orthopsychiat.*, 1957, 27, 117–133.
9. Horney, Karen. Finding the Real Self. *Amer. J. Psychoanal.*, 9, 1949.
10. Jourard, Sidney. *The Transparent Self*. Princeton, New Jersey: D. Van Nostrand Co., 1964.
11. Kneller, George. *The Art and Science of Creativity* New York: Holt, Rinehart, and Winston, Inc., 1965.
12. Marx, Karl and Engels, Friedrich. On Alienation. In *Images of Man*. C. Wright Mills (Ed.). New York: George Braziller, Inc., 1960.

13. Moustakas, Clark. *Creativity and Conformity.* Princeton, New Jersey: D. Van Nostrand Co. (In Press).
14. Moustakas, Clark. Education, Alienation, and Existential Life. In *Essays Toward A Humanistic Psychology.* Henry Winthrop (Ed.) (In Press).
15. Moustakas, Clark. *Loneliness.* Englewood Cliffs, New Jersey: Prentice Hall Inc., 1961.
16. Murphy, Gardner. *Human Potentialities.* New York: Basic Books, Inc., 1958.
17. Neill, A. S. *Summerhill,* New York: Hart Publishing Co., 1960.
18. Rogers, Carl. A Theory of Therapy, Personality, and Interpersonal Relations As Developed in the Client-Centered Framework. In *Psychology: A Study of Science,* Vol. 3, Sigmund Koch (Ed.). New York: McGraw-Hill Book Co., Inc., 1959.
19. Rogers, Carl. Toward A Modern Approach To Values: The Valuing Process in the Mature Person. *J. Ab. and Soc. Psychol.,* 1964, 68, 160–167.
20. Smillie, David. The Roots of Personal Existence. *J. of Humanistic Psychol.,* 1961, 1, 89–93.
21. Weiss, Frederich A. Self-Alienation: Dynamics and Therapy. *Amer. J. Psychoanal.,* 1961, 21, 207–218.
22. Winthrop, Henry. Empathy and Self-Identity Versus Role Playing and Alienation. *J. Existentialism,* 1964, 5, 37–50.

CHAPTER 2

Creating
The Authentic Relationship

The elementary and secondary grades offer a challenge and opportunity to teachers who wish to make teaching and learning a vital and personally meaningful experience. In these grades teachers must often follow a prescribed curriculum which focuses almost entirely on intellectual functions and abilities. The teacher is likely to be greatly restricted in time. Frequently every period of the day is scheduled for reading, social studies, arithmetic, English, handwriting, and other subject areas. Strong pressures to conform to prescribed standards and goals are sometimes encouraged by school administrators. The teacher who is eager to pursue values and beliefs which represent his personal philosophy and his talents and interests must often depart from external demands and meet the child as an individual.

In spite of the divisional curriculum, many teachers realize that the child's entire self comes to school and is involved in every activity and experience. Every child wants to be known as a unique person, yet most teachers find it difficult or impossible to respect individual differences. With so many other pressures and responsibilities, with such large groups, with prescribed curriculum requirements, the teacher's time and energies are almost completely used up. Creative thought, imagination, and better human relations in the classroom are, too often, ideals and dreams.

Only the most unusual teacher refuses to be defeated by pressures from parents, administrators, specialists, and other teachers. The task of finding a way of reaching the vast potential of each child, of responding warmly, humanly, and tenderly, of being sensitive, is almost insurmountable. Yet there are teachers who, in spite of all obstacles, manage to live with the child emotionally as he explores his total self and attempts to discover his own reality.

For the teacher burdened with the requirements of teaching and deadened by pressures, the attitudes, principles, and concepts of mental hygiene will have little meaning or value. But perhaps they will encourage teachers to try out some of the approaches presented in this book. At least they are concrete and real and have been worked out by teachers themselves, within all the realities and limitations of larger classes, limited resources, and professional pressures.

Those teachers who participated more deeply in the emotional experiences of their children in school found the going difficult at times, confusing and stressful, but most of them felt their contribution to the child's total life and their own growth were rewarding experiences. Seeing a frightened, timid, struggling child move forward toward freer expression and spontaneity, toward richer self-achievement, is an incomparable gratification.

Every teacher faces the disturbing problem of helping unhappy, dissatisfied children to find a positive way of living in the classroom. Every teacher must in some way meet the variety of emotions that children bring with them to school. How the teacher does this depends on the type of person he is and what he believes. But when we work with children who need help, it is hard to ignore the need before us in favor of something less meaningful and less real.

This book gives an account of how teachers recognized and responded to children in significant personal relationships. The special relationships presented are based on the teacher's belief that the best way to know the child is through his own perceptions of experience. Understanding of the child and his experience of reality comes from his inner world which is expressed directly in personal interaction with the teacher.

Confrontation and Encounter[*]

Two ways in which teachers may establish significant bonds in their relations with children are the confrontation and the encounter. The confrontation is a meeting between persons who are involved in a conflict or controversy and who remain together, face-to-face, until feelings of divisiveness and alienation are resolved and replaced by genuine acceptance and respect, even though differences in belief and attitude may continue to exist. The encounter is a sudden, spontaneous, intuitive meeting between teacher and child in which there is an immediate sense of relatedness and a feeling of harmony and communion.

The Confrontation

In their meetings with children teachers experience frustration and conflict, sometimes so severely that they do not feel they can continue their work on any constructive basis. Then, either the relationships will deteriorate or the persons will face each other and struggle with the issues and problems. The confrontation is not an intellectually planned session which requires an audience and a referee. It is a private, intimate conflict between persons which happens, often spontaneously and unexpectedly, when a crisis arises in a relationship and the persons must either reach a new level of life together or face the consequences of a broken relationship, evasiveness, distortion, and alienation.

The confrontation may last only a brief time or it may be of long duration depending on the depth and intensity of the dispute. It requires that the persons remain together until there is a resolution of feeling. The individuals may terminate the confrontation, still at odds as far as the issue is concerned, but not at odds with each other. This is the important point for the teacher to realize—the child must be free to maintain his

[*] This section is a revised excerpt from the author's article (26), Confrontation and Encounter. *J. of Existential Psychiatry*, Vol. 2, No. 7, Winter 1962, 263–290.

own identity, to trust his own senses if a relationship is to have any valid meaning at all.

In the classroom confrontation, the child must have the right to be in disagreement with his teacher. Paradoxical as this seems, only when persons can openly disagree, if this is the reality of their experience, is it possible for them to establish genuine bonds. When the teacher forces the child, through repetitious phrases and commands, through conditioning, belittling, and group pressures, when the teacher uses subtle, brainwashing devices, and cuts the child off or beats him down, the child soon realizes that the only acceptable way is the path of conformity, taking on the words and ways of the one in authority. Increasingly, the child becomes insensitive to his own self and unresponsive to his own experience. He becomes numb to criticism and rebuke, develops a suspicious and mechanical approach against further attacks, and comes to be unfeeling in his associations with others.

The confrontation is a way to an authentic life between persons, but each person must maintain a living awareness of his feelings and must be honest enough and courageous enough to let the initial breach heal through the silent, sacred, covenant of love, and strong enough to maintain the human sense whatever else may be cancelled out in the issue or dispute.

In the creative disputation, each person must be aware of the other's full legitimacy. Neither must lose sight of the fact that he is seeking in his own way, with whatever talents and skills he possesses, to find a meaningful way to live, to express the truth as he sees it.

The teacher is sometimes afraid to confront a child who is hostile, caustic, or vengeful. Such a teacher avoids and avoids until the accumulation of feelings becomes so unbearable an explosion occurs, and the teacher loses control. Once the self is out of control, there is no possibility to bring about a positive resolution of the problem. But when the hateful, rejecting emotions subside, there is always hope that the teacher can come to terms with the child and reach a depth of relatedness and mutuality. The threat of anxiety in facing an embittered, destructive child can be eliminated only in an actual confrontation with the dreaded child because until we actually meet him, we cannot know him. We cannot know whether we can live with him, whether we can face the issue or crisis and maintain our own identity with love.

Two illustrations involving conflicts between teachers and children in the classroom are presented below. The experiences are narrated by the teachers themselves.

Mrs. Lawrence Confronts Her Group

Over a period of many months, a fairly successful teacher-indoctrination or "brainwashing" had been executed in this group on the joys of research study and the woeful disadvantages of using just one textbook for their work. But, someplace along the line another job of "thinking and speaking for yourself, expressing your own convictions" had been running a strong counter course! Like a regiment in ambush they sprung one quiet day; almost united to a man on the pleasure they would derive from having a text, a single book, with discussion questions and problem exercises, "like the other kids." Being kicked in the stomach might have been less painful to me at that moment; and to save the sinking ship and the drowning crew, I pulled out all the stops.

"Have you no appreciation of the value of looking at things more than one way? Can't you see the *fun* you could have putting ideas together from many phases of American life and from many different sources? What about the legends, literature, art, music, and dances of your people," I stormed. "Can't you draw some conclusions of your own? Must you have it crammed down your throats from the pages of one little book; and one dictating teacher?" And for a final "piece de resistance", in words to this effect, or more accurately, in these very words, I said, "You are all just plain lazy! You want to be spoon fed."

Well, there was hardly a dry eye in the house, the little scene I had staged had brought about the desired effect! Proud? Well, at that moment perhaps, but still rational enough to add: "You needn't decide now what you want to do; but tomorrow I will expect you to indicate on a slip of paper if you prefer to have the text book for the year, or if you would prefer to work together from many resources and research methods toward some meaningful insights and conclusions."

When my shaking stopped, and I sat in my empty classroom, I began thinking of the ugliness of the whole thing! This is teaching? Victory at any cost? It didn't take too long for me to realize that some of the very people who mattered most must now wonder if they really know me as an honest self. Where was the consistency of my values now?

I can't honestly say that I knew what I was going to do about it when I walked in to class the next day; in spite of the long night's struggle and post-mortem of the confrontation, but I applied, through no advanced plan of my own, the age old principle of apologizing when you know you have done something wrong. I held to my belief in the value of the resources, methods and principles we had used in the past months, but I admitted temporary irrationalism and professed that my lack of respect for their opinions was inexcusable! If it would afford them a better opportunity to state their views, and if it wasn't too late, I suggested a discussion. Everyone had something to say and the cleansing power of my words resulted in a completely different classroom atmosphere and a heightened sense of group solidarity. My pleasure in being a part of this was only commensurate with the knowledge that I had learned far more than any child in the room from this experience.

RICHARD AND MRS. KING

I received Ricky in first grade with the fore-knowledge that as a kindergartener he had been able to antagonize and successfully fight several second and third graders. This gave him something of a personal standing, if not a social one, in the eyes of his class and his teacher. He was also introduced to the principal many times.

I discounted his infamous first year. I was not sure which child he was during the first few days of school but he set about

enlightening me soon afterwards. Whenever there was an unusual amount of loud talking I would ask, "Who's shouting?"
Ricky would always answer, "It's me, Ricky Holway." After a
few days of instruction I knew Ricky well. He was usually
sliding, running, or galloping around the room. And he always
kept his eyes on me while he created the furor. As soon as I
looked up and noticed him, he stopped.

In straightening out names and learning who the children
were, I found that I had two boys named Ricky. The children
identified Ricky Holway as "the one who fights." I said that
I hadn't seen any fighting so that wasn't going to help me to
know the boys. Ricky said he would start a fight and then I
would know. I laughed and told him that I'd remember now
because he was the Ricky who had such a good sense of humor.
He seemed to think that over suspiciously.

In the beginning, I had asked the children to do a set of
big and small drawings. Ricky was quick to point out that that
was kindergarten work. He said loudly, "Aw, that's baby stuff.
We did that in kindergarten." I answered lightly, "Of course
it's kindergarten work. I want to be sure you can do it before
we can go on to reading and writing." Ricky drew—all in purple,
as I remember.

The next day, while we were practicing writing names, Ricky
asked for a new name tag. He said he wanted Richard on it,
not Ricky. He said he didn't like the name Ricky any more.
Besides, there was another Ricky in the class. Since he had
previously shown a marked tendency to take short cuts in his
work, I pointed out that Richard was longer and more difficult
to write. He said, "That's all right, I want my own name." I
made the tag for him. I thought he wrote his name very well
and told him so. I have had good neat papers from him ever
since. From that day I called him Richard instead of Ricky.

Following the christening, for many days Richard finished his
work so quickly that I asked to see his papers and then con-
gratulated him on work well done. Someone announced that
Richard was not finished because he had not made the drawing.
I asked the others if they liked to draw. Everyone nodded,
shouted in the affirmative. I told them that Richard did not like

to draw just then but one day he might wish to. The class accepted this gracefully. All except Mike, who impishly asked, "Is Richard your pet?"

Richard spun around to Mike and yelled,

"Do you want to fight?"

"No," answered Mike, "I'm littler than you."

Richard was the first to laugh and we all joined him.

I can't tell you when, but sometime during the first six or eight weeks of school, Richard stopped hitting. I can recall no scrimmages on the playground during the past month and a half.

Richard has had a special "privilege" since the second week of school. That privilege consists of coming into the building and into the room as soon as he arrives at school. The reason for this is that invariably he created chaos standing in line before the bell. Three or more times a week a service girl would usher him in and report that he had been calling them names under his breath, but so softly that his invectives could not be heard.

A few weeks ago he came in again, or was brought in, for the same name calling and shoving. I sat down with him this time. I had not made an issue of it before. I talked to him about his "privilege". I told him it was no privilege at all and he knew it. He knew he had to come in early because he was not big enough to restrain himself outside. I added that, although he had told us often that he hated kindergarten, he should have learned some better ways of getting along with others, but since he hadn't, he would have to learn in the first grade. I don't remember what else I said, but Richard listened. We decided together that beginning the next day he would no longer have the privilege of coming into the building early. He would come in with the other children.

One morning, many weeks later, he came in with his class, stopped at my desk and said,

"The service girls said I was to tell you I'm doing better in line."

I told him, "Good for you. I knew you could cooperate if you wanted to."

I cannot say when our relationship changed significantly but there is a major difference since the early weeks of school. He used to challenge everything I had to say. This was all right. We differed. I had my ideas which I argued and he argued his. I sometimes told him, "Richard, you got up before I did this morning now quiet down until I catch up with you." Sometimes he did, other times I was on my own. Occasionally I told him he had been most annoying and that if he could think of anything on his own to help the situation to go ahead and do it. At the time he was tolerantly accepting of me. But now we are friends and we both know it.

One last incident. He was asked to step out of the room one day, "Just until you can settle down and relax." While he was out in the hall he switched all the boots around. When he came back in, he told me what he had done. I said "good," playing the game with him. But at lunch time I discovered it was no game.

From many voices, I heard, "Mrs. King, I can't find my boots. I have two for the same foot and I can't find the other. Richard mixed them all up."

I called, "Richard, come here and straighten out these boots, please."

By this time everyone was complaining, even children whose boots he hadn't touched. It took Richard about three minutes and he had them all matched, but the accusations were still being voiced loudly. So I announced,

"If there's anything I like, it's a boy who can straighten out his own messes." "And that's me," said Richard.

The Encounter

The encounter is a direct meeting between two persons who happen to come together. It may be an exchange of brief duration or last a long time, a meeting with a friend or with a total stranger. In such a meeting there is full human intimacy and depth. Although every confrontation is an encounter not every encounter involves a dispute or controversy. Sometimes the encounter is a simple coming together of two faces or pairs of eyes, a sudden sense of knowing and being within the other, a feeling of harmony, unity, and continuity where subject-object, self-other, individual-universal dichotomies disappear. The encounter is an immediate, imminent reality between two persons engaged in a living communion, where there is an absolute relatedness and a sense of mutuality.

The encounter is a creative experience, in which there is a dropping off of conventions, systems, and rubrics, and a letting go so that one enters into the reality of a situation in terms of the conditions and requirements intrinsic to that situation. Openness, receptiveness, and relatedness are significant aspects of the encounter. The encounter is not a fortuitous meeting of two individuals, but rather a decisive inner experience in which something totally new is revealed, in which new horizons are opened (6, p. 119). Martin Buber (1, p. 112–113) relates an encounter between an educator and student, a vital meeting which occurs when a young teacher faces his class for the first time. Vacillating between issuing orders immediately and setting up rules and standards of conduct, the teacher suddenly encounters a face in the crowd, a face which strikes him. It is not a beautiful face, but a real face and, though it contains an expression of chaos, on the face, the teacher reads a question: "Who are you? Do you know something that concerns me?"

I quote now the passage which presents this encounter:

In some such way he reads the question. And he, the young teacher, addresses this face. He says nothing very ponderous or important, he puts an ordinary introductory question: "What did you talk about last in geography? The Dead Sea? Well, what about the Dead Sea?" But there was obviously something not quite usual in the question, for the answer he gets is not the ordinary school-boy answer; the boy begins *to tell a story.* Some months earlier he had stayed for a few hours on the shores of the Dead Sea and it is of this he tells. He adds: "Everything looked to me as if it had been created a day before the rest of creation." Quite unmistakably he had only in this moment made up his mind to talk about it. In the meantime his face has changed. It is no longer quite as chaotic as before. And the class has fallen silent. They all listen. The class, too, is no longer a chaos. Something has happened. The young teacher has started from above.

No matter how complicated or restricted or frightening life appears to be, the opportunity for encounter is always present.

However heavy the pressures and responsibilities of life, there is nothing that can completely prevent genuine meetings between teacher and child. The encounter can become a reality if the teacher is willing to make the required commitment.

Principles in Creating
The Authentic Relationship

Adler (1) once wrote that the only people who really know human nature are those who have experienced the worth and value of others through their own empathy, that is, through the fact that they have also lived through crises or have been able fully to recognize themselves in others. Correspondence of personal experience is perhaps the best basis for knowing what an experience means to another person, but without such identity of experience, we can still understand the meanings that experiences have for children through listening with objectivity and warmth and through maintaining an attitude of acceptance and trust.

A special kind of objectivity is required in the teacher's approach to the child in the personal classroom relationship. It is the completely unbiased attitude of seeing what an experience means to the child, not how it fits into or relates to other experiences, not what causes it, why it exists, or for what purpose. It is an attempt to know attitudes and concepts, beliefs and values of the child as they are perceived by him alone. The experience of the child as he perceives it is sufficient unto itself. Any kind of evaluation or diagnosis of the child's behavior breaks up the child's experience, treats him as an object, and interferes with the establishment of a genuine relationship.

Selecting material reported as fact in the child's past record may set up expectations and prejudices in the mind of the teacher. Even if the "facts" are accurate they are still but fragments, and dead fragments at that, of the world in which the child lives, a unique personal world of color and potential life. Knowing the content of the child's experience does not explain the underlying meaning of his behavior.

When teachers ignore the child's own account of his experience and fail to recognize that facts have special meanings for different children, they make generalizations and plans which distort the true nature of the child's experience. For example, the fact that a child withdraws from his neighbors in school does not tell us what this means. Overtly it may look as though he is rejecting others but actually he may be so engrossed in exploring his own interest or developing an idea or just wondering that he is completely unaware that he has departed from others and remains alone. A closer attempt to understand the child from his own point of view may indicate that he does interact socially with other children when social behavior is meaningful to him.

The teacher does not recognize the otherness of a child as a reality by projecting into him someone else. And when one sees in a person his father, mother, sibling, or anyone else, one ignores the person as he really is. Angyal (3) regards this as a fundamental disregard for, and destructive attitude toward, the other person. He points out that real understanding of the other person is not some sort of shrewd analysis which has a keen eye for the weaknesses of people but is a deep perception of the core, of the essential nature, of the other person as he is.

Resistance is a way for the child to maintain his own sense of self in the light of external pressures to manipulate and change him. It is a healthy response, an effort of the individual to sustain the integrity of the self (22). When the individual submits without wanting to submit, he is weakened and unable to function effectively. Conformity blocks creativity, while freedom and spontaneity foster growth.

Rank (29) stressed the importance of positive will expression, that is, the expression of one's own feelings and convictions, as a basis for decision and action. He believed that the denial of personal expression is the essence of neurosis. His aim was to strengthen the person's belief in himself. In the light of external pressures, attempts to force the person to submit to symbols, standards, and values outside himself, the individual must often call upon hidden potentials within himself, follow his own internal cues, maintain his position, and assert himself in order to remain an authentic person. When the individual submits and distorts his own feelings the health of the person is impaired and he becomes alienated from the very people who make up his world.

It is within the nature of the child to realize his individual potential as fully as possible (17, 19). The child will defend himself against all attempts to change him that threaten his own perceptions, beliefs, attitudes, and values. He will respond favorably to people who permit him to enhance the self by expressing and exploring his interests and by developing skills which enable him to have personally satisfying and meaningful experiences. The child will not respond positively to teachers who are manipulating him. Such teachers can be effective only if they are very strong and force themselves upon him. Then the child is driven into a painful situation, not only because he is unable to respond in a healthy way, but also because he is shocked and disturbed, sometimes so severely that he becomes what they want him to be. When we force an individual to behave according to external or authoritarian values, we impair his creativity and his desire to grow as a unique person.

The real self is the central inner core within each child which is the deep source of growth (19). It is the most stable and consistent value in life. To live in terms of the persons we are is the only way to health and self-fulfillment. Being authentic permits us to establish a personal identity, and fosters genuine human relations.

Given the opportunity to grow and to actualize one's self provides the best basis for interacting with others, and within the framework of groups and society. When individuals are free to be themselves, they do not violate the trust that is conveyed to them. In such an atmosphere individual integrity is maintained and fostered and society is enriched. We must not accept as intrinsic an antagonism between individual interests and social interests. Maslow (24) has strongly emphasized that this kind of antagonism exists only in a sick society. But it need not be true. Creative individual expression, that is, expression of one's own intrinsic nature, results in social creativity and growth, which in turn encourages and frees the individual to further self-expression and discovery.

Personal interaction between teacher and child means that differences in children are recognized and valued. Expression and exploration of the child's uniqueness and distinctiveness are encouraged. Only what is true and therefore of value to society can emerge from individual interests which are expressions of one's true nature. Adults may offer resources, make available opportunities, and give information and help when it is meaningful to the child; but, in a personal relationship, to force standards, social values, and concepts on the child is to stifle his potential creativity and difference.

Relations must be such that the child is free to recognize, express, actualize, and experience his own uniqueness. Teachers help to make this possible when they show they deeply care for the child, respect his individuality, and accept the child's being without qualification. To permit the child to be and become is not to promote selfishness, but to affirm his truly human self.

CONCLUSION

The illustrations of personal classroom relations presented in this book were selected from materials gathered by ninety-two elementary and secondary school teachers. All these teachers have had some special preparation for their work. In addition to visiting teachers in their schools, a psychologist was available for consultation. The teachers came from a variety of school systems to discuss their experiences both in the classroom and in the community. They met in small groups with other teachers, principals, and counselors, over a period of one year. In the course of these discussions they often explored problems of their own, difficulties in relations with parents, with other teachers, and with principals and other administrators. As each of these groups met, they tended to find the group itself was the most valuable resource for clarifying and solving classroom problems.

All the approaches described were planned by the teachers either as individuals or from suggestions by the group. Each teacher kept careful notes or made tape recordings over the year. The teacher was encouraged to explore difficulties that were encountered in establishing and fostering the personal relationship, as well as questions and reports of progress.

For a number of weeks, before any approaches were attempted, the teachers studied and discussed the theory and principles of individual psychology and creative teaching. They explored problems in their interpersonal relations and became more sensitive and accepting of each other.

The school administrators assisted teachers in various ways. Tape recorders were available to teachers who wanted to use them. A flexible curriculum plan was made possible. In each of the groups some principals were members, so that the philosophy and its implications for classroom teaching were developed through interaction between teachers and principals. The emphasis on the personal classroom relationship and on assisting individual children to be free from threat and grow in their own ways received the full support of the various school administrations. Each teacher also was enrolled in an extension course on interpersonal relations offered by The Merrill-Palmer Institute. The group met for approximately three hours each week throughout the academic year.

The teachers came to believe that children grow through creative, spontaneous experiences which have personal meaning and value. They provided opportunities and resources to make these experiences possible within the classroom. Their work showed movement in the direction of healthier, happier, and more authentic interpersonal interaction between the teacher and the child.

REFERENCES

1. Adler, Alfred. *Understanding Human Nature.* New York: Greenberg Publisher, Inc., 1927.
2. Allport, Gordon W. *Pattern and Growth in Personality.* New York: Holt, Rinehart, and Winston, 1962.
3. Angyal, Andras. A Theoretical Model for Personality Studies. *J. Pers.*, 1951, 20 (1), 131–141.
4. Arbuckle, Dugald S. *Teacher Counseling.* Cambridge, Mass.: Addison-Wesley Publishing Co., 1950.

5. Axline, Virginia M. Morale on the School Front. *J. Educ. Res.*, 1944, 37 (7), 521–533.

6. Axline, Virginia M. Nondirective Therapy for Poor Readers. *J. Consult. Psychol.*, 1947, 11 (2), 61–69.

7. Axline, Virginia. *Play Therapy*. Boston: Houghton Mifflin, 1947.

8. Baruch, Dorothy. *New Ways in Discipline: You and Your Child Today*. New York: McGraw-Hill Book Co., Inc., 1949.

9. Buber, Martin. *Between Man and Man*. Translated by Ronald G. Smith. Boston: Beacon Press, 1955.

10. Buber, Martin. *Hasidism and Modern Man*. Edited and Trans. by Maurice Friedman. New York: Horizon Press, 1958.

11. Buber, Martin. *I and Thou*. Trans. by Ronald G. Smith. New York: Charles Scribner's Sons, 1937.

12. Cantor, Nathaniel. *The Dynamics of Learning*. Buffalo, N. Y.: Foster and Stewart, 1946.

13. Eiserer, Paul E. The Implications of Nondirective Counseling for Classroom Teaching. *Growing Points in Educational Research*, 1949. Official Report. Washington: American Educational Research Association.

14. Faw, Volney E. A Psychotherapeutic Method of Teaching Psychology. *Amer. Psychologist*, 1949, 4, 104–109.

15. Fiedler, Fred E. The Concept of an Ideal Therapeutic Relationship. *J. Consult. Psychol.*, 1950, 14 (4), 239–245.

16. Fromm, Erich. *Man for Himself: An Inquiry into the Psychology of Ethics*. New York: Rinehart & Co., Inc., 1947.

17. Goldstein, Kurt. *Human Nature: In the Light of Psychotherapy*. Cambridge, Mass.: Harvard University Press, 1940.

18. Gross, L. An Experimental Study of the Validity of the Nondirective Method of Teaching. *J. Psychol.*, 1948, 26, 243–248.

19. Horney, Karen. *Neurosis and Human Growth*. New York: W. W. Norton & Co., Inc., 1950.

20. Jersild, Arthur T. *In Search of Self*. New York: Bureau of Publications, Teachers College, Columbia University, 1952.

21. Kelley, Earl C. *Education for What Is Real*. New York: Harper & Brothers, 1947.

22. Lecky, Prescott. *Self-Consistency: A Theory of Personality*. Frederick C. Thorne (Ed.). New York: Island Press Co-operative, Inc., 1951.

23. Lee, Dorothy. *Freedom and Culture*. Englewood Cliffs, New Jersey: Prentice-Hall, 1959.

24. Maslow, A. H. *The Psychology of Being.* Princeton, New Jersey: D. Van Nostrand Co., 1962.
25. Moustakas, Clark. *Psychotherapy With Children.* New York: Harper and Row, 1959.
26. Moustakas, Clark. Confrontation and Encounter. *J. of Existential Psychiatry,* 1962, 2 (7), 263–290.
27. Moustakas, Clark. (Ed.). *The Self.* New York: Harper and Row, 1956.
28. Myerson, Abraham. *Speaking of Man.* New York: Alfred A. Knopf, Inc., 1950.
29. Rank, Otto. *Will Therapy.* New York: Alfred A. Knopf, Inc., 1950.
30. Rasey, Marie. *It Takes Time.* New York: Harper and Brothers, 1953.
31. Rogers, Carl R. *Client-centered Therapy.* Boston: Houghton Mifflin Co., 1951.
32. Rogers, Carl R. *On Becoming A Person.* Boston: Houghton Mifflin Co., 1961.
33. Schwebel, M., and Asch, M. J. Research Possibilities in Non-directive Teaching. *J. Educ. Psychol.,* 1948, 39, 359–369.
34. Snygg, Donald, and Combs, Arthur W. *Individual Behavior: A New Frame of Reference for Psychology.* New York: Harper and Brothers, 1949.

CHAPTER 3

The Individual Child and His Emotions in the Classroom

Feelings and attitudes are learned at an early age. Children bring to the classroom a variety and intensity of emotions, ranging from feelings of fear, anxiety, and failure to self-confidence, self-reliance, and success; from feelings of rejection and insecurity to belongingness and security; from attitudes of prejudice and intolerance to acceptance and respect for differences. Some of these emotions are situational or temporary, others are persistent and chronic. Some are submerged, some are superficial, and others are natural and spontaneous. All emotions influence the child's attitudes toward himself, other children, and his teachers. They affect his ability to read, to spell, and to think.

Every teacher wants to be a good teacher and to provide the kind of environment which enables children to grow optimally. There is no greater joy in teaching than to see growing children be themselves and explore their potentialities. Prescott (3) has emphasized that a primary condition to the establishment of an effective interpersonal relationship with a child is the recognition by the teacher of feelings and attitudes peculiar to him and influenced by the special conditions of his life.

Unfortunately, not all teachers are aware of the significant influence they have on the children in their classrooms. All children respond to the teacher as a person. The teacher's attitudes toward them, though perhaps only subtly expressed, are conveyed to children and influence their behavior. This influence can be very penetrating and pervasive, and may materially affect the child's behavior.

Some time ago an incident occurred which helped a teacher to modify her perspective on teaching and children. Mrs. Lenore assumed she understood all the children in her class. One day a most tragic and traumatic incident occurred. She tells about it in her own words.

Marion appeared very pleased with all arrangements made for her in her new school and responded well to the teaching. I considered her a normal, well-adjusted child and more or less let her move along on her own, without paying too much attention to her. She came to school regularly for five weeks. Then she was absent for a period of days. The counselor finally made a home call. Marion was in the detention home. The police had picked her up at the request of the neighbors and her own family. There had been a terrific battle at home which resulted in almost complete annihilation of interior decoration, furniture, and dishes. Marion had severely attacked her two small sisters and attempted to kill them. The house itself, the doors, windowpanes, and walls were thoroughly damaged.

Marion's mother told the counselor that Marion had always been resentful, incorrigible, uncontrollable, and filled with hatred for her stepfather and half sister.

The upheaval was so violent and dramatic it didn't seem possible that it could have been created by the same child I had always considered so normal and well disciplined.

How did it happen? Why did it happen? Had I missed her strong feelings of inadequacy, unhappiness, and frustration? Did they really exist in the classroom? Was Marion so clever she was able to completely conceal them?

I do not know the answers to these questions, but perhaps this disaster could have been prevented if I had been more alert, more sensitive to Marion, if I hadn't just let her go along because she was so quiet and compliant. Certainly Marion is not the child I originally thought her to be. I hope she returns. I know my relationship with her will change and be influenced more by her real attitudes and needs. This experience made me examine myself as a teacher and my methods more closely. I have been in service a long time and have tended to judge more by outward appearances rather than by getting beneath the surface to the root of the child's feelings. I believe I have allowed routine classroom procedures to dim my perceptions of the children as individuals. With age should come wisdom, but is it always true?

Those of us who have worked with children in play therapy have had a chance to hear children express feelings about classroom experiences. Some children have indicated their strong resentment toward teachers. Others, like eight-year-old Marion, have shown that their teachers misunderstood them and had inadequate perceptions of them.

In her fifth play session Mary burst out laughing, shrilly and nervously, "You know what I do in school? Just sit and peel crayons and it makes me happy. One-two-three-four-five. That's what she makes us do all the time."

Barbara, who had been very nice in her manners and polite in her expressions, suddenly began to show some of her hostile feelings toward home and school. Her teacher had given Barbara a number of important classroom responsibilities. Barbara had always accepted them, apparently with satisfaction, but in one of her middle play sessions she analyzed the situation as follows: "Now she's given me something else to do. She makes me take charge when she goes out. I got so much stuff to do already. I wish someone else would take my place. I never get any of the treats, just hard work. And I miss too many good things. At home there is art, music, and tap, and I had a horrible dream last week. Too ugly to tell."

Then there was Donald, thirteen, laughed at, criticized, made to feel stupid in school. Everything he did ended in failure. The pressures were overwhelming both at school and at home. He ended up with migraine headaches and a severe stomach disorder. He told about it in his first play session.

You see, I'm in the 6A, and at the end of the semester, well, we go to junior high. My teacher said that junior high is tough. You have to be smart and everything and the 6A is the most important thing in school, and the most important grade. And I had trouble. I couldn't do my work. One thing I had trouble with was arithmetic. I tried to do it, but I was sick and it got me down. My arithmetic dropped and I didn't know what was happening to me.

I had these headaches and I couldn't do my work. And so I had another thing I couldn't do either. I can't do my spelling. I used to be real good. I used to get hundreds. But I had these headaches. And this trouble with my vision—my right eye. I was sick. It was hurting me. And I threw up and everything. And now I'm so worried. I started worrying about the kids in school. I didn't know what to do. And now I think . . . . And now I think . . . . I don't know what is the matter. Anyway, the teacher thinks I'm nuts or something and the kids think so too. They don't know that I'm feeling this way. They think I'm nuts. See, if they think you are doing something stupid or something like that, you know, make a mistake or something, they think you're nuts. . . .

But they're always after me. I like to draw in school. They don't think I can do anything, but I can draw better than any of them. And they tell me, "Say, listen, don't you know you're supposed to do your arithmetic?" Or something like that. And I get mad at them. I don't like it. But they do a lot of silly stuff. No one calls them nuts to their face. Anyway, I never had that feeling before of worrying. I started to worry and I wasn't doing so well in school and none of the kids like me so I worried and I . . . I . . . I . . . took these aspirins to feel better. And when I'm asleep I have these bad dreams. . . .

Anyway, the teacher don't think I'm good at anything. I'm good at mechanical things and stuff like that, but I don't have the chance to build things. I like to make things but they cost a lot of money, like model airplanes. I want to make them from balsa wood. I like to experiment with chemicals and mix things . . . .

Some traumatic experiences in school are remembered a long time. Children tend to remember vividly the teacher's emotional responses, the teacher himself, long after they have forgotten the school skills and lessons. William, at twenty, was still deeply troubled by painful classroom experiences, so greatly that in college classes he often became violently ill. Excerpts from his interviews are presented.

Underneath I feel if I don't achieve, I won't be approved of . . . . There's one area—arithmetic. When I was in grade school, the teacher would stand over me all the time and she told my father I wasn't doing as well as I could. He used to make me come home. The teacher I had was very authoritarian and she was just like my dad. And when I came home, I used to have to sit three and one-half to four hours a night, in the sixth grade, doing division problems, and he'd stand right there watching everything I did and showing me every step of the way where I was wrong. I can remember my physical reaction at the time. I'd sweat and sweat and chew off my nails. That went on for the whole year. My father and my teacher always over me, and that's the same sort of thing that goes on now. I'm more used to it, this standing-over-my-shoulder business. And it isn't all my imagination because it still happens every day.

How can teachers understand the individual child and his emotions? How can teachers be more aware and more sensitive to the feelings of children in the classroom? How can they help children such as William and Donald to feel more worthy?

Answers to these questions cannot be prescribed. Somehow each teacher must work out for himself the kind of relationship with children that will help the child as well as the teacher to be more honest and more genuine. Certainly the teacher must provide an emotional atmosphere which permits children to express their feelings. When given the opportunity to express feelings without fear of punishment, children often attack the teacher and point out his injustices, peculiarities, and biases. Sometimes this will be hard to take. But the important thing is that once these feelings are out in the open, once children know they have the right to express them, their intensity of negative feeling will often be lessened. The teacher, as well as the children, will then be in a position to explore their interests and develop their potentialities more fully. Expressing negative feelings paves the way for mutual understanding and growth in the relationship. Through expression there is possibility for change both in feelings and in behavior. Suppressing these feelings does not eliminate them. They may originate in one situation with one teacher but soon generalize to many situations and many teachers. No teacher wants to be attacked, but the submerged feelings of resentment and injustice are much more dangerous and harmful than those openly expressed.

No one can tell a teacher how to relate to the individual child and his emotions. The teacher must discover for himself the ways to deeper sensitivity to children's feelings. In his own relations with individual children the teacher must learn to respect unique perceptions and to live authentically with the child on the basis of these perceptions.

The potentiality for real understanding of children exists only when they are in an atmosphere which permits and encourages them to be themselves. Every child wants to be accepted as a person, to feel that others care for him.

Sometimes as adults we believe that our more extensive experiences automatically provide us with the understandings children should have. Too often this gives us a picture of the child from our own point of view, but not necessarily from the child's point of view. We miss understanding the child's perceptions when we focus on our own.

When we try to see the child as he sees himself, we can understand the particular meanings and values that he attaches to his experiences. A child's play and his verbal expressions, anything the child does that comes from himself, provide opportunities for understanding his inner world of feelings and emotions.

Listening to children as they express themselves, without trying to press our thinking and feelings upon them, is perhaps one of the most fundamental ways of promoting mental health in the classroom. Some time ago a writer (4) who had discovered the value of listening in all interpersonal relations summarized her experiences as follows*:

Listening is a magnetic and strange thing, a creative force . . . . The friends that listen to us are the ones we move toward, and we want to sit in their radius as though it did us good, like ultraviolet rays . . . . When we are listened to, it creates us, makes us unfold and expand. Ideas actually begin to grow within us and come to life . . . . It makes people happy and free when they are listened to . . . . When we listen to people there is an alternating current, and this recharges us so that we never get tired of each other. We are constantly being re-created.

Now there are brilliant people who cannot listen much. They have no ingoing wires on their apparatus. They are entertaining but exhausting too. I think it is because these lecturers, these brilliant performers, by not giving us a chance to talk, do not let us express our thoughts and expand; and it is this expressing and expanding that makes the little creative fountain inside us begin to spring and cast up new thoughts and unexpected laughter and wisdom.

* Appreciation is expressed to Brenda Ueland, *The Ladies' Home Journal*, and Curtis Publishing Company, copyright 1941, for permission.

I discovered all this about three years ago, and truly it made a revolutionary change in my life. Before that, when I went to a party I would think anxiously: "Now try hard. Be lively. Say bright things. Talk. Don't let down." And when tired, I would have to drink a lot of coffee to keep this up. But now before going to a party, I just tell myself to listen with affection to anyone who talks to me, *to be in their shoes when they talk;* to try to know them without my mind pressing against theirs, or arguing, or changing the subject. No! My attitude is: "Tell me more. This person is showing me his soul. It is a little dry and meager and full of grinding talk just now, but presently he will begin to think, not just automatically to talk. He will show his true self. Then he will be wonderfully alive . . . ."

Effective listening does not come automatically and easily. It comes only through continued practice and the desire really to understand the perceptual expressions of the other person.

Children want to feel they are talking with, not to, someone. They want to know they are understood and accepted. A child can be deeply understood only if he can be comfortable enough to be himself and only if we attempt to see how he perceives his relations with others, how he interprets his experiences. The child must feel that what he says is worth while. Then he can look at himself more completely and more fully explore his attitudes toward others.

When the child feels free to be himself and comfortable in his relations with his teacher and his classmates, he has the opportunity to grow toward fulfillment of his potentialities. He has the kind of inner peace and outer security that he needs to enable him to strive toward more complete self-fulfillment. He can make greater use of all the resources in his environment.

The motivation for exploration and expression of potentialities, in the final analysis, lies within the child himself. He needs a warm, accepting environment. He needs a teacher to respect him, accept him as unique and worth while, and believe in his capacities for continued growth. Once these conditions are present, and facilities and materials are available, he will be able to explore his interests and develop his potentialities in his own way.

Every child needs the opportunity to express his feelings without censure. We sometimes think that if we suppress anger or fear, if we shut it out, deny it, or change the subject, its influence on the child will be minimized. More often than not, when we respond to children in this way, the feelings remain, become intensified, and more strongly influence the child's behavior. Though it is sometimes difficult to permit children to express their feelings, there should be regular opportunities in the school

Photo by Merrill-Palmer

The Teacher's Human Presence. Marcia is totally absorbed in an experience in nature, sharing her sense of wonder with her teacher. It is a moment of aesthetic harmony between teacher and child that gives human meaning to school life.

for children to talk about their experiences in their own way. Many teachers who feel they cannot permit children to express themselves any time they wish, find that setting aside a regular time once or twice a week has special value for individual children and does not jeopardize the over-all school program. Whenever it is possible to permit expression of feelings, the strength of the feeling may be lessened and perhaps its influence will be modified or removed, particularly when there is continued acceptance and respect for the child.

Exploring an Individual Interest. Marion is engrossed in toothpick sculpture. She has spent several hours working alone and planned the design of the geometric structure completely on her own before beginning the construction.

NED—MISS MORTON'S REPORT

The first five weeks of school were unhappy ones for Ned and me as well. He did everything to cause trouble, struck youngsters, broke toys, scribbled on other children's pictures, ruined others' work, screamed all the time at everyone, and always did the opposite of what he was supposed to do. One day he got so mad at me he went into the coatroom and threw all the boots in one pile and pulled all the coats and hats off the hooks onto the floor. He hit anyone who came near him, or if any of the youngsters tried to help him do anything. Eventually he was left alone in the group, and was blamed for everything that happened. I punished him every day and it rolled off his back like water off a duck's back. If I had had the time, I could have been at him every minute of every morning.

I tried everything I had heard of in working with him; nothing seemed successful. He had nothing to do with me, there was nothing but a negative relationship between us. Then it occurred to me that I might make a more honest effort to understand the meaning of Ned's behavior. I learned that Ned had been left completely alone during the day since he was two. His lunch had been left on the table for him. One incident occurred when he was about two and a half which helps to explain his home situation. Ned was outside playing. The yard next door had been roped off to protect the new grass. Ned went over and carefully leaned over the rope to feel the soft green that was there. He toppled over and fell on the grass. His father saw him, came out of the house, got the garden hose, and turned it on him full blast. After soaking Ned completely, his father turned without a word and went back into the house. Ned was left crying on the grass. His mother has been desirous of having other children but the father says, "One brat around the house is enough."

Ned's mother has spent more time with him than his father has. She took two days off work when he entered school. This was the first time she had been home with him in several months.

Ned has been kicked out or asked to leave several nursery schools. Most people who have worked with him have found him hard to handle.

Ned has been beaten and subjected to every type of punishment possible, not only by his parents but by the neighbors as well. They have resented him. They say he is mean and nasty. They won't let their children play with Ned. So Ned has become a very lonely child. He sits on his front-porch steps waiting for something to happen.

One day at school Ned was hurt. He had bumped into a table. I saw it happen. Ned ran off into the closet by himself. I wandered in and talked to him for awhile and told him I was sorry he had hurt himself. I told him I realized how much it must have hurt. For the first time, perhaps, I tried to show Ned I really cared, and maybe for the first time I did care. He stopped crying and hobbled over and shoved his leg at me. I rubbed it and kidded with him a little. Then he took my hand and we left the coatroom together. Before this he had never come to me for anything.

This was the beginning of a new relationship with Ned. For the first time his teacher really felt kindly and sympathetic toward him. She showed Ned that she could understand his feelings. The report continues:

Up until this time Ned had not entered into play with anyone, and during our telling and showing time had contributed only disturbance. On October 21, a few days after the being-hurt episode, Ned started talking and playing with other children. For a number of days his play was friendly and constructive. The following type of expression occurred several consecutive days during discussion time:

Ned: Did you know I had a fire at my house?

Miss Morton: Oh?

Ned: The firemen came. It was in the basement. The furnace burned all up. There was lots of smoke and everything.

Miss Morton: Were you home?

Ned: I was sleeping. My mom, she saw the fire and screamed. I ran out of the house. Mother was crying. I helped her to get out of the house, then I ran in and saved my dad. He is a fireman now.

Miss Morton: Your dad is a fireman?

Ned: He knows what to do if we have another accident. He didn't even know what to do. I did, though. And if the big giant comes again, he will kill him. I had a great big knife. (*Shows with his hands.*) I cut his head off. I cut him and I hit him lots of times. Then I cut off his legs and he couldn't get away. There was lots of blood everywhere. Gooey red blood—blood. He couldn't get away because I cut off his legs. I killed him.

The group accepted what Ned said and seemed impressed. They waited for a reaction from me, but there was none, except interest in Ned's story. And, difficult as it was, full acceptance. We went on with the telling time in the usual manner.

In the next two weeks Ned told many gruesome stories. Gradually his behavior improved. He spent a great deal of time with me, bringing his work to my desk when I was there. He didn't want to talk much, just be near. If anyone came and wanted to have a shoe tied or a sash on a dress tied, he jumped at the chance to help.

On November 1 Ned came out of the coatroom with two blankets. He saw me looking at him. He said, "I got Nancy's blanket; the kids shove so in the coatroom, I wouldn't want her to get hurt. She's my friend. She likes me. So I get her blanket for her." "It's nice to have a friend," I responded.

A few days later during telling time Ned said it was his birthday. He came up and stood next to me and we all sang birthday songs to him. He seemed very happy and leaned over and gave me a hug.

Ned: Golly, you're nice.
Miss Morton: Why, thank you, Ned. I think you're nice too.

On November 11 Ned got to school early in the morning. He came up and stood at my desk. I happened to be writing.

Ned: Miss Morton.
Miss Morton: Yes, Ned.
Ned: You're my friend?
Miss Morton: Yes, I am.
Ned: You know what?
Miss Morton: No, what?
Ned: Yesterday wasn't (*A pause.*) wasn't my birthday.
Miss Morton: Oh?
Ned: No, I wanted to play a joke on you, but it wasn't so funny, 'cause you're my friend.
Miss Morton: You don't like to play jokes on your friends?
Ned: I make jokes with my mother lots of times and she gets mad at me. I wouldn't want you mad at me, 'cause you're my pal.

A few days later Ned painted a picture and followed the painting rules for the first time this year, being careful not to get paint all over the floor. He hollered to me to come and take his painting off the easel and said, "This one I take home, but I want to paint one for you." "You can, Ned, after everyone has had a chance to paint once." "OK, you call me when I can." Ned dashed off to play with the blocks. Later there was a free easel, so Ned started in. He said in a loud voice, "This one is for you. I want to leave this one here for you." "Fine, Ned, I would like one of your pictures."

Abandoning all the painting rules that I had set down, Ned took two brushes and slopped the paint on the easel. Laughing, he put more and more paint on the paper. Then he replaced the brushes, shoved back his sleeves, and rubbed his hands in the paint, all over the paper.

Ned: This one is for my pal Miss Morton. Ha-ha, this one is for
    you. I think it's prettier than the one for my mother. I want
    you to keep this one forever and ever.

Miss Morton: You want me to keep it always.

Ned: Yes, 'cause, its the best one. (*When he finishes, he starts to
    leave the mess he made on the floor.*)

Miss Morton: Ned, I'm glad you gave me the picture, but I
    can't let you leave the floor like that. It has to be cleaned up.

Ned: Oh yeah, where's the rag?

Miss Morton: You know where we keep it.

Ned: OK, I'll get it.

Ned got the rag, put lots of water on it, and slopped the rag down on the floor. He made three trips to the bathroom, bringing lots of water each time. Finally he got the mess cleaned up.

It is interesting that the carefully drawn painting which Ned felt would please his mother gave him little personal satisfaction. The painting he liked best was messy, without structure or form, and did not convey anything intelligible. Yet it was made with satisfaction, freely and naturally. There was more of Ned in the second painting, so he chose to give it to Miss Morton, who he knew would accept it and be pleased with it. Miss Morton's report continues:

During "Open House" I had an opportunity to talk with Ned's mother. The following discussion took place:

Mother: I suppose Ned has been causing a lot of trouble.

Miss Morton: Oh, we are getting along fine.

Mother: He always has caused a lot of trouble and was very
    unhappy in nursery school. We had him in four different
    schools but he never liked it. He doesn't say much about
    school but he does like you, I know that.

Then I asked Ned's mother if she was able to spend any time with him. She said she was off one day a week, but when she was home, Ned was always outside. He didn't seem to want to be with her.

I suggested planning something together, just the two of them, maybe a trip uptown or shopping, or anything when they could be together. She hastened to say, "Oh, Tuesday is the only day I have to get my housework done. I wouldn't be able to do anything like that." So I suggested reading a story before bedtime. She said she had done that every once in a while, but not much lately because she was so busy. I told her I thought it would help if he knew that he could have a few minutes every day that were just his, either to talk with her or listen. She left saying she would try to work something out. She seemed willing and concerned but very busy.

The first aggressive outburst in two weeks occurred one day when Robert showed Ned a jet plane he had made from construction toys. Ned slammed it out of Robert's hands and to the floor. "That stinks," he shouted. The jet fell apart. Robert began to cry; Ned stormed off. I told Ned I could not permit him to destroy children's things and asked him to remain in one corner of the room by himself. Ned seemed hurt that he was unable to play with other children. Ned stood in the center of the room, threw the clock into the playhouse corner, and sulked off to get his rug. After awhile I walked over to talk to him. "You are mad at everyone today, huh?" "Yes, I'm mad, mad, mad." "Ned, you know I get mad at things too, and I know how you feel, but you can't go on making everyone unhappy that way. When we are alone early in the morning you can do almost anything you want to, but I can't let you do that when the others are here. I just can't let you." Ned settled down again and played constructively for a number of weeks.

On November 17 Ned played house with another little boy. He called me on the play phone, and, shouting over all the other voices in the room, asked me to dinner at his house (playhouse). They were having turkey, dressing, cranberries, coffee, and black-and-blue cherry pie. I said that I would be glad to come. I hung up on my play phone, got my coat and hat, went over, and knocked on the door. Ned met me. He helped me off with my coat. He pushed my chair in under the table and we all sat down. Before we ate dinner Ned leaned over and whispered, "Would you like a drink before dinner?" I answered, "No thank you." "Well then, we will eat," he said with delight. He proceeded to cut the turkey. Flip, his friend, served the dressing and cranberries. Ned said, "You can have seconds if you want them." I took more. Flip said, "Ned made the whole dinner, I made the pie. It is black-and-blue cherry pie, you know." I said, "I think everything is delicious." Ned jumped up, saying he had forgotten the coffee. He poured our cups full. Then he got up after we were through eating and said he must take off, the airport had just called him. "Stack the dishes, Flip, and save me a piece of pie. I'll help you with the dishes when I land again," he yelled. Off went Ned. Flip said, "Golly, Ned is a lot of fun to play with."

This ends the contacts I have had with Ned. But to me many changes have taken place. From a child who outwardly hated everyone, he has started to have successful play experiences with others in the room. He still has bad days and seems to slip back easily. But I feel much has been accomplished. I too have changed in my feeling for him; I don't fight him any more, and his fights with me have stopped. He still is far from being adjusted to the room situation. However, I feel that he knows me and feels that I am an understanding friend who wants to help him grow in ways that will make him happy.

Discussion*

In this relationship, when the teacher discovered the meaning of Ned's hostile behavior, when she attempted to help him feel more important and happier at school a noticeable change in his behavior took place. He participated in the activities of the kindergarten. He began to make new friends. Though his attacks continued, they diminished considerably. He was less feared by other children. The teacher's attitude and behavior changed too. Miss Morton now began to appreciate Ned, whereas earlier he irritated and upset her. She began to value him and enjoy being with him. She gave him more attention, listened to his feelings, and accepted him as he was. Together Ned and his teacher achieved a more honest and free relationship.

Ned needed someone who could help him feel he was not entirely bad, someone who felt and believed he had potentialities for constructive behavior. His teacher needed a better understanding of him and knowledge of the world in which he lived. She needed to feel successful as a teacher. When these needs were met, the barriers to a harmonious relationship were removed and teacher and child were able to begin a new relationship, with new perceptions of each other. They could begin to trust and value each other as unique persons.

* The discussions are presented as tentative observations, reflecting the author's experience with the teachers involved.

MARY

Mary had been referred to the mental hygiene service for stealing. Her parents were distressed, since she had recently stolen money from her teacher. Her father was a lawyer and had attempted without success to lecture her on the consequences of stealing. During her first three play sessions Mary spent most of her time making things for her parents and her little brother. She wanted everything to be "nice for them." Throughout each of these interviews she was anxious about the time and whether she could finish her pictures just the way she wanted them. Her characteristic attitude of anxiety about time pressures was repeated again and again, as in the following excerpt:

Mary: Now let's see, one, two, three. Make these flowers here. I want to make a nice booklet for Jimmy. Look here. See? And now do I have time? I am worried badly. (*Continues coloring industriously.*) Do I have time, Mr. Stanley? Do I, do I, have time? I must hurry, hurry, hurry. I am so nervous. Do I have time? Do I have time to color all this in? (*Mumbles to herself.*) I hope so. I hope I have time. What shall I put on this page for Uncle John? Will I have time to make a little cat and dog, a little puppy dog? Will I have time? Do I have time? Tell me, please tell me, Will I have time?

A feeling of hostility is expressed indirectly:

Mary: Sometimes Mamma says, "Come on, Mary, let's get it done," and I say, why, I just burst out laughing. (*Laughs shrilly and nervously.*) You know what I do in school? Just sit and peel crayons and it makes me happy. One, two, three, four, five. That's what she makes us do all the time. (*After making three booklets, one for each member of the family, she writes "Jimmy" on one booklet, "Father" on the third, and then she speaks to the therapist.*) I know how to write "Father" but I don't know how to do "Mother." Could you help me? (*The therapist spells "Mother" and Mary scribbles*

the letters on the booklet, whereas she had printed her
father's and brother's names very carefully.)

Hostile feelings are expressed directly with much intensity:

Mary: Is it all right if I paint their hair?

Therapist: If you want to, it is up to you. (*Mary takes red paint*
and with an expression of intense anger on her face, begins
to paint the doll's hair.)

T: Maybe you just feel like smearing their faces. (*Mary looks*
up at the therapist and screams "Yes!" She smears gobs of
thick red paint on the faces of the dolls, then clutches them
in her hands and walks over to a tub of water. She dips their
heads in the tub.)

M: (*With angry sarcasm.*) Their hair should be lighter. (*Does*
this again and holds them under the water a little longer.)

T: Maybe you want to fix them so they can't even breathe.

M: (*Becomes very intense in her play. She gets all the family*
figures and sticks each one alternately down headfirst into
the bottle of red paint. She moves them around in the
bottle.) Now I will let them up for a little fresh air. Can't
breathe down there. Now they're back in the water. Back
with your head. Now up. (*Repeats this sequence of behavior*
for the next twenty minutes of the interview, then takes all
the figures but the mother-doll and puts them back on the
shelf.)

M: Because I don't like you. You stay down, now. You can't
breathe. I hate you. Stay.

In the fifth interview Mary continues this type of play.

M: Look at all these people I have. Here, I'll take the baby.
Have to get their tonsils out. Te-hee, he-eee-hee-he. Oh, look
what the people have to do. Oh boy, hee-hee-hee. (*Is pleased*
when T places the bottle of red paint on the table.) Where's
that tub? Oh, I'll take this and I'll go get some water (*Dips*
up water from bucket into bathtublike boat.) I'll get some
water just like I had last time. Where shall I put this pretty
picture? Shall I put it over here? (*Places it on small chair*
by dollhouse.) OK? 'Cause I don't want to get it in all this

stuff. Oh, eee, eee. (*Becoming enthusiastic for what is next to come.*)

T: You can hardly wait to do that, can you?

M: Ooooh, which one shall I dump in first? *Oooh!* (*Dips mother-doll figure into bathtub.*) Hee, eee, down she goes. Dee, dee, dee. Oh, this is fun! Now I'll dip her in the red. (*Dips figure feet first into bottle of red paint, then reverses her and puts her head in.*) And then we're going to dip 'em back in the can. (*Runs over to bucket.*) Goin' to *throw* 'em in. Then we'll get 'em all in.

T: You'll just get rid of them all right.

M: Now this one. Now the Father in the nose.

T: There goes the Father down in the water.

M: Now in there. (*Bottle of paint.*)

T: There he goes, down.

M: Now we just throw the father in (*Dashes him down into bucket of water.*) Just throw him right down in.

T: Just get rid of him, huh?

M: Yes. This sure is fun. (*Sighing, blowing through teeth.*)

T: Just makes you feel good, huh?

M: Um-hmm. (*Goes through same process with another figure.*) Now he can't even breathe. Now he goes in. Just throw him in. Do I have time? I surely do have time!

T: None of them can breathe. Just get rid of 'em, huh?

M: Yeah. (*In whispered voice.*) . . . . (*Does another the same way. Returns to table.*) Do I have time? I surely do have time!

CHILDREN'S EMOTIONAL EXPRESSIONS AT SCHOOL

Teachers have recorded several excerpts of emotional expressions at school and their attempts to respond to these expressions in terms of the principles of individual psychology. For the most part the teacher listened as children described their experiences, accepted the feelings involved, tried to show understanding, and encouraged children to explore the experience further. The teachers were more interested in how children felt about their experiences than in the content of the experience itself. Some of

Feelings for the Baby. Mary and Jane are washing babies, expressing different feelings. Mary handles the baby with tender care and elicits the teacher's help. Jane squeezes the eyes and face of the baby figure. Later she hugs
the baby and carefully puts on a diaper.

these episodes of behavior are presented briefly to illustrate the
teacher's approach and how it helped in the release of pent-up
feelings.

Mother-Sibling Conflicts

Billy seemed sullen and quiet as he approached the teacher.

Billy: (*On the verge of tears.*) Do you know what? My big
sister made my mommy sad this morning. My sister even
sweared at her.

Mrs. Johnson: And that made you sad too?

Billy: Yes. My little sister cried and I cried. My big sister
slammed the door when she left for school and my mommy
cried and cried.

Mrs. Johnson: Your big sister upset all of you, didn't she?
Billy: Uh-huh. (*Sits down beside Mrs. Johnson, plays quietly.*)

Father-Mother Conflicts

Virginia: My daddy really is in trouble. He hasn't been home for four nights. We don't even know where he is. My mother is sure mad at him.
Mrs. Williams: You miss your daddy, don't you?
Virginia: Yes. I hardly remember what he looks like. And boy! My mother is going to 'splode one of these times.
Mrs. Williams: You are worried that your mother will get very angry?
Virginia: You can say that again! When she gets mad, you just better get out of her way.
Mrs. Williams: Mothers get mad just like anyone else, don't they?
Virginia: Yes. She got mad at me yesterday and I got spanked. I wore my party shoes out to play and got a little bit of mud on them.
Mrs. Williams: You got them all dirty.
Virginia: A boy pushed me on purpose and I stepped in the mud. It wasn't my fault, but my mother spanked me.
Mrs. Williams: You thought it wasn't fair for your mother to spank you?
Virginia: No. It wasn't my fault.

Children's Perceptions of War and Injury

When the play time began, the children were scattered about the room engaging in various activities. Seven boys chose blocks and two boys and two girls chose the play corner. Suddenly Miss Ellen heard a great commotion in the playhouse. Screams and groans came from several children lying on the floor.

Patty: You know what? Our playhouse was just bombed. I've got a broken leg. Oh, it hurts!
Kathy: I've got a broken head and I'm all bloody. (*Pretends to faint.*)
Virginia: I'll get the doctor. (*Runs around the room yelling.*) Help! Help! We need a doctor.

Duddy: (*Stops working a puzzle to watch the commotion.*) I will. But wait till I get a hat. Our doctor always has a hat when he comes to see us. (*Chooses an old army hat from the dress-up collection.*)

Patty: Now I'm a nurse. We need some more hurt people. Come on, Jeff.

Jeff: No. Davy and I are bombing you, silly. We can't be in your hospital. We're on the other side.

Before the end of the playtime everybody in the group joined in this dramatic play. There were many screams, bruises, broken bones, and a variety of medical treatments. Some children responded favorably to doctors and nurses, others negatively.

Children's Perceptions of Marital Conflicts

Carol and Virginia were playing dress-up.

Virginia: I'll be the Mother and you be my neighbor.

Carol: OK. Let's pretend I just dropped by for coffee.

Virginia: I haven't time. I'm going out—and *not* with my husband. I'm mad at him. I'm going out with another man.

Carol: Who is your husband? Let's get Duddy.

Virginia: Now, you sit in this rocking chair and snooze instead of doing work. (*Duddy promptly snores.*)

Virginia: (To Carol.) All he does is sit on his fanny. I'm going out with another man. But don't tell my husband.

Duddy: I heard you. Where did you say you were going?

Virginia: Oh! Out!

Carol: You said you'd beat his brains out.

Virginia: OK. (*Duddy and Virginia have quite a scuffle.*) Now you walk out and slam the door and I'll cry. (*Duddy leaves; Virginia moans.*)

CONCLUDING COMMENTS

Ultimately, every teacher wants to meet the child on a significant basis; every teacher wants to feel that what he does in his contacts with children makes an important difference, brings about significant events and experiences. Many teachers have no technical preparation for facilitating and enabling personal growth in the classroom but the desire to evolve genuine life and the awareness of the importance of meaning in learning are important first steps. From this desire and awareness, moments of personal interaction emerge and through the relationship the teacher can enable the child to discover his real self, to develop his real interests and special talents and thus find a way to self-realization as an individual and to rich life with other children. Of course, the teacher too must become increasingly himself and pursue activities which have meaning for him. When conditions of freedom, openness, trust, love, and opportunity to make choices and be responsible for them, exist in the classroom, real life emerges and the teacher perceives each child as a unique individual, who cannot be measured or compared. The teacher regards the child's difference as an essential attribute in learning, and values the child as a person to be recognized, honored, and approached with respect rather than as someone to be molded and manipulated, controlled and changed. In the significant classroom relationship, the teacher enters into a bond with a child, a bond that has vitality and realness between the persons. In such a relationship, opportunities and resources emerge which enable both child and teacher to realize hidden potentials, to release creative capacities, and to stretch to new horizons of experience, together and alone, where learning has an impact on total being and where life has a passionate, enduring character.

REFERENCES

1. Axline, Virginia M. *Play Therapy*. Boston: Houghton Mifflin Co., 1947.
2. Moustakas, Clark. *Psychotherapy With Children*. New York: Harper and Row, 1959.
3. Prescott, Daniel A. (Chairman). *Emotions and the Educative Process*. Washington: American Council on Education, 1938.
4. Ueland, Brenda. Tell Me More. *The Ladies' Home Journal*, November, 1941, 51, 53.

CHAPTER 4

Sensitive Listening
to Emotional Expressions
of Kindergarten Children*

The kindergarten presents an opportunity for teachers to help children grow both as unique individuals and as important members of the group, to help them feel comfortable in expressing themselves, and to help them develop a positive attitude toward school. The flexibility of the program enables the teacher to try out new approaches and to help children resolve their tensions and conflicts.

In the kindergarten there should be no requirements to cover specified amounts of subject matter and the teacher should be free to put her talents to creative use. One way the teacher can relate significantly to children is through sensitive listening to their emotional expressions.

The teacher has numerous opportunities to observe and respond to the feelings and attitudes of children. While children play in the playhouse, the sandbox, or build with blocks, the teacher may sit by one of these groups, observe the exchange of feelings, and try to understand what they mean for the individual child. Since children frequently vary their choice of playmates and play activities, the teacher may find it difficult to consistently explore a child's particular attitudes or emotional patterns.

* This material is based partly on anecdotal and verbatim records kept by twenty kindergarten teachers in four school systems. The illustrations were selected from these reports.

Though it is a complex problem for the teacher to follow shifting patterns and expressions of large groups of moving children in the vicissitudes of their play, whatever understanding and acceptance the teacher can convey, even in fleeting moments, will have some value to the individual child.

The teacher may provide a regular time where a consistent relationship with a small or large group is established in an atmosphere of warmth and acceptance. In some instances where the teacher had planned on one or two periods a week, the children themselves requested regular daily opportunities for verbal expression in an organized group. In this relationship children may ultimately feel free to talk about their most significant feelings and to release the influence of anxiety and hostility.

Mrs. Anderson's Kindergarten Group

This kindergarten group came from a variety of family backgrounds, economically, educationally, and culturally. At the first session of this experimental program Mrs. Anderson said, "You may use this time to talk about anything you feel like talking about." The teacher recorded the children's verbal expressions during or immediately after the session. Some of the material was informative or factual, based on daily experiences. Some children expressed imaginative material stimulated by facts in the discussion. Frequently children would express attitudes and feelings toward siblings and other members of the family.

This was a first-semester kindergarten group and thus had to go through the process of learning to listen to one another. Initially the attention span of the children was relatively brief and the sessions had to be limited to fifteen or twenty minutes each time. It was not possible to give every child a turn to speak every day. As the situations arose, the teacher frequently had to remind children that only one child could talk at a time. Though this problem did not disappear completely, it diminished considerably with the passage of time and the consistent adherence to the limit.

Ultimately this procedure motivated every child with a desire to express himself. The child who initially seemed to find the most difficulty in verbal expression later used this medium as an outlet and an aid in improving his relations with other children. The story of Bonnie illustrates this.

Bonnie was an unfriendly child, quiet and withdrawing. She spoke rarely with other children and seldom played with them. In the beginning Bonnie did not respond to the opportunity for

Listening with Children. The teacher provides an opportunity for children to talk over their experiences. She accepts the child's perception exactly as it is presented and does not give information at this time.

verbal expression. She remained at the edge of the group, saying nothing, though her facial gestures indicated that she was responding to comments of the others. Gradually she began to talk about her baby sister with more conviction, repeating over and over again the same resentment and bitterness. As her feelings toward her sister were recognized and accepted, they were expressed less frequently and less intensely. There was an accompanying change in her feelings toward other children. Bonnie for the first time began to play with others and had a much more friendly attitude.

Through this medium children were assisted to utilize speech in their relations with other children, and there was a general decrease of physical aggression such as punching and slapping. Teddy and George, for example, were among the great fighters in the kindergarten. As they learned to express their aggressive feelings in the discussion group meetings, their conflicts at other times were handled more often with words than with blows. The teacher was delighted one day after two months of frequent battles between these two children to hear the following conversation:

Teddy: I am mad at you. You took my place.
George: And I am mad at you. I want to paint.
Teddy: I do, too.
George: I do, too.
Teddy: Let's take turns. I'll paint now and give you a turn after.
George: OK.

The experimental procedure under discussion should be distinguished from the often used "news time." The teacher does not direct attention to the facts about the child's life experiences, nor does he ask questions or correct the child's expressions. The teacher is concerned with the meanings that facts have for individual children in the context of children's experience, and must forgo imparting information or correcting false ideas until another time.

In the "news time," if the child repeats the same material daily, the teacher reminds him that he told that story yesterday; but in this experiment it may be significant that the child frequently expresses the same feelings and desires. The repetition actually is never exactly the same, and repeated expression in an accepting atmosphere may ultimately aid the child to live more comfortably with his emotions.

Expressed attitudes of the group toward a particular child may influence his behavior. Roger, for example, had a notorious reputation not only in kindergarten but in the entire school. He habitually sank his teeth into any person he could reach. During

Personal Interaction with the Group. The teacher listens to the children's expressions and responds with interest and acceptance. She tries to understand the child's experience exactly as the child sees it.

63

one of the experimental sessions there was a sharp cry. Roger had attacked his neighbor. One of the children shouted, "Why don't you give him his milk now, maybe he is hungry." Another child responded, "Dogs bark for food, they don't bite for it." Other comments followed. In their own way the children showed they understood Roger's need for warmth and affection. In essence, the children told Roger there were more acceptable ways of seeking attention. The teacher made it clear that other children generally liked Roger but not when he attacked them. This session proved of much value to Roger. Though he continued to express his anger in attacks on others, these attacks occurred less frequently and often in more acceptable ways.

In the experimental sessions many of the children established a kind of role in the group. Bruce typified the moralist, revealing a pattern of practicality and seriousness. On one occasion, when two children were marking up each other's papers, Bruce was heard saying, "Two wrongs don't make a right." Several times during the discussions Bruce made similar observations. George portrayed the dreamer, weaving fantastic tales of folk and fairyland. This was George's approach throughout the discussion sessions.

The teacher's role during these discussions with children is that of a sincerely interested person who finds that everything the child says is important and acceptable to him. In empathy the teacher puts himself in the child's place and tries to understand the experience exactly as the child sees it.

Sensitive listening to emotional expressions of kindergarten children only during the spontaneous discussion periods would not be enough to help children be more comfortable emotionally and explore their potentialities. The teacher must be aware of these feelings at all possible times and convey his awareness, understanding, and acceptance to children.

Some Excerpts from Children's Expressions

To show more clearly the process of interaction among children and their teacher during the discussions periods, the following excerpts from Mrs. Anderson's group are presented. Not every comment was meaningful to the teacher, but some of the remarks had dramatic influence on the teacher's understanding and helped bring about a more satisfactory school experience for the child.

Excerpt 1

Becky: I saw a monkey on a tightrope.

Joanne: I saw a little girl dress as a monkey and climb on a black rope, she took a pocketbook and threw everything on the floor. She threw it down hard. She was sorry.

Mrs. Anderson: You wish she hadn't done it?

Bruce: Do you know that my brother has a log cabin at home? Not a real one, a little one. I let him play with my brick house and he won't let me play with his log cabin. He never lets me play with his things.

Mrs. Anderson: He doesn't want to share his things with you.

Bruce: No.

Mrs. Anderson: And you don't think that's fair.

Teddie: You know what I saw? Seven men standing on a ball. A ball standing on seven men, big tall men, too.

Rodger: Yesterday my mom got me things for a house. We have two television sets, a bedroom, a stove with a real hot fire, a refrigerator, a couch. Now we have two of everything. A real house inside of our house. Even a toilet and a toothbrush for me too. (*Roger has experienced living with three different fathers and in two different homes, both meager in affection as well as material objects.*)

Robert H: I have some news for you. We have a new house now. We don't have to go down the basement to go to the bathroom any more. My Bill has a bathroom in his own room. Bill is big. He can drive a car. My baby is going to live in my room.

Helen: I saw some animals in the air, they were elephants.

George: I saw monkeys going teeter-totter. I saw monkeys fly a plane. (*This is only one of George's frequent happy fantasies.*)

The feelings expressed in this session included fellings of guilt over some misdemeanor of the past, resentment toward brothers and sisters, feelings of family pressures, need for martial security and affection, and positive family feelings.

Excerpt 2

Joanne: My sister is going to have a birthday. She is going to be two years old. *She screams her head off.* She screams! That is how she says please (*Considerable tension in Joanne's voice as she conveys these feelings toward her sister.*)

Mrs. Anderson: It bothers you to hear her scream like that.

Donald: I jumped off our porch one time. That was when we lived upstairs. Now we live downstairs.

Bruce S: If I could get into the lake, guess what I would do?

Mrs. Anderson: What would you do?

Bruce: I would jump into the water and dunk my head and catch little minnows.

Judy: I wonder why Billy screams when he wants to get off the toilet?

Mrs. Anderson: You want to know why he screams?

Judy: 'Cause he wants to get off. Mommy puts a strap on him and when he gets off, he wants to get on again. (*Frank bewilderment over the toilet-training process.*)

Mrs. Anderson: He doesn't seem to be able to make up his mind.

In this session the following feelings were expressed: resentment toward baby sister, recall of pleasant past experiences, confusion about toilet training, and difficulties with younger sibling.

Excerpt 3

Patricia D: My dolly hit her head.

Mrs. Anderson: It must have hurt her.

Patricia D: Yes, it did. I fell down too once and it hurt.

George: One time I was making a wooden ball with wings like an airplane. I got hurt, my finger bled. A nail slammed into my finger and made it bleed. (*Said with strong feeling. It sometimes helps to tell about a painful experience.*)

Mrs. Anderson: That must have hurt terribly.

Patricia D: My daddy works at Plymouth and makes cars.

Linda J: My dad has the flu and a cold. I thought we were going to see a movie but we couldn't go.

George: My father had a new rocking chair and a button came off. All my friends came over and we teeter-tottered on the chair. Now we haven't got it any more.

Bonnie: One time I rolled off the bed. That was when I was four. (*This is the first time Bonnie has said anything in the group.*)

George: My mother had the chickenpox and had to stay home for a week. My father had it too.

Bruce Y: Both at the same time? Who cooked and washed the clothes?

George: Don't you know that I can make scrambled eggs?

Donald: My brother woke up and one of his eyes were stuck together. I tried to help him open them. (*Donald often speaks of his protective feeling toward his younger brother.*)

John B: My brother and his friend went to the show on the streetcar and walked home all alone.

Bruce Y: My dog has the mumps. One time we had a cat and he knocked down everything and we got a dog. Now we want a cat again.

Others: What did you say?

Bruce Y: I can't understand myself. (*Said sadly and with feeling. Bruce shows some of his own concern over his speech difficulty.*)

Some of the major feelings expressed on this day were description of painful past experiences, pleasant family relations, and positive sibling feelings.

Excerpt 4

Ronnie: My brother hit me in the eye with a slingshot. It hurt me.

Mrs. Anderson: This hurt you and you were frightened.

Linda: I have a cold now. It's only a little cold. It is going to be Easter. I like Easter.

Teddie: You like Easter. It's fun, it's fun looking for eggs. (*Teddie takes Mrs. Anderson's role and empathizes with Linda's feelings.*)

Photo by Merrill-Palmer

Empathy in the Classroom. Jim is really with Larry in a moment of precarious block-building. Jane, in the background, is also very much in the experience.

Joanne: I stumbled two times when I was doing a jig.

Teddie: You stumbled two times. (*Again Teddie takes Mrs. Anderson's role.*)

Joanne: Yes, my daddy had to pull me up.

Becky: My uncle said not to drink milk before going for a ride in a car. It makes you sick.

Mrs. Anderson: Your uncle thinks it makes you sick to drink before going for a ride.

Becky: Yes, one time I drank a big glass of milk. We went for a ride and my mommy spanked me and I cried. I threw up. She said I was naughty. My uncle said it was because I drank the milk. Now I don't drink milk any more. (*Mrs. Anderson thought Becky became sick when her mother spanked her and called her naughty. She was tempted to offer Becky an explanation and support.*)

Helen: I fell down the stairs yesterday.

Mrs. Anderson: It hurts when you fall down.

Roger: We have a television. We have a drive-in right in our house. That is what my grandma says.

Collette: Some kids pushed me right through some glass.

Mrs. Anderson: That must have hurt a lot.

Becky: (*Holding her doll.*) My baby wants to go wherever I go.

Mrs. Anderson: Your baby wants to be where you are.

Linda T: My mamma can go where she likes if she leaves someone with me. (*Linda shows her independence in other ways.*)

Bonnie: I don't like to be left alone. (*Bonnie constantly follows the teacher around the room.*)

The feelings expressed in this session were hostility toward brother, reports of happy times, and assertions of independence.

Excerpt 5

Donald: I'm glad that Bruce isn't here. He is so mean.

Joanne: I think he is nice. He said that he would invite me to his party.

Collette: I think he is nice. He picks up my snow pants off the floor. (*Several other children made positive comments about Bruce.*)

Bruce Y: Do you know that I have a bank? Not the kind that robbers get into, a little one.

Gail: I have a bank and I have two dollars in it.

Joanne: One day my sister scratched me and bit me. I wanted to scratch her back. She is one year old. I wanted to scratch her, I wanted to scratch her. (*She expresses these feelings with considerable intensity.*)

Mrs. Anderson: You didn't like what she did, and you felt like scratching her back.

Joanne: I didn't. My mother was there. (*Joanne expresses bitter feelings toward her younger sister. This resentment has not been expressed as directly and forcefully before. She indicates also feelings of anxiety in her relations with her mother.*)

Excerpt 6

Lois: (*Holding her doll.*) He wants to come to school because he wants to come with me.

Bruce Y: (*Excitedly.*) She says "he" and he isn't a boy. The doll is a girl. (*Bruce tries to give information but Lois maintains her feeling.*)

Lois: Well, he likes to.

Bruce: Yes, but it is a girl. (*Bruce persists.*)

Lois: Well, he likes to.

George: I have a boy doll and he likes to come to school. Sometimes he kisses the girls. He falls in love and feels like he is married. (*George expresses premature feelings of courtship and marriage. Perhaps a happy portrayal of his own family life.*)

Mrs. Anderson: Feels just like he's married.

Roger: You know what we have in our house? A hundred Easter baskets, yes sir, a hundred Easter baskets. Easter morning they were everywhere you walked.

Teddie: Why didn't you put them in the stairway so people would step on them?

Roger: You know what we have in our house? A hundred Easter know we have a new house now. We have three new beds. You know that one of the beds is in the living room.

Bruce Y: Is it a davenport and when you open it up it is a bed?

Roger: Yes, in the daytime we sit on it.

Bruce Y: My dad said to my mom, "Would you like to play golf?" And my mamma said, "How can I? I have no sticks?"

Bruce Y: One time we went to a circus and the elephant was acting like a teacher. There was a blackboard and the baby elephants were the kids.

Linda J: My dad has a cold today. Skippy didn't go to school today. He didn't want to go.

Joanne: I saw a bird nest in our tree. It was a robin's nest.

Linda T: When I was walking here, I saw two birds.

Dennis: My dad got his car crashed into a tree. (*Dennis frequently talks about things that have been destroyed.*)

Teddie: A long time ago Butch was here, and he had no place to sleep, and we moved a bed into the living room for him.

Bruce Y: Butch is my dog.

Teddie: Butch is my nephew. (*Each child perceives words in terms of his own particular experiences.*)

Joanne: (*Sobbing very hard.*) I bought a licorice today and told the lady I'd pay her back later, and I don't have any money. (*Joanne got candy on credit and expresses her troubled feelings.*)

Mrs. Anderson: You are worried that you can't keep your promise and pay the lady.

Joanne: I don't have any money.

Mrs. Anderson: Do you feel you have to pay her back today?

Joanne: (*Wipes away the tears.*) Maybe I can get the money tomorrow.

Mrs. Anderson: Maybe you can and it would be all right.

Perhaps the most important feelings in this session were the accounts of happy family experiences and Joanne's guilt reactions to lying. Mrs. Anderson attempted to support her emotionally while suggesting a possible solution.

Excerpt 7

Bonnie: Sometimes I don't feel like getting up. Sometimes I feel like a baby, but then I couldn't come to school and I want to come to school. (*Bonnie has a baby sister at home. She sometimes resents the attention and preferential treatment given her younger sister.*)

Dennis: My brother kept my mom from waiting on me. He wasted my mom's time so I couldn't come to school. My brother was bothering me so I couldn't get ready for school. (*Dennis never gets to school until about nine-thirty or later. He has considerable difficulty in getting along with his brother at home.*)

Bruce Y: This morning my mom told me to take the dog out, and when I got there, he had made a mess. She was mad, real mad. (*Bruce has a good grasp of his mother's feelings. Sometimes she expects him to move more quickly than he can.*)

Steven: My sister is always mean to me. She jerks me by the neck and pulls me down, and knocks me down.

Joanne: Does she bite? My sister bites.

Steven: No, she doesn't. My mom and dad won't do anything about it.

Mrs. Anderson: You feel she should be punished.

Jean: Don't let her have what she wants. That is how my mother punishes us. (*Steven has presented his angry feelings toward his sister for the first time. He is relieved to hear the sympathetic comments of other children.*)

In this session a number of children discussed family conflicts. It was especially heartening to Joanne to discover that other children have strong feelings about brothers and sisters. It seems to many of these children that mothers always favor younger siblings.

Excerpt 8

Bruce Y: I didn't go to sleep until my mom came home. My dog barked and barked, and I heard someone coming in so I jumped up. I was alone and I was scared. (*Bruce expresses his frightened feelings.*)

Mrs. Anderson: You were glad to see your mother and dad when they came home.

Roger: I am getting big. I don't hit any more. (*Roger's attacks on other children have lessened considerably in school.*)

Helen: My mom got her dress all dirty and she had to wash it all over. (*Mothers spill and mess too sometimes.*)

Collette: I am giving my mother a white dress.

Joanne: Linda, your eyes are so blue.

Mrs. Anderson: Joanne, you like blue eyes, and think Linda's are very pretty.

As time went on, the children found it easier to talk about their experiences. The discussions helped to bring a greater spirit of friendliness and inner peace to the kindergarten and promoted a happier experience for everyone.

The authentic teacher is in a position to help children find the courage to be themselves by encouraging individual children to express their feelings openly and freely. By being genuinely present to the child, the child feels the welcome spirit and can take the first step in honest expression of feeling.

Certainly the teacher cannot always remain calm when he is being threatened and challenged but he can continue to strive for acceptance of the child even though he may not always be able to accept the child's behavior. When a child deliberately attacks another child and threatens his safety, the teacher must step in and remind the child of the limit. This can be done in a constructive way. "I know you feel like hitting, John, but I can't let you do that." The teacher has responded to two aspects of the situation: the actions and the feelings. The attack is stopped but not John's right to his feelings of anger. The harmful or the dangerous has been denied, but the feelings are permitted outward expression. Thus, the channels of communication are open for teacher and child to meet on an authentic basis, rather than via make-believe and pretense.

Sometimes the teacher is forced to reject the behavior of the child and therefore to reject the child. This rejection may be less severe if the teacher focuses on the behavior itself. If the rejection occurs *only occasionally* in a relationship and is limited to the behavioral act, while at the same time the feelings are recognized and accepted, a general attitude of acceptance can still exist and be conveyed.

When children are permitted to express their real feelings, eventually they gain a release from them. Many children will repeatedly relate painful past experiences or hostile feelings toward some important person. These feelings may at times seem almost unending to the teacher of kindergarten children, but in a warm, accepting atmosphere, the frequency and depth of feeling lessens and often disappears. Sometimes feelings are more situational and temporary and lose their significance the first time they are expressed to an empathic listener.

Teachers also must be themselves, for only when they have the courage to be, and live by their convictions, can they fully participate in children's growth.

MISS QUEEN'S KINDERGARTEN GROUP

From the beginning of the year several members of Miss Queen's kindergarten group showed hostility toward each other and to any form of regimentation. Though the entire group was quick and alert, the children were strongly influenced by Jerry, who had an amazing degree of social skill. His large physical stature and his good ideas made him the leader of the group. If there was a question about his leadership, he would remind others that he was the boss. Jerry's friends were loyal and faithful.

Early in the school year, but some time after the children were well acquainted, Miss Queen told the group that many times things happened to people that they wanted to talk over with others. She made it clear that any time someone wanted to talk about something, the group would be interested listeners.

This was all Dirk needed to hear. He had been waiting for just such an opportunity. He said that he was tired of being bossed by Jerry. Miss Queen tried to accept and empathize with these feelings.

Miss Queen: You wish that Jerry wasn't always the boss, is that it, Dirk?

Dirk: He just makes me mad sometimes when I always have to be the man what starts the rocket and I never get to drive it.

Miss Queen: He really angers you. You never get the best job.

Jerry: Sure, Dirk, you can do it, but when you count backwards from five, the rocket starts real fast and shakes the driver. If you count backwards from ten, its a slower take-off. I'll count now and you drive.

Dirk's mother was concerned, too, because of Jerry's rudeness and domineering attitude. She felt that Dirk was picking up some bad habits. She tried to convince Miss Queen that Jerry was a harmful playmate and should not be permitted to play with Dirk at school. Miss Queen, however, felt that Jerry needed a chance to express his dominant qualities. At home he was rigidly restricted. She felt, too, that the more positive aspects of his self could flourish only if the negative expressions were accepted. Dirk also needed the relationship to become more assertive himself and to learn how to manage a dominant personality. This was something Jerry and Dirk had to work out in their own way. Miss Queen therefore did not isolate them. At home, however, Dirk's mother did not permit Dirk to play with Jerry. At first it was difficult for Dirk. At times he seemed lost. Finally he himself decided to avoid Jerry in school. The group became divided between followers of Jerry and followers of Dirk.

Then came the day when Miss Queen announced to the group that the children could pretend there were no grownups at school. Miss Queen said that this might make some happy, some sad, and others might not care. The group was asked to draw a picture to tell what they would do or how they would feel. Jerry made drawings of fuses and said he had the power to blow up the school if he wanted to. The same day Jerry had brought a box of fuses to school to show the group. He had explained that they had power and could do things. Many of the children had been keenly interested in the fuses. Jerry went on to tell that sometimes he felt like blowing up the teachers. Then he added, "The real reason is I want to blow up the school to find oil under the school." David, Gordon, and Jim started to show signs of great excitement.

David: Come on, Jerry, Let's start.

Gordon: Fuses make electricity and I'll help.

Kathy: Those boys will go to reform school where they won't let you out.

Dirk: Sit down, Kathy, or you'll get blown up.

Jerry: I'll blow up the school and the fire department and all the policemen and then there wouldn't be anyone to help.

Miss Queen: You just feel like blowing up everything, is that it, Jerry?"

Jerry: Yeah, and people will be electrocuted stiff.

Dirk: Put the fuse in a gun and aim it at that house. (*Points out window.*)

The group laughed. This was the first time in several days that Dirk had joined Jerry. Soon they were playing together regularly again. Dirk's mother continued to keep them apart at home.

Vickie got up one day and asked who would like to be the bad baby in her play. Sandy and several others offered. Sandy was chosen for the part. Vickie was the sister and Claudine the mother. Vickie prefaced the play by saying the baby is very bad. Vickie has a baby brother at home. Vickie tells the group the baby has picked on his sister for two days. Thus the play began.

Vickie: Mother, Mother! Dickie is pulling my bangs and he won't let go.

Claudine: This baby is very bad and he will have to be spanked, but first I'll take your bangs out of his hands. (*Mother then spanks the baby and the baby cries.*)

Vickie: He's just a rascal. He's always hurting me.

Several other incidents occurred during the special approaches. Some of these are presented below.

Excerpt 1

Dirk: When we were at my dad's friend's, I found a golf ball. When we went home, I made up an excuse and took the golf ball. Then my mom tried to take it away from me so I kicked her. (*Dirk often mentions his resentment of his mother's interference.*)

Miss Queen: You don't like her to take things from you and you kicked her.

Dirk: Yeah, but not very hard.

Sandy: My brother was playing near the railroad tracks and he got all muddy. I went to get him and I got all muddy. We both came home. Then Mamma spanked me but not him. My brother called, "Sandy, Sandy," but I had to stay in bed. (*Children recognize unfair treatment at an early age.*)

Miss Queen: You must have been angry to be punished after helping your brother.

Sandy: Yeah, but Mamma let us get up after a while. (*Children often make allowances for their parents.*)

Excerpt 2

Dirk: We got bikes at our house. It was my birthday and both my sister and me got 'em. It was really my birthday, but my sister got a horn and a carrier on her bike. My bike has training wheels but no horn or carrier.

Miss Queen: You wish you had a horn and a carrier like your sister's, is that it, Dirk?

Dirk: Yes, but maybe when my sister has a birthday I will get a surprise, and besides, the man didn't make us pay very much money for our bikes, my mom and dad said.

Sandy: My mother had two teeth out way back. She has to have more out, but not till these get well. She was sick last night.

Linda: Jay Vernon, my brother, fell and hurt his head, and if he doesn't have stitches, he will have a scar over his eye. My mother was mad at us. She said it was my fault.

Sandy: My mother wears rubber gloves and now she has sore hands and one sore foot, but she's getting better.

Kathy: My mother is a cripple. She stays in bed and only eats bread and water.

Jerry: That's what they feed ya in jail. She'll die.

Kathy: She does eat breakfast and chicken and chili for lunch, but no grease in her food. And she won't die!

Excerpt 3

Dirk: I had a bad dream. A lion and a tiger climbed up my house. They killed my baby and then an elephant threw the baby over the school. Then my dad shot the elephant. Sometimes I have worse dreams than that.

Miss Queen: Sometimes dreams are awfully scary.

Dirk: Sometimes I have good ones too and sometimes I can't remember them.

Miss Queen: The bad dreams are easier to remember.

JoJo: I had a dream and I talked right out loud. My sister told me about it. She heard it through the walls.

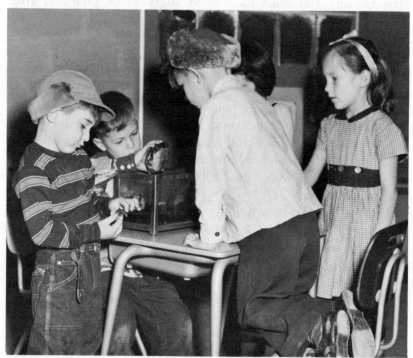

Other Children Given Support. Richard is not yet ready to take the large turtle and examines one of comfortable size.

Excerpt 4

Sandy: My mother still has sore hands so she can't wash the dishes. My dad does them and I help him. *Sandy always expresses positive feelings toward his family.*)

Miss Queen: It's nice for you to have him home.

Dirk: I might not live at our house any more, cause we are going to move. My mom say there are too many brats around our street and lots of trucks on it. We can't find a new house and

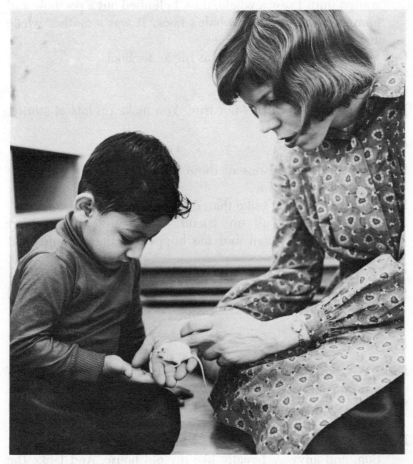

Photo by Merrill-Palmer

Child's Fear. Purna has always been afraid of mice. The teacher accepts this fear and respects Purna's own readiness to come to terms with it. Though still apprehensive, with the teacher's support, Purna is taking a major step in resolving his fear.

    no one wants our house to live in. When people look in our house, I don't tell them about the brats.

Miss Queen: You don't think people like brats.

Dirk: Yes. (*A pause.*) It might be an apartment near a creek.

Jerry: I felt like taking a swim, so I got on a submarine, and when we got in deep water, I watched through the periscope and waited until I saw a whale, then I climbed out a porthole and jumped on the mother whale's back. It was a mother whale and I played with her babies.

Dirk: That's not true. A whale is as big as a school.

Jerry: It might have been a shark.

Dirk: They have teeth.

Jerry: Well, so what if it's not true. You make up lots of stories.

Excerpt 5

Dirk: My sister pulled one of those dirty tricks today. She came to school without me.

Miss Queen: You didn't like that, did you, Dirk?

Dirk: And she took all my friends—Adele and all my other friends. So my mom and me hopped in the car and beat them all.

Miss Queen: You fooled her after all.

Jerry: I'm bringing five mother birds to school. They are all going to have babies. Then each person can take one home.

Excerpt 6

Dirk: We found a house—a new house. It is lovely and it's near a crystal pool.

Miss Queen: You are glad your family has found a new place to live.

Dirk: Yet, but my dad can't go swimming 'cause of that operation, and anyway I really like my old house. And I like the kids.

Miss Queen: Even though your mother doesn't like them, you do.

Dirk: But my mom says I can invite some new kids to come to my new house and go swimming.

Jerry: I got in some mud at Easter time, but it was really quicksand.

Dirk: Now listen, you know there isn't quicksand around here.

Jerry: Yes, there is, and you can get covered up with it.

David: Do you live near a jungle, Jerry?

Jerry: Nope, I just live a little way from the school.

Jim: I saw a picture of a boy stuck in the mud and he was
there a long time.

Jerry: So was I, and I almost sank out of sight.

Miss Queen: You really did have an experience.

Jerry continues to gain status in the group by making up
fantastic stories. Dirk has used discussion time to explore a per-
plexing problem—the problem of having to move. At first his
attitude seemed to be similar to his mother's, but as he discusses
the problem he realizes that the children his mother calls "brats"
are actually his friends. He decides that moving will be extremely difficult when the time comes to make a change. Several
children during the sessions discussed illnesses, painful experiences, and conflicts with brothers and sisters.

In late April Miss Queen noticed that Mark, a child usually
quite anxious to conform and always very adaptable, was becoming aggressive in his play with other children. He had trouble
completing one thing before going on to another. This was not
like him. He would leave a trail of unfinished work and dash on
to something new.

Later he announced to the group that someday he would not
be at school because he would be having his tonsils out. He explained that he didn't know what day it would be, because the
people at the hospital were going to call his mother when he
could come. Miss Queen sensed that Mark was feeling quite
anxious over the impending operation. She encouraged a group
discussion. Jim spoke up. "My brother just came home from the
hospital. He had his tonsils out. He gets dressed but he stays on
the couch and watches television. He wants to gargle all the time,
but mom says it's no good. His throat feels scratchy and he
talks funny. He took his guns to the hospital with him."

The discussion led to the construction of a "hospital." Mark
helped build it but said nothing. One room was for new babies
and one room for the entire group participating in this play.
Girls called from the playhouse to report household accidents.
Pedestrians were hit by cars. Mark said that he was in his house
waiting for the hospital to call so that he could have his tonsils
out. Dirk, a doctor, called on the phone and told him to come

to the hospital and bring his mother too. Mark went to the hospital and sat in the waiting room. Soon he jumped up and said, "These nurses need hats and white dresses, and the doctors should wear white coats." A discussion followed about how the group could make nurses' hats. The hospital play stopped for the day. Mark seemed relieved.

The next day, however, Mark went directly to the "hospital" and stayed there during the entire period at playtime. He went through the operation experience several times. One day he was absent from school. When he returned, he had little to say about the experience.

Mark: I was starting to go to school and the wind blew the door so hard that it knocked me down. I fell down the steps and got these two black eyes. I went back to the hospital for X-rays. I know lots about the hospital now.

Miss Queen: You had two trips to the hospital?

Mark: Yeah! After a while it was fun. We ran all around.

Later Mark's mother told Miss Queen he had expressed fears several weeks before the operation but just prior to it they had suddenly vanished. It seemed that as Mark expressed more and more of his anxiety about the operation in the play period, as he underwent the operation several times, his anxiety diminished considerably.

One day Claudine fell in the mud and was literally covered from head to toe. She was dripping wet as well as muddy. Miss Queen told her that since it was nearly dismissal time, she would drive her home. Jerry, Dirk, and several other children in the group overheard Miss Queen.

Jerry: That isn't fair. All the kids should get to ride with you.

Miss Queen: You want all the children in the kindergarten to ride home.

Dirk: Now listen, Jerry, you stinker, Claudine is all wet. If you were wet, then Miss Queen would take you home.

Jerry: Shut up, Dirk.

Miss Queen: Yes, Jerry, I would take you home if you ever needed me to do it.

Jerry: OK. (*Laughing.*) Boy, you sure did get in the mud and it's lucky you didn't get hurt falling from 'way up there.

When Jerry had the opportunity to express his feeling that Miss Queen was unjust he was better able to accept her decision.

Miss Queen never found enough time to hear all that the children wanted to talk about in a day. She arranged her schedule so that she could sit and "visit" with children as they arrived in the morning. Not all the children wanted to talk. Sometimes a child would chat for awhile and then go on to make a picture or talk with other children. Sometimes the discussion involved a small group of children. The shy, quiet children seemed to find it easier to talk early in the morning when not too many others were around. Later, these same children found it easier to express themselves during the regular school day.

Two particularly withdrawn children early in the year were Cheryl and Jennifer. During September and October Cheryl remained constantly at Miss Queen's side. She was quiet and withdrawn, cried easily, and refused to play with other children. One day Miss Queen mentioned to Cheryl that she usually arrived at school fifteen or twenty minutes before the bell rang, and invited Cheryl to join her. Cheryl came to school early every day during the next few weeks. The first morning she talked mostly about her brother Larry, describing numerous pleasant experiences with him. Then she began to tell about incidents in which her parents had treated her unjustly. As she established a comfortable relationship with Miss Queen during these morning sessions, she expressed more personal concerns and problems. This experience seemed to release emotional tensions in Cheryl, and she became more and more secure during the regular kindergarten sessions. She began to express herself in the group and to play with other children. Dramatic play seemed to help her to become spontaneous and cheerful in her school relationships.

Jennifer's shyness lasted much longer. As late as January, she was a withdrawn, tense little girl. She had missed several weeks of school during the first semester, but after a tonsillectomy, began attending regularly. In February Miss Queen told Jennifer that if she wanted to come early in the morning, they could have that special time to talk together. Jennifer was excited and giggled violently. She frequently wore dress-up clothes, especially animal costumes. She preferred playing with the materials and toys. She seemed to be portraying difficulties at home, expressing strong negative feelings toward her older brother and sister. Beginning early in March Jennifer and Cheryl came together for the early morning sessions. Gradually a friendship developed between them which carried over to most activities in the kindergarten program. For the most part these children played together happily, but one day the following discussion too place:

Cheryl: (*Lips pale and quivering.*) Miss Queen, poor little Larry! He had to go to the hospital. Jennifer and I were playing in her car parked in the driveway. She pulled the controls and the car started rolling backward. We jumped out, but the car went right over Larry's leg. It's all Jennifer's fault, too.

Jennifer: (*Starting to cry.*) I didn't mean to!

Cheryl: You did too. And now maybe Larry won't be able to walk. He already has to wear one brace. My mother said it was your fault.

Miss Queen: Jennifer is sorry about it. She never realized what would happen.

Cheryl: Well, we're just lucky it didn't go over his tum-tum. I guess he'll be all right. I want to tell all the kids not to play in cars. It's very dangerous.

Jennifer: I won't do it any more.

The following day Cheryl entered the kindergarten very excited.

Cheryl: Larry is all right. He just has a bruised leg. He didn't even have to stay at the hospital.

Miss Queen: Then you don't think Jennifer needs to worry any more.

Cheryl: No, and anyway, I was with her. I didn't even get a spanking.

Given the opportunity to tell about the accident, Cheryl expressed considerable feeling toward Jennifer, whom she held responsible. Miss Queen might have tried to show Cheryl where she was at fault too and partly responsible. However, Miss Queen accepted Cheryl's perception, even encouraged her to talk more about it. Once Cheryl realized that Miss Queen would make no accusations, she was able to admit what she probably already felt—that she had contributed to her brother's injury. Cheryl had previously expressed hostility toward her brother, and it is possible she felt considerably anxious and guilty. When she saw that in her relationship with Miss Queen there was no need for her to defend herself, she could assume her responsibility and imply that perhaps she should have been punished. Jennifer, of course, felt considerably relieved by this admission and was able to resume her growing friendship with Cheryl.

Miss Queen felt that she had helped these girls develop their first social relationship at school. Seeing them play together and support each other emotionally was a great joy and personal satisfaction for her.

Miss Queen scheduled a part of each day for children to choose something they wanted to do. The only limitation was that they must decide for themselves. Since it is impossible to follow the expressions of every group, the teacher must move to different groups on different days. Miss Queen felt it extremely valuable to stay with a group long enough really to understand what the activity meant to the child.

Bobby is a tiny, wiry little fellow, full of fun and mischief, and always in a hurry. He has a severe speech defect and dislikes all rules and regimentation. He has excellent coordination and likes to appear bigger than he is. He likes a good fight. He will usually do what is expected of him if supervised by an adult. Independently, he tries to set a record for breaking all the rules he knows.

Excerpt 1

For several days Bobby had the boys build blocks around him, and when they had built quite an elaborate building, he seemed to enjoy jumping up and destroying it.

Miss Queen: You like to hear the blocks crash.

Bobby: Yeah. I like to wreck it. I always like to wreck things.

Miss Queen: You just feel like wrecking things?

Bobby: I even wreck the kids' hut over by Chrissie's house. Them kids get so mad. I wreck it and then run. They can't catch me. I'm too fast. Some of them are big guys too. And they can't even catch a little six-year-old.

Miss Queen: You aren't afraid of boys bigger than you?

Bobby: No. I like to make them mad. It serves them right, because they won't let Chrissie and me play in their hut.

Miss Queen: And if they did, you wouldn't try to wreck their place.

Bobby: Yeah.

Excerpt 2

Jeff: I had my first lesson in getting on a bike today.

Miss Queen: You feel proud to be learning how to get on your bike.

Jeff: I can do it all alone now. It only took one lesson.

Bobby: What's so good about that? I could ride a two-wheeler when I was only five.

Chris: Sure! He rode my brother's bike when he was only five. So did I. And I can ride even a bigger bike now. That's simple!

Bobby: My bike is about 16 inches high. I don't have any trouble getting on it.

Miss Queen: Getting on a bike is easy for you. Some other things are hard for you. That's the way it is for all of us.

Bobby: No, everything is simple for me.

Jeff: (*Who speaks very distinctly.*) Talking isn't easy for you. You have to go to see Mrs. Kline because your S's aren't so good. S's are easy for me.

Bobby: Oh, S's don't count.

Excerpt 3

Bobby: Yesterday I saw an airplane with its wings folded back.

Donnie: That probably was a jet.

Bobby: Yeah. It was a jet. It ran out of gas and landed in the field right next to our house. It went crash. (*Makes sound of the airplane landing.*)

Chris: When?

Bobby: Yesterday.

Chris: I mean what time yesterday?

Bobby: In the afternoon, right after school.

Chris: I didn't see it and I was with you until you had to go home for dinner.

Bobby: Oh yeah. I forgot. That happened at our old house up in Florida.

Excerpt 4

Bobby: My daddy and I went hunting for rattlers once up in Florida at my old house. We didn't want to waste our BB shots, so we took along a lot of big rocks. Boy! We found some big snakes. One was as long as from the top of the piano down to the floor.

Johnny: Whew! That's pretty big.

Bobby: We threw rocks at the rattlers and killed them.

Jeff: I doubt if a BB shot would kill a snake that big anyway.

Bobby: They were extra big BB shots.

Chris: How many rattlers did you get?

Bobby: About 500. (*Everyone impressed by this big number.*)

Bobby: My daddy and I went fishing up at my old house last summer. My daddy is a good fisherman. He has all kinds of medals and prizes for fishing. And this time he caught a huge northern pike. It really made the pole bend. And just as he got it up to the boat, it jumped out of the water and I grabbed it by the tail and pulled it into the boat.

Miss Queen: I'll bet your daddy was glad to have you along to help him land that fish.

Bobby: Yeah. And my daddy got so excited that he fell out of the boat, and I had to pull him in too. And then I had to start the motor and drive the boat back to our house.

Miss Queen: You were a hero, weren't you?

Bobby: (*Brief pause, then sadly.*) My daddy never takes me anywhere.

Miss Queen: And if he would, you'd be a big help to him.
Bobby: Yeah.

Excerpt 5

Bobby: I brought two packages of Chiclets, so everybody can
    have some. (*Bobby's first generous impulse.*)
Miss Queen: Fine! Are there enough pieces for everyone?
Bobby: There are twenty-four.
Miss Queen: Let's count them to be sure. Choose someone to
    help you.
Bobby: OK. I choose Chris.

After the count was made it was revealed that the boxes contained twenty-four pieces of gum and that there were twenty-
four children present. Bobby was delighted. Just then, in walked
Donnie, tardy. Bobby rushed up to him.

Bobby: Go home. Why did you have to come? You just spoiled
    everything. (*Very angry and almost in tears.*)
Miss Queen: You are sorry that Donnie came, but he didn't know
    about the Chiclets.
Bobby: Let's not let him have one because he is late.
Patty: You probably couldn't help it, could you, Donnie?
Donnie: No. The oilman came just when we were ready to leave,
    and Mother had to wait until he filled the tank.
David: That's a good reason.
Bobby: Maybe Betsy can't have the gum because she is allergic
    to chocolate.
Betsy: Gum's not chocolate. I can have gum.
Bobby: Say, I have an idea. It's really fair too. Let's put this gum
    on the shelf until tomorrow and I'll bring another package.
Miss Queen: That's a good idea, Bobby. We can have our gum
    party tomorrow.

In time the frequency of Bobby's fantasies lessened. Miss
Queen did not attempt to point out realities to him but permitted
him to experience his own reality and be influenced by it in his
own way.

Some excerpts from the later part of the school year involving other children follow.

Excerpt 1

Jimmy: My daddy and I went to Canada yesterday. My sisters didn't even get to go. Just us men.

Miss Queen: Just you and your daddy.

Jimmy: My sisters were mad too. Sometimes they get to go and I don't and it makes me mad too.

Miss Queen: You understood how they felt when they couldn't go yesterday.

Jimmy: Yes. We went through a tunnel, and we saw where a bus hit a truck. And then we saw a lot of people. My daddy talked and talked to them, and I got tired and told him to go home, and we did.

Miss Queen: You were tired and were glad to be on your way home again.

Jimmy: Uh-huh. And my mommy was glad to see us too.

Excerpt 2

George: I have two things to tell you today. One will make you sad and one will make you glad. I'll tell the sad one first. When we were on our way home from Florida, there was an accident. My mother got a bloody nose and a cut hand, and my daddy got a scratched finger. And our car was all scratched up. I was scared to death.

Miss Queen: I guess it must have been a terrible accident.

George: Yes. Only I liked one thing. When we were at the hospital waiting for my mom and dad to get fixed up, someone saw us and brought us ice-cream cones. Wasn't that nice of them?

Miss Queen: That was thoughtful of them.

George: Now I'll tell you the glad part. We had to leave our car there, and we got to fly home on a big four-engine plane. The houses and the roads all looked so little. But one time we went up 5,000 feet, and we couldn't see anything on the ground.

Miss Queen: You were glad to have a chance to fly in an airplane.
George: Yes. That was my first time up.

Excerpt 3

Nadine: Bobby is coming to my house for lunch today and we
are going to play all afternoon.
Jenny: Well, I hope you don't act awful, the way you did yesterday when you came to my house. She got into everything
and my mother made her go home.
Nadine: I don't care. I don't like to play with you anyway, and I
hate your mother. (*A pause.*)
Miss Queen: You two girls didn't have much fun yesterday, did
you?
Jenny: No. And she hit me too.
Nadine: She hit me first. Bobby never hits me, so we'll have lots
of fun today, won't we, Bobby?
Bobby: Uh-huh. I'm glad you asked me to come.

Excerpt 4

Nadine: My mother and daddy went to Florida yesterday and I
cried.
Miss Queen: It made you feel sad to have them go away.
Nadine: I told them they had to bring me something if I couldn't
go, and they said they would.
Miss Queen: Does that make you feel happier, to know they
will bring you something?
Nadine: Sure! But I wish I could go too.
Miss Queen: That would be best of all.

Excerpt 5

Nadine: I got mad at my sitter last night because she turned
out the light in my room. Mommy always leaves it on.
Miss Queen: And were you scared to have the light off?
Nadine: Yes.
Katie: Maybe the sitter just doesn't know.
Nadine: My sitter really is awfully nice. She tells me stories, and
last night we popped popcorn.

Miss Queen: She's helping to make you happy, isn't she?

Nadine: Yes. She just loves my kitty too.

Excerpt 6

Phillip: (*A child who rarely talks.*) Gramp brought me a rubber policeman on a motorcycle. I was going to bring it for showing today, but my little brother bit his head off.

Miss Queen: He bit the policeman's head off?

Phillip: Yes. He chewed on it until it came off. It made me mad and I cried.

Miss Queen: You felt very bad that your brother spoiled your new policeman.

Phillip: Yes.

Jimmy: Why don't you bring it anyway? We could just pretend he has a head.

Phillip: OK, I will.

Excerpt 7

Phillip: Here is the policeman I was telling you about.

Katie: What policeman?

Phillip: The one my brother wrecked when he chewed off its head.

Billy: That's a nice toy, Phillip. We can just pretend he had an accident and got his head chopped off.

Phillip: OK. I'll choose you to play with him.

Billy: Why don't you play with me? Let's make a police station with the blocks.

Phillip: OK.

In addition to work with groups, many teachers in the kindergarten have found it quite helpful to select one child for more concentrated work. Usually the child is chosen because he presents a special type of interest or problem to the teacher. He may be withdrawn, fearful, and aloof from other children. He may show considerable resentment toward the teacher and indifference to the program. The child may show hostility toward other children. He may be nervous, hyperactive, and wild. He may refuse to follow directions or participate in the activities. The teacher may select a child with whom he does not have a good relationship or whose mannerisms irritate and annoy him. What-ever the background, the teacher selects the child because he sincerely wants to improve and strengthen his relationship with him.

Most of the teachers who participated in the Merrill-Palmer experiment felt that it was important to begin with one or two or a small group of children first and concentrate on having more

Personal Interaction with a Child. The teacher's presence assists the child in exploring experiences and arriving at strengthening self-perceptions.

effective relations with this group before attempting procedures with the total class. The reports of teachers, though not all of them were successful in work with individual children, showed the values of this approach in helping children to be happier in the kindergarten. Frequently the teachers themselves indicated a change in their own attitudes. A few of these cases are pre-sented in detail to show how the special relationship is developed and the type of experiences which help to bring it about.

JIM AND MISS WARREN

Jim is an attractive, dark-haired boy, five years of age. He is small in stature, but sturdy, alert, and best described as having a little pixy face with shining black eyes that often reveal his emotions.

During the first few days of school Jim presented no real problems, though he would often stand and wring his hands and purse his lips in a nervous sort of way. He was brought to school and called for by his mother and two younger brothers. The younger brothers were about a year-and-a-half and three-and-a-half years of age. His mother left him hesitantly at first, but after being assured that it was best to leave Jim, she went on her way. At this time Jim appeared to be anxious to conform to the necessary rules and regulations in kindergarten, and usually busied himself at the sand table when he was free to decide for himself what he wanted to do. However, when the entire group was called to the piano to sing, participate in rhythms, hear a story, or have discussions, Jim went off to the farthest spot from the gathering place. During the first month of school Miss Warren frequently explained to the other children in the group that Jim did not care to sit with a lot of other children but preferred to be alone. She mentioned that perhaps someday he would want to sit with the group. One day, as Miss Warren read a story, Jim came closer to the group so that he could see the pictures in the book. The other children encouraged him with their approval of this new venture on his part. But this was a temporary move, for the next day Jim was back in his old corner, apart from the group.

By the end of the fifth week of school Jim was interested in the stories but still listened to them from his distant spot. During other activities he was absorbed with his own thoughts. Gradually he began to use kindergarten materials other than the sandbox.

The first important contact between Miss Warren and Jim occurred after he had completed cutting out a large picture of himself. He made it by lying on a large piece of paper and then having Miss Warren draw around him. He colored the clothes in the picture so that they duplicated those he had on, then made a face and colored some hair. Miss Warren hung the picture on a bulletin board with some others. Jim was apparently pleased, and stood looking at the picture as he nervously wrung his hands

Photo by Merrill-Palmer

A Child Works Alone. Bill is conducting an experiment in electricity, while a number of group projects are underway around him. It is important that Bill have resources to explore his interests. At this moment, he is unaware of others, and is engaged in exploring and discovering.

and pursed his lips. Miss Warren said, "Jim, you have done a nice job. Would you like to take it home with you?" In response Jim said, "Yeah, I could tell my mom someone else has come to live with us."

Later that day Jim began hitting the legs of his picture. Since it was on the blackboard, he was hitting his own hand with each blow.

Miss Warren: I see you want to hit your picture, Jim.

Jim: Yes, I wish I could reach the head, but maybe someday I can take my long arm and hit it altogether.

Miss Warren: I see you feel like hitting, but doesn't that hurt your hand?

Jim: No, it only hurts the legs. (*Laughs and skips over to the sandbox.*)

The next contact came when some of the children in the group had built a large aircraft carrier with blocks. The ship had guns, lifeboats, and a landing deck for planes. Jim contributed ideas to the building of the ship, but when it was completed, and everyone went aboard, he said he would be the enemy. His was an enemy aircraft, and Jim took great delight in having various members of the group drop as he "killed" them. When one child did not drop to the floor after Jim had supposedly killed him, Jim picked up a large square block and intended to throw it at him. Just as he raised his hand to throw the block, Miss Warren picked him up, looked at him directly, and said, "At school I can't let you throw the blocks at anyone. I know that you want to throw the blocks, Jim, but I can't let you do it."

Standing rigidly, every muscle in his body tense, Jim yelled, "It isn't a block, it's a bomb." Then he kicked at Miss Warren and ran off, screaming, "I hate all those dumb kids, they're just dumb. I hate you too, and I hate this sappy school." Jim threw himself on the floor, cried hard for a long time, but said no more. Miss Warren went over to him and drew up a chair, saying, "Jim, would you like to come up here and sit on my lap?" Jim did this reluctantly, saying nothing. After a while he got up and went off to play quietly alone.

The next contact was three days later, when Jim's mother arrived at school at noon to take him home. His mother continued to do this after Jim had been in school for five months. Twice each day she bundled up the two younger children to take Jim to school and take him home, explaining that he was not responsible enough to walk the four blocks alone. As the mother appeared in the coatroom on this day, Jim, who had been minding his own business, spied his three-and-a-half-year-old brother, walked over to him, sprang on him, and gave him a poke. After the mother had separated the two brothers, Miss Warren asked her if that was a common occurrence. She said that it was, and added that Jim was always tired when school was out. She said that all the children took naps, though, because the father did not get home from work until ten o'clock at night, and the children stayed up until he arrived. Recently Jim had not been taking naps, and he was usually awake at six each morning. She ended the conversation by saying that schedules were not the only thing that Jim upset at their house. He was always in trouble.

The next meeting with the mother was initiated by her. She wanted to know why Jim never brought home any of the things he made at school. Miss Warren explained that none of the children were compelled to make things at school, and that Jim always made good use of his time in other ways. Miss Warren said that she was encouraged by Jim's progress. He was more aware of other children in the group.

Three days later Jim's mother brought him to school and stayed for thirty-five minutes. Jim remained in the coatroom the entire time his mother was at school. She watched while Miss Warren gave some group directions for making crepe-paper jack-o'-lanterns, but among those who chose not to make one was Jim. Instead, he made a map, showing exactly how to get to his house. When he finished, he said, "Here. This is for you to keep, so you can come to my house." His mother left the kindergarten room irritated by Jim's behavior. She said that his father really had control over the children, and she would have him speak to Jim about doing what he was supposed to do at school. Miss Warren indicated that she understood how Jim's behavior could be annoying, but repeated that she was satisfied with the progress he was making. Miss Warren said that it did not really matter whether Jim made the jack-o'-lantern or not; that the important thing was for him to do what was satisfying to him. When Jim's mother expressed fear that Jim would fail if he did not do the work, Miss Warren assured her that Jim was a capable, intelligent child, and added that the most important thing was for Jim to find school a happy experience where he could be himself. Jim's mother left with a more accepting attitude toward Jim's school behavior.

A few days later the kindergarten group made applesauce and invited another group in the school to come for midmorning dessert. One child suggested making place mats, and another suggested singing a song for them.

Jim: Since we are having a party, we really should have a game.
Miss Warren: Good idea, Jim. Could you think of a game?
Jim: Yes, I will make a game for these kids.

The finished product was a piece of paper with two slits in it, called the tunnel. Then trees, bridges, and houses were colored on the paper, with a railroad track which went in and out of the tunnel. A small train was made to fit the track. Each child was to have a turn taking the train in and out of the tunnel. The game was put on a table for the children to use after they had finished eating their crackers and applesauce. Jim was glad to explain how the game was to be played.

The children were delighted with the game. They all enjoyed it, and Jim had his first successful social experience.

The following day Jim played with another child during play period. He approached Miss Warren.

Jim: I want a big piece of paper so that I can paint a picture about that turkey story. Adele is going to help me, 'cause she knows how to make good turkeys.
Miss Warren: Fine, Jim, I'm glad you want Adele to help you.

Jim made a picture of the people who could come to his house for dinner on Thanksgiving Day. Then he invited Adele to sit at one end of the table and Miss Warren at the other. Both of these guests were served white meat. Several other children were asked to join the group, and Jim served each person his choice.

At this point it seemed that Jim was happier with other children in the group. It was a regular thing for him to join the others for games, stories, or group-play projects, although at discussion time he still went off by himself. The hand-wringing appeared less frequently, as did his preoccupied look, but he still had several nervous gestures. His mother had told Miss Warren that he was punished at home when he wrung his hands, shrugged his shoulders, or sat and daydreamed. She indicated that these nervous patterns had decreased considerably, and she thought punishment helped. Miss Warren, however, wondered whether Jim's greater acceptance of himself in his relationships with other children had not been a factor in the change.

With the onset of winter weather, Jim started wearing more cumbersome outdoor wraps to school. He could put on his own snowsuit and galoshes, but each day when the group went outdoors, Jim had excuses for staying inside. Even when he had help, he managed to be the last one out. He explained this by saying, "I like it outdoors with our kids, but those others get in my way." Here he had reference to children in other grades in the school, who used the playground at the same time. At these times Miss Warren encouraged Jim to play with the others.

Miss Warren: You like to be outdoors with your friends that you know in our room. I see Adele and Billy over there on the slide all by themselves.
Jim: I can play with them. (*Off he goes.*)

The day of the Christmas party the mothers came to have Christmas cookies that the children had baked and decorated at school. Jim's mother and two brothers came, and Jim did a good job of taking care of them. He showed them where to put their coats and where to sit, and then showed them some things of interest to him in the room, such as narcissus bulbs, a map showing where the children in the group lived, and the children's work. This behavior was in complete contrast to his earlier hostile attitude when his family came to school. Jim joined other children for songs and helped serve refreshments. It was his most socially effective behavior in the presence of adults. His mother was proud of him.

At the end of the year Jim still needed approval and reassurance, but he had grown considerably. Miss Warren worked toward getting some special privileges for Jim at home, so that he would not have to conform to all the limitations put upon the younger children. When Miss Warren's relationship with Jim's mother became more secure, she was able to convince her that Jim's age entitled him to a different kind of status in the home.

Miss Warren was pleased one day when Jim's mother approached her and remarked, "We never did things like this when I was in school. I really didn't know how to prepare Jim for school, because I didn't know what they did in kindergarten. I guess, after all, if he's happy in school, that's what really counts."

Discussion

What were some of the factors that improved the relationship with Jim? What aspects of the relationship helped Jim to a more positive experience in kindergarten?

Jim's mother was unable to free Jim to grow in his own way. She refused to permit him to make choices because she was afraid he could not act in a responsible way and thus increased his feelings of dependency and inadequacy. Jim found it necessary to overconform to rules and regulations at home to please his mother. His hostile feelings, however, accumulated inside and began to spill out in destructive behavior. His growing feelings of anxiety were expressed outwardly in the frequent wringing of his hands and pursing of his lips. At school he withdrew from activities and other children. Because he had to fit into a tight schedule at home, it was frightening for him to have freedom in school. Fortunately, Miss Warren understood Jim's anxiety and was patient and understanding when he was unable to make choices. She accepted his decision not to participate in group activities until he was ready. Jim could move in and out of group functions at will. He could decide for himself when he wanted to make greater use of kindergarten materials and resources. He could complete activities or not, as he wished. Again and again Miss Warren attempted to show Jim she was interested mainly in his happiness and the type of activity which Jim himself found personally satisfying. Miss Warren was interested in Jim's growth, but she realized that only Jim could choose to pursue his own real interests and wishes.

Miss Warren responded to Jim individually whenever possible and attempted to help him feel important and worth while. She let him know frequently that his presence was recognized and felt. She encouraged Jim to express his ideas and indicated to him that his suggestions were always important. She encouraged Jim's interaction with other children when he wanted to play and made suggestions that would help him move comfortably in group relations. Miss Warren accepted Jim's aggression when it occurred and permitted him to express hostile feelings toward her, other children, and the school. She indicated to Jim that he had a right to feel as he did. Jim could express his feelings in destructive behavior as long as health and safety rules were maintained and important school property was not destroyed.

Miss Warren worked toward a positive relationship with Jim's mother too, in spite of their different points of view. She accepted the mother's ideas and attitudes, while at the same time trying to show that school philosophy and practice had changed. She helped the mother to understand that Jim's happiness and security at school were important and would have a strong influence on his school achievement. Miss Warren gradually gained the mother's aid in helping Jim to have a more rewarding experience at school. His personal security increased, and his relationships with other children and his teacher were enriched.

Chris and Miss Thomas

Chris is five years old. In some situations he is extremely aggressive. At other times he appears shy, self-conscious, and anxious. During the month of September and the first part of October Chris had little to do with Miss Thomas and ignored her friendly overtures. Often he would turn and walk off when she approached him. He seldom offered to participate during telling or showing time. But when he did participate, he giggled nervously, covered his face with his hands, and told of incidents which he hoped might shock the group. The children did not listen attentively when Chris was the speaker. They were bored and disgusted with his performance.

During choosing time Chris displayed a disorganized kind of

behavior. If he chose clay, before long it was in his or some other child's hair. If he chose crayons, they were soon in his nose or ears. If he chose blocks, he enjoyed crashing them into another child's building. This behavior was accompanied by a silly, nervous giggle. Finally all the other children rejected him.

Neighbors of Chris's family came to school as a group one day and commiserated with Miss Thomas when they discovered Chris was in her room. Chris was one of the "bad boys" on the street. Miss Thomas was shocked at the strong, bitter feelings the neighbors expressed. They outlined a long list of misdemeanors and said they hoped she would keep Chris away from their children at school. Feelings of sympathy for Chris arose in her when she realized that, in a sense, she too had rejected him. Her relationship with him could stand improvement, she thought, so she set to work. The following excerpts emphasize the changing nature of Miss Thomas' relationship with Chris and her efforts to help him to be happy at school.

Excerpt 1 (*Time: Before School.*)

Chris was the first child to arrive at school. A big boy accompanied him to the door, looked in, and quickly walked on when he noticed that a teacher was in the room.

Miss Thomas: Was that one of your brothers, Chris?
Chris: Yep. (*Walking on into the coatroom.*)
Miss Thomas: What is his name?
Chris: I don't remember. (*Silly giggle, self-conscious.*)
Miss Thomas: Now you are teasing me. (*Laughs too.*) You don't want to tell me his name?
Chris: Nope. (*Walks off toward the blocks.*)
Miss Thomas: All right. He looks like a nice boy. Next time he comes to school with you, would you like to invite him to come in to see our room?
Chris: Nope. (*And then, with much feeling, and also the self-conscious giggle.*) God, no! (*Playing with the trucks.*)
Miss Thomas: You don't want him to see our room?
Chris: Nope. *Period!* (*Runs over to greet Bobby, who has just arrived. Bobby turns away from him.*)

Miss Thomas: Bobby, maybe you and Chris could help me tack these pictures on the bulletin board. (*Both children agree simultaneously and chat as they work.*)

Excerpt 2 (*Time: Next Day.*)

The class walked to the gym for music assembly. Chris was the leader, walking beside Miss Thomas. Suddenly he darted behind her, holding on to her skirt and giggling furiously. Five upper-grade children, including Chris's brother, walked past. The latter just shook his head and grinned, then walked on.

Miss Thomas: You are hiding from someone, is that it, Chris?
Chris: Sort of.
Miss Thomas: You don't want someone to see you?
Chris: Nope. My brother.
Miss Thomas: You don't want him to see you walking with your friends.
Chris: Uh-huh. He always laughs at me.
Miss Thomas: Well, I don't think he saw you this time. Shall we go on to the gym?
Chris: Uh-huh.

Excerpt 3 (*Choosing Time.*)

Chris was playing with a little racer and crashed it into the wall. It broke into four pieces. Children came running to report that Chris had broken another car. Chris had a self-conscious giggle and grin, but Miss Thomas knew that he was frightened.

Miss Thomas: Come over here and tell me about it, Chris.
Chris: (*Cockily.*) I just wanted to break it. That's all.
Miss Thomas: You just like to break our cars and trucks.
Chris: Yes. It's fun to make them go crash, bang, crash.
Miss Thomas: You like to make lots of noise and smash things.
Chris: Sometimes. (*Starts to walk off.*)
Miss Thomas: (*Walking along with him.*) Chris, I can't let you break our toys. I've told you that before. The cars don't belong to you. They belong to our school. No one may crash them into the walls and break them. I know how you feel, but I can't let you break our trucks.
Chris: OK, OK. (*Sullen.*)

Excerpt 4 (Next Week—Choosing Time.)

The following week Miss Thomas put Chris in charge of the trucks and blocks, "since he was so interested in them." The crashing of trucks stopped, but his hostility began to come out in other ways. During choosing time he usually played with trucks and blocks. He built very complicated structures, usually by himself. He was hostile if anyone came near "his" blocks. One day he threw a block at Randy, who came too close to his building. Fortunately his aim was bad. Miss Thomas approached Chris.

Miss Thomas: You don't want other children to touch your building, Chris.

Chris: No. It's all mine. They will wreck it.

Miss Thomas: I think Randy likes your building. Would you like to show it to him?

Chris: No. He's just in the way.

Miss Thomas: OK. I understand how you feel.

Chris: Well, maybe he can watch. Would you like to, Randy? (*In a short while the children were playing together.*)

Excerpt 5 (Time: Same Week.)

About this time the class began to have an epidemic of what Chris termed "dirty words." Chris was the instigator. For two weeks he injected his vocabulary into everything the group did. A few children admired him for his boldness and enlarged their own vocabularies too. Many rejected both him and his language. Others were completely astonished. Up to this point Chris had not been an active participant in music activities. During this horrible two weeks he sat and whispered dirty words to those within hearing distance. The songs were interrupted by a fit of giggles from his admirers and shouts of disgust from others.

Miss Thomas recognized Chris's new behavior as another outburst of hostility and anxiety. Although she was ready to give up at times, she accepted this behavior, wondering if it would ever cease. The epidemic finally blew over with the approach of Halloween.

Excerpt 6 (Time: Just before Halloween—after School.)

One day after school some fourth-grade children came to the room to report that Chris was walking on top of the principal's car. Miss Thomas was ready to leave, so she went outdoors to investigate. Chris, a smaller boy, and a dog were sitting inside the car.

Miss Thomas: Hi, Chris! Is that your mother's red car?
Chris: Yep.
Miss Thomas: It looks a lot like Mr. Bond's.
Chris: Yes. Some boys said they would report me for being in
    Mr. Bond's car. They wouldn't believe me when I said it
    was mine.
Miss Thomas: They just didn't know. (*The smaller boy climbs
    out and walks around on the hood of the car.*)
Miss Thomas: Is this your little brother?
Chris: Yeah. That's Andy. He always does bad things. He always
    copies me.
Miss Thomas: You both like to do bad things, huh?
Chris: Sure! So what, if we scratch it! We'll just get another car.
    (*The dog jumps out of the car window and runs across the
    field chasing some other dogs.*)
Chris: Oh! (*Slapping the seat of the car in nervous excitement.*)
    He's a stinky old dog. Who cares if he gets lost and never
    comes home?
Miss Thomas: You don't like your dog.
Chris: Oh, he's all right. But he always does bad things. I can't
    go after him. I have to stay with Andy.
Miss Thomas: I'll watch Andy if you want to get your dog.
Chris: Would you? OK. (*Chris runs after the dog.*)

Excerpt 7 (Time: Next Day—Before School.)

The class was collecting orange crates to build a car sales and gasoline station. Chris and Bobby came in with two big crates; they were out of wind but beaming. Miss Thomas had encouraged at every opportunity this friendship between Chris and Bobby.

Chris: Here, Miss Thomas, I brought two of them. Boy! Are they ever heavy!

Miss Thomas: Wonderful! Did you and Bobby carry them all alone?

Chris: No. My brother helped us. He's the boy you saw looking in our room. Mom drove us to school so we wouldn't have to carry them so far. My brother says our room is neat. Can he come in after school and see our stuff?

Miss Thomas: Sure he can. It's always nice to have visitors. It was nice of your brother to help you.

Chris: Yeah. I've got two other brothers too. Andy is the cutest one. You saw him yesterday. Remember?

Miss Thomas. Of course I remember.

Chris: Everybody thinks he's best.

Miss Thomas: Is Andy your favorite too, Chris?

Chris: Well, he's awfully little and cute, but he fights with me a lot. He's mad when I go to school. (*With a chuckle.*) He takes my toys and breaks them when I'm not home.

Miss Thomas: You don't like to have your toys broken, do you, Chris?

Chris: No. He breaks my toys at home, so I used to break these at school.

Miss Thomas: I see. (*A long pause.*) We have almost enough crates now. Since it was your idea, would you like to be in charge of the building?

Chris: Sure! (*Beaming.*)

Excerpt 8 (Next Day—Choosing Time.)

Chris: Say, Miss Thomas, this car is neat. See? This is where the people walk in. And here is where the door rolls up and down to let the trucks and cars go in. And see over here. Here's where we keep the stuff. All the cars are parked in a row. Nobody can walk on them here. We protect them.

Miss Thomas: You like to keep our trucks and cars from being broken, don't you?

Chris: Yeah. Some of the kids aren't very careful. They bash them into things.

Excerpt 9 (Several Days Later—Choosing Time.)

Chris: Miss Thomas, Miss Thomas. Come and see our big bed. Me and Randy made it. He's a good builder. But nobody else can touch it except you and him. See! We can get into it.

Miss Thomas: You and Randy are having lots of fun building together. (*Chris's friendship with other children has grown steadily.*)

Excerpt 10 (Time: Following Monday—before School.)

A picture of Chris's family appeared on the first page of the society section of the local paper. Andy's picture, larger than the others, was featured in a prominent spot.

Miss Thomas: That's a good picture of you, Chris.

Chris: Yeah. But did you see Andy's? The man who took the picture thought he was the best.

Miss Thomas: He liked him better than you and your older brothers?

Chris: Yes. His is the biggest. But he is awfully cute.

Miss Thomas: You like him too, don't you, Chris?

Chris: Yeah. He's a neat little guy. I don't get so mad at him any more.

Miss Thomas: Sometimes little boys don't know any better.

Chris: No. Sometimes little boys don't know any better.

Excerpt 11 (Time: Halloween Party.)

The children were telling stories. The shades were down. The only light was from the big jack-o'-lantern. Until this time Chris had been self-conscious and nervous at telling time. He usually put his hands on his head or over his face, wriggled, and looked thoroughly miserable. His "news" was nearly always accompanied by a silly giggle, although he no longer chose subject matter that would shock his audience. The result was that the children couldn't hear him and didn't listen to him with much interest.

In the darkened room, however, he felt more comfortable and offered to tell a story. He was much more poised than usual. He did slip on and off a chair, over and over, while he was talking, but the group could hear every word. The story was about a number of witches who repeatedly came to his house on Halloween night and finally killed everyone but Andy and Chris. He convinced the witches that Andy was "the cutest one, and such a little boy." The witches were all his friends. The children accepted Chris's story with much hilarity. And Chris was so delighted that he might still be adding to the story if the children had let him.

Miss Thomas: You are a fine storyteller, Chris.
Chris: Yeah. That was fun.

.   .   .

Chris: (*The following week.*) Miss Thomas, you know that Halloween story I told. Well, that was the first time I ever told a story. I didn't know I could do it so good.
Miss Thomas: Maybe you can tell us another story soon.
Chris: Well, maybe. But I'll do it at resttime, when our shades are down. I can think better when it's dark.

Excerpt 12 (Just before Thanksgiving—Choosing Time.)

Chris: Miss Thomas, see our big bed. Eight of us can sleep in it all at once. Watch me count the kids. Now lie still, all of you. One, two, three, four, five, six, seven, eight, nine, ten. We're having fun!
Miss Thomas: Ten boys all having fun playing together. How nice!

Excerpt 13 (Time: Next Day—Choosing Time.)

Chris: Miss Thomas, did you know that I can sing "There's a Big Fat Turkey Out at Grandpa's Farm" all by myself?
Miss Thomas: We'd like to hear you. Good for you! (*Chris is nervous but gets through it.*)

Discussion

Miss Thomas' attempts to help Chris have a happier, more effective kindergarten experience were initially motivated by her troubled feeling that Chris was a disturbed little boy who was rejected by most people, including herself. She began by accepting Chris' rejection of her. She observed that the more other children rejected Chris, the more hostile and destructive he became, until there was a constant feeling of antagonism toward him in the group. Miss Thomas was aware, too, that the development of her own relationship with Chris was not satisfactory. She tended in the beginning to react as the children did. It was only after some adults in the neighborhood came to school to malign Chris that Miss Thomas realized that he was a child in constant trouble in all his relationships. Only then did Miss Thomas "go to work" to establish a good relationship with Chris. She learned to respect his judgment and regarded him highly. She showed a keen interest in him and his family. She encouraged a positive relationship between Chris and other children at every opportunity and let other children know that he was an important person to her. She helped Chris express his hostile, frightened feelings openly and directly rather than through destruction of toys and other children's work. She listened and accepted his feelings, and when necessary explained the limitations of the school setting. Miss Thomas accepted the epidemic of bad language instigated by Chris, though it was not easy for her to do so. However, this seemed to be a turning point in her relationship with him. The epidemic blew over, and for the first time Chris showed positive feelings toward Miss Thomas and a friendly attitude toward other children. He even expressed concern at times that some children did not treat school materials and equipment with care. He gained insight into his own behavior in concrete situations, e.g., he explained that he broke playthings at school because his younger brother destroyed his toys at home. Miss Thomas' positive relationship with Chris continued to grow. Chris established friendships with several children and participated in school activities with a greater feeling of self-confidence.

By focusing on one individual child, attempting to understand the child, helping the child feel more comfortable and more acceptable, these teachers modified their own attitudes and brought about a happier, more effective personal relationship. Once these teachers had experienced a significant relationship with one child, they were able to see possibilities not only for helping other individual children but also for working with groups. They explored ways of assisting all children to express their feelings, so that their first major contact with school would be honest and worthwhile. Each teacher worked out her own approaches and endeavored in her own way to improve and promote genuine, intimate relationships with the children in her classroom. Each teacher moved toward increasing authenticity, sensitivity and awareness in her relationships with children.

CHAPTER 5

Mental Health Approaches
in the Early Elementary Grades

The various mental health approaches described in this chapter are not presented as prescriptions for teachers to follow. They are suggestive of ways teachers have discovered for themselves as effective in helping children openly to express and explore feelings in the early elementary grades. The reports which follow are taken from exploratory materials gathered by twenty-eight teachers in four different school systems. While emphasizing mental health approaches, these teachers maintained an objective attitude, neither criticizing nor praising, but attempting to relate with children honestly and authentically and to convey acceptance and respect for the child's own perception of his experience. An atmosphere of warmth and trust was created where children were free to be themselves and where teachers could meet children on a deep and meaningful basis.

Mrs. Stanley and Her Second-Graders [*]

Children are often reprimanded for, or forced to inhibit, an expression of their real feelings. If they express such negative

[*] This section is a revision of the author's paper (with Nancy Strohm), Free Emotional Expression in the Classroom. *Progr. Educ.*, 1953, 30, 118–122. The sections appearing in the original paper are reprinted here by permission of the editor, Lawrence E. Metcalf.

emotions as anger, hostility, hatred, and envy, they are usually not accepted. If, on the other hand, these emotions are turned inward and do not find some outlet, they are likely to grow until the child is so involved in them that he is unable to think or act free from their influence.

Perhaps one of the most valuable experiences the school can provide for many children is that of opening to them an acceptable, yet effective, means of expressing their feelings. In an attempt to do this, a second-grade teacher in a public school undertook the following experiment.

Introducing Children to Their Feelings

In order to introduce the experiment, the children were offered an opportunity to discuss some of their more common feelings. As they talked, a number of children mentioned that they had seen anger in others and were sometimes angry themselves. They agreed that it was best not to get angry, but that at times it was nearly impossible not to do so. Many children thought that getting angry was not wrong, but that some ways of expressing anger were undesirable. In talking about constructive ways of expressing angry feelings, they mentioned stamping their feet, walking away from the person or thing, striking an inanimate object, and yelling. The teacher suggested that feelings can sometimes be explored by talking to an understanding person or in drawing and playing. In time other feelings were discussed by the group, but anger was the most pervasive attitude expressed and received the most attention.

How the Experiment Was Conducted

The experiment was carried on with a class of twenty-nine second-graders, largely from the lower socioeconomic group. The class had about an equal number of Negro and white children, but there were twenty boys and only nine girls. Most of the children were of about average intelligence, but there were more slow than rapid learners.

Five procedures were used, four definitely structured, in which the children were asked about particular attitudes or thoughts, and one clearly unstructured, in which the children were free to do as they wished. The time allotted to these procedures varied. Some were completed in two forty-minute sessions in a week, others were carried on for longer periods. The first, second, fourth, and fifth periods were structured, the third and several others were not. Directions were given during the structured sessions and all the children did the same thing. During the non-structured sessions the children were told they were free to use any materials in the room and to do as they pleased, as long as they were fairly quiet and did not bother one another or children in other classrooms. They were usually free to talk to the teacher or tell about the pictures they had made. Only the stories concerning the pictures were recorded during these periods.

The teacher showed interest in, and complete acceptance of, what the children were doing and saying, and expressed neither praise nor condemnation of the children's attitudes. The opportunities to teach ideas or facts during these periods were by-passed in an attempt to keep the time free for the expression and exploration of feelings.

The Wish

In introducing this procedure the teacher gave the following instructions: "Close your eyes and listen. There is a fairy on your shoulder. She is whispering to you and this is what she is saying: If you could do anything or be anyone you wanted to be, what would you wish? Don't tell anyone, and when you finish, I'll be back and you can tell me. We must work quietly so that we will have time to finish by the time the fairy comes back."

The children were enthusiastic and set to work on their drawings. Children who drew quickly and finished early were told they could turn their papers over and draw anything they wished on the other side or use the library or other materials in the room quietly. The same procedure was followed in subsequent experiments for those who finished quickly. When the drawings were completed, the children gathered around the teacher's desk and were told the fairy was inside a tape recorder waiting to hear their wishes.

The attitudes expressed by the children in drawing and describing their pictures fell into three categories: of the twenty-two children participating, five expressed a desire for some material object, money, puppets, boats, a vehicle, or a dog; four wished to go somewhere, to a farm, to Texas, to New York, or to a show; three wanted to be someone else, a millionaire, a cowboy, or a nurse. Of the ten who did not draw a wish, five just drew and described a picture, two others drew about school, and three drew pictures of war and fighting.

The Picture Story

In this procedure the children were told they could draw about anything they wished, and when all had finished, they could take turns showing their pictures and telling a story about them. A tape recorder was used to record their stories.

Twenty-two children participated. Five boys who made and cut out houses each described his house as that of "The Three Bears," but their stories differed, ranging from a simple statement that the house belonged to the three bears to a long, involved story of fighting and fantasy. The stories of six children dealt with Indians, monkeys, a junkman, a boy, and people in the jungle. Others told about themselves or their families. Two carried over the idea of a wish, two did not care to tell a story about their pictures, and one modeled money in clay.

The "Free-play" Sessions

For several periods the children were told they could make whatever they desired and could go to the teacher to talk about it if they wished. The materials available included paste, scissors, paints, paper, clay, chalk, and a doll corner. As children expressed themselves through these activities, recordings were made by the teacher. Some children made frequent use of these periods to draw and describe their pictures, some drew and told long stories, but others, not wishing to participate, drew or played alone or in small groups. Their feelings could not, of course, be recorded, since they did not offer to talk about them.

Feelings about School

In these sessions some children requested more definite directions than "drawing their feelings about school," so the teacher suggested that they draw what they would do if they came to school one day and found only children, no teachers, principal, maintenance people, or any adults. Of the twenty-three children who drew pictures, eleven drew school activities, drawing, reading, having a puppet show, and playing. Two drew but did not know what they would do. One child did not want to tell about her picture. Several children drew pictures portraying family difficulties, and the rest talked about going on trips, a bomb, a big man fighting, and jumping and climbing.

Being Bad

During a reading period a story was read about a boy who did something bad. In the discussion that followed the children suggested things they thought were bad, and some described things they had done that they or others considered bad. The teacher suggested that each child think of something bad he had done. When several children complained that they could think of nothing, the teacher modified her instructions and suggested that they draw something for which they had been punished. The group was cautioned not to tell anyone about the pictures. Later they were told they could take turns showing them and choosing people to guess what they had drawn.

Most of the twenty-two children drew something they had done for which they had been reprimanded: breaking, losing, taking, spilling things, and doing things they were asked not to do. Five continued to tell fanciful stories of fighting and adventure, one girl continued to refuse to tell about her pictures, and one related how badly he felt when he saw a turtle killed. Many seemed freer in expressing themselves by the time they drew their last picture. Only one child refused to say anything at all, though she had drawn a picture for each session.

How Three Children Responded

Three selected cases are presented to illustrate individual responses to the experiment.

JAKE

Jake is a repeater in the second grade. He is capable of good behavior but has been inattentive in school and aggressive toward other children in the class. He has continually bothered other children and struck out at them on the slightest provocation. Jake even fights with larger boys and seldom complains when hurt.

When Jake first joined the class, most of the children refused to play with him and several girls often teased him. Jake was greatly angered and much strife resulted. He admitted having a bad temper but protested that he could do nothing about it. He reacted seriously and belligerently to teasing and slight affronts, fancied or real, and usually retaliated promptly.

In the early stages of the experiment Jake was very dilatory about drawing and habitually made a line or two on a sheet of paper and then discarded it, using five or six sheets of paper at each session without completing anything. Finally the teacher set a limit for him, telling him that he could have no more paper until he finished his drawing. This proved effective, for Jake not only finished the drawing but found that he could express and explore feelings on relatively few sheets of paper.

Jake's first picture required that he draw a wish. He drew quickly and even more quickly destroyed what he had made. He began a second picture but destroyed this too. When he discovered that he could tell the story of his wish over a tape recorder, he ran back to his table, found someone else's picture, and awaited his turn anxiously. The picture showed a boat with three figures in it, shooting at a plane. In describing the picture Jake used the names of three of the boys in the class, with only one of whom he seemed to be at all friendly. The description: "Here is G and here is old R. He said that he is trying to shoot G's plane down, and old M, he's trying to shoot at the plane too."

In his second drawing, allowing him to make anything he wished, Jake started scribbling and stuffing paper into the wastebasket. The teacher at this time limited the amount of paper he could use, and Jake then, surprisingly, drew very carefully. When his turn came to talk about his drawing, he displayed a profile of a man's head and shoulders and said, "This is the junkman and this is a wagon. He is going to get the garbage pail and empty it."

Jake did not attempt to draw during the next session. Then he missed a few days of school, during which the class discussed anger, self-control, and possible means of expressing anger without harming oneself or others. Jake was mentioned by a number of children and they attempted to understand the motives for his behavior. The class put paper in a special place, to be used when any of them felt angry and wished to work through their anger by scribbling, tearing, cutting, drawing, or in some other way that required the use of paper. Jake often used this paper after his return, even when not noticeably angry. He began to control himself and his temper better and reacted to teasing more with humor than venom. Certainly the group's understanding of Jake from his own point of view and acceptance of him contributed to the modification of his behavior.

Jake's final picture was again the head and shoulders of a man, but he was facing full front this time. At one side was a small record player. He said, "That's me in a restaurant, and I put a nickel in to play music and be happy. That's me right there." So Jake, who had never identified himself with his drawings, was finally free enough to point with pride and assurance to his picture and say, "That's me right there."

GEORGE

George is a quiet, shy, rather passive boy. Children report that on the playground he is more aggressive, especially when there are no teachers around. His attention span is short compared to that of the average second-grader. George is accepted by the other boys and girls and is regularly chosen in games and other class activities.

George was not present during the first experimental sessions. His first picture, in which he could draw anything he wished, represented two figures, a large one dressed in a boy scout uniform and a much smaller one colored in solid black, with a green triangle between the two. In telling about them he said, "This is a picture of a boy scout, and here is a man, and there is where they sleep in the house."

Several weeks later George drew a picture of a large red house with a green background, an apple tree, two small figures on swings, and two larger figures on the roof of the house. His description: "Here is an apple tree and a swing. The mother and father are coming. The children are frightened."

In his picture of what he would do if there were no adults in school, George drew four large red chairs with a small brown figure sitting in each chair, each figure holding what seemed to be a yellow-and-black-striped book. After two children had guessed what they thought the picture was, George said, "I don't know myself."

George's final picture, on "being bad," was more carefully drawn and more detailed. Across the top was written "The Office and Books." At the bottom he made an orange desk with books on top, an orange figure with a book in his hand, and a red shelf with books on it. After two children had guessed about the picture, George smiled and said, "I'm stealing a book from the library." He seemed pleased that he could say this to the group.

Though apparently of minor importance, this incident takes on significance in that George revealed a troubled attitude, which he explored further in talks with the teacher. These talks seemed to enable him to be more himself, more outgoing, and more expressive in the classroom.

JANICE

Janice is an attractive little girl with much imagination and vitality. She especially enjoys dancing, singing, talking, and reading before the class. The boys in the class often complain to the teacher that Janice deliberately pulls up her dress in front of them. The teacher told Janice of their complaints and explained why it would be better not to do this in class.

Janice's pictures showed how she turned to drawing to express some of these feelings about herself. In the drawing representing whatever she wanted to show, she made a small booklet in which three pages were covered with indecipherable printing, which she did not talk about, and three pages showed first a boy and his mother, then a boy on the floor with his mother above him, and finally a boy riding an animal. Janice described it: "This is a book I made. The mother called the little boy, and he didn't come, so he got spanked. Here he is on the floor crying. Then this is the next day and he is riding his pony."

For Janice drawing seems to be a valuable experience at which she spends much time both at home and at school. She often brings to school, and describes to the teacher, pictures she has drawn at home the previous evening. When the opportunity to draw and talk about anything she wished was presented, Janice produced at least eight pictures each time. The common theme was love and robbery. One of these drawings portrayed scenes of young love, with considerable detail of figures embracing in a background of elaborate furnishings. Her story began: "A man and lady went hunting and caught a fox, and now they are going to eat pancakes. The love heart on the wall means they will get engaged. There are two snowmen in the cupboard and a coffee pot still on the stove. There is the bathroom. Whenever they go in, no one can see them. There is the moon, it's nighttime. The woman has dropped her gun on the floor."

For another drawing Janice told this story: "This is a cowboy and a cattle rustler. He beat the cowboy to the cattle and stole them. This is the sheriff's house. He forgot they were coming to steal the cattle. He is in town talking to the deputy. The cattle rustler comes to steal some money."

Shortly after this session Janice brought the teacher a picture in which appeared three figures, two girls and a boy. One girl was standing, one sitting. The boy was juggling green balls and apparently urinating. Janice told her story excitedly: "I'm taking my clothes out of my drawer and throwing them into a pile because Mother is washing them. My brother is sitting under a hole, dripping, and he is juggling. Susan (*A sister*) is playing in the electric chair. She thinks she can kill me. She thinks it's a real chair, but it's only a play one. We are playing. My brother is dancing because he has a girl's dress on."

Several days later Janice made two large pictures, one showing a boy and girl on swings, done partly with chalk and partly
with crayons, the other, done entirely with crayons, showing
three buildings, two figures, and a horse. Janice told this story:
" 'The Texas Ranger' is the name. A boy and girl lived together.
They were swinging one day. The mother is calling them because they are going to move into the West where the cowboys
are. Now me and R. C. are there. Then the day after that they
get married. I'm at the drugstore, and while I'm at the drugstore
a bad man creeps up on the sheriff and shoots him. I'm buying
bullets and a cowboy suit, because when I came to town we
didn't have anything to wear, just my pants. But the whole town
was empty. They were all sleeping. At the same time the candy
store got robbed. We decided, since there were so many hold-
ups, that we would go back to the city. It's more comfortable
there. We went back wearing our cowboy suits."

To illustrate what she would do if there were no adults in
school, Janice made a girl in red slacks, walking toward a desk,
a door, and a cupboard. On the other side of her picture Janice
drew a figure going through a brown door. Across the top was
printed "I'd come in the room and play games."

Janice's picture of bad behavior showed an Indian tent in a
cornfield, with table and chairs, a rabbit on one side and a girl
on the other. She told this story: "One day I was playing in a
cornfield, and my brother put a girl's dress on and a ribbon in
his hair. And a rabbit came into the field and ate an ear of corn,
and I took an ear of corn and threw it at an Indian's head. And
I thought my grandpa wouldn't know because he was inside the
tent. And I ate an ear of corn and my grandpa spanked me on
the b-u-t."

Janice no longer pulls up her dress in class, nor does she
arouse disturbed feelings in the group. Apparently she expresses
these feelings in her drawings and has thereby gained greater
understanding and acceptance of them.

Summary

Of the twenty-six children who participated, fourteen seemed
to follow a definite pattern throughout the experiment. For ex-

ample, three boys who began by drawing and talking of war and fighting carried the same theme through to the last picture. Seven children who said little at first were quite vocal by the last drawing and often revealed certain feelings and attitudes more clearly. Five children, three of whom seemed quite happy and well adjusted, drew and described their pictures, then sat down without expressing much feeling. Those who were most aggressive and unsettled in the classroom usually reflected these qualities in their pictures and stories.

Since many of these children are aggressive and unsettled, perhaps one of the greatest values of this activity is to provide an acceptable outlet for expressing their hostile feelings. The children are beginning to understand that it often helps to express these feelings, and that by expressing them in imagination and fantasy, and talking about them in a totally accepting atmosphere, they are no longer so strongly impelled to act them out in everyday life. Other more immediate values gained are the release of tense emotions, making room for more positive and pleasant feelings, and the greater understanding gained by teacher and children of how people feel and how their feelings affect their behavior.

Mrs. Sells and Her First-graders

Mrs. Sells approached personal interaction with the first-grade group with some reluctance and many questions regarding its value. She wondered whether anything significant or even different could come from such an experience. Mrs. Sells started by permitting the children to express themselves through expanding boundaries in the classroom, particularly during a free-play period. At this time they were given the privilege of choosing any materials they wished that were available in the room, such as paper, scissors, games, puzzles, clay, writing paper, and books. They were permitted to talk aloud in a conversational tone and could organize any game they wished to play. They were free to use this time any way they wished, to pursue interests and goals that had personal value to the individual child.

In the beginning bedlam reigned for a few minutes each time

Mutuality of Individual and Group Projects. Here the children are pursuing individual interests. Social interaction occurs naturally in the context of personal exploration.

while children made decisions. The same items and materials were generally selected during this free time. At first many children in the group seemed unable to cope with the additional freedom and screamed loudly in the midst of wild activity. Frequently they looked to Mrs. Sells, evidently wondering just how much noise and confusion she could take and when she would stop it. Always there had been definite limits as to how much noise and moving about was permitted before the child would be hushed or reprimanded in some way. Three or four children said they didn't like the noise and wished Mrs. Sells would make the children stop, but Mrs. Sells did not interfere, and the children had to settle this problem on their own.

Mrs. Sells walked around, trying to listen to the children's expressions. The first incidents did not impress her as particularly startling or revealing. In one corner a group of boys had made an airport out of clay. Their conversation was mostly about types of planes and how fast they could go. There was one crash-landing. A child was literally pushed out of the group because he wrecked two planes. He sought Mrs. Sells's help. She listened and talked with him but did not interfere. Finally he told the group he would not crash any more if they would let him stay and play. They allowed him to play again and the zooming and humming of the planes resumed.

A group of girls played beauty parlor. Their conversation consisted mostly of how glamorous they wanted to look. Mrs. Sells felt she had to curb this activity, as one little girl had a lipstick and was generously applying it to all her customers, as she called them, for one dollar extra. However, they continued to play beauty shop, combing their hair, looking at themselves in a small pocketbook mirror, and giggling loudly.

Several children chose puzzles, others paper, paste, and scissors, and another group chose games and toys from the table. Some children in the room were interested in an alphabet game using letter cards. Soon most of the groups disintegrated and the children went to the cupboard for a box of letter cards. Before the free period was over practically the entire group worked with the alphabet cards. An unusual hush came over the room and everyone seemed to be quietly occupied.

This was a new experience for Mrs. Sells. In the past, free play meant just that for the whole period. It was hard for her to understand why, now that the children had much more real freedom, they were so quietly engrossed. This pattern of quiet involvement continued over many sessions.

One day Mrs. Sells asked the children to draw pictures of the

thing that bothered them most. The children responded immediately, and eagerly worked on their drawings. Some of them
portrayed minor irritations, such as having to walk to school,
making their own beds, neighbors who did not like their dogs,
and having bossy friends. However, Martha's picture provoked
a considerable amount of emotional expression and discussion.

Conflicts. When children have the freedom to move about the room, exploring individual interests and using available resources,. conflicts sometimes
occur. In most instances these conflicts are resolved by the children themselves. The teacher stands by, if possible permitting the children to work
out their difficulties.

The drawing showed the teacher with arms outstretched and
mouth wide open. Martha told about it in her own way: "This is
a picture of Mrs. Sells yelling at us. I don't like it. It makes me
nervous. I know it isn't her fault. Billy causes all the trouble. It
scares me when she has to holler or run after him. I wish he
would learn to behave." Other children responded to Martha's
cue.

David: He bothers me too. I can't do any work when he is so
noisy.

Michael: Mrs. Sells, I don't want to hurt your feelings, but can I
tell you something?

Mrs. Sells: Yes, if you want to. I'd like to hear it.

A Moment of Anger and Discouragement. Plans are sometimes thwarted.
John feels free to be angry and discouraged. He decides to sit and watch for
a while.

Michael: You just don't know how to handle Billy.

Mrs. Sells: What would you do if you were me?

Michael: There are three things I'd do if I were you. I'd put him
back in kindergarten, and if he didn't behave there, I'd send

him to nursery school, and if he didn't behave there, I'd make him stay home until he learned to behave.

At this point Billy, who had been rolling on the floor, climbed up onto Mrs. Sells's lap, looked sad, and just sat and listened.

David: Billy is a liar and a poor sport. I gave him a brand-new penny one day if he wouldn't bother me while I was reading. He yelled in my ear and grabbed my book away. He is a liar, that's what he is.

John: Don't say "liar," just say he doesn't tell the truth.

David: But Mrs. Sells, he really is one. He says he never starts anything, and every day he does start all the fights. My dad told me to hit him back. I'm sorry I called him a liar, but I get mad at Billy.

Michael: Mrs. Sells, why don't you take Billy to Sunday school? He doesn't love God.

Tom: Billy is a baby, always sitting on your lap.

Billy: (*With tears.*) I do love God! I do love God!

Michael: No, you don't. I can tell the way you act. You don't love Mrs. Sells either. She is nice to you, and when she tries to make you behave, you kick her. I don't believe you even like your mother. Your mother is nice. When I was at your house for lunch your mother had the bestest lunch for us, and all you want to do is fight with me when I am at school.

Carolyn: Let me handle Billy. He should be told off.

Billy: (*Jumping off Mrs. Sells's lap and starting after Carolyn, doubling his fists and yelling.*) "I'll handle you, too."

Carolyn: Down, boy. Down, boy. You get back to your seat and stay there.

Billy: (*Stopping just as he reaches Carolyn, and returning to his seat.*) I do go to Sunday school! I do love God! And I love Mrs. Sells and my mother! Carolyn, I hate you, and I'm not going to grow up and marry you. Martha, you started this with that old picture of yours and I hate you!

Carolyn: I don't want to marry you, Billy. I thought if I said that, maybe you would behave and not bother me.

At this point there was a period of silence, then the criticisms of Billy continued.

Alan: Mrs. Sells, I know what is wrong with Billy. He doesn't have any brothers or sisters, and he doesn't know how to play with other children. My mom says we should be kind to Billy and teach him how to play. But she isn't kind to him. She won't take him to school in our riding group any more. The other mothers won't either. Every day he hits my baby brother, and my mom almost had an accident because he hit her when she was driving one day.

Tom: My mother said Billy shouldn't be allowed to come to school.

Helen: Billy shouldn't come to school until he is eight or nine years old. Maybe he wouldn't act like a baby by then.

Michael: Mrs. Sells, you are too nice to him. He'll never learn unless you punish him. You really should tell Mr. Black. (*The principal.*)

On this critical note the discussion ended and the children were given an arithmetic assignment. Mrs. Sells approached Billy and told him that the children really wanted to help him, regardless of what they had said, and that she liked him and was glad he was in her group. For the next several weeks Billy did not disturb anyone, and the children gradually began to play with him and show other ways of accepting him.

Another interesting incident occurred in Mrs. Sells's group one day during a discussion in one of the special sessions. Duane had drawn a picture which aroused much interest and feeling in the group.

Duane: This is a picture of my little brother when he broke my speedometer. I wish I could have chopped his head off. He breaks something of mine every day. I'd like to chop off his head, but my mother always tells me to be patient. Bobby would soon learn not to do it if I could just hit him once, and we might someday be good friends, but most of the days I hate him. He always gets me into trouble.

Hugh: My big sister always gets me into trouble. My mother won't interfere. She says we should fight our own battles. She is bigger, but I'm tougher.

Cindy: I hate my brother when he chases me and hits me.

Peggy: My sister is four years old and she brings home friends from the nursery school and they get too bossy. Mother says I'm older and I shouldn't pay any attention. My sister's friends are brats.

Warren: My big sister lays down on my bed, and then my mother blames me for not smoothing my covers. She never tells my mother it is her fault. She won't rest on her own bed, she doesn't want to muss it, so I get into trouble.

Helen: My sister Ebba thinks she's smart. She says first-grade children are nuisances, that we don't know anything, and she tells my mother every little thing I do.

Jay: I hate it when my brother doesn't eat. My mother tries to make him eat. He won't, and he starts to cry. Then my dad gets mad, so does my mother. Then they say, "Jay, you eat what's left on Craig's plate," and I have to eat it.

Gary: Whenever I'm playing with my little brother and he yells and screams, my mom always yells, "Gary, stop it!" I tell her its Bruce. She says, "You're bigger," and that I should take care of him and not make him holler. My sister Caroline blames me for everything too. I hate my sister sometimes. She thinks she is pretty.

Jan: I hate it when my brother does something at the table. He is always spilling his milk or throwing his food. It bothers my dad too. He takes Jimmie upstairs and mother and I have to eat alone. I always like to talk to my father, and I can't because he gets upset and mad when this happens.

Several other children had made pictures showing resentment toward brothers and sisters, nearly all adding "And Mother always blames it on me, when I didn't start it."

Another approach was having all the children draw pictures of the things they wished for most. The pictures were interesting. Most of them wanted toys, two a larger house, one a hatchet, and two or three wished to take a trip to fairyland. Almost all the pictures depicted joy and fun. In the discussion period children told about these happy experiences.

In another session the children drew pictures of experiences in the hospital or doctor's office. No one seemed to mind the "shots."

All expressed positive feeling for their pediatrician. However, the hospital patients did not like the smell of ether, but all seemed eager to tell about their experience. Most of them enjoyed the sensation because they saw pretty pictures. Some heard fairy bells and some saw everything turn to silky waves. Two or three said it felt like being "konked" on the head.

One child said he hated to go for a checkup because the doctor made him take off his clothes, in front of a nurse too. The children all snickered and some laughed aloud. Warren blushed and tried hard to keep back the tears. He is very reserved and dignified. He whispered in Mrs. Sells's ear, "I wished I wouldn't have said that." Mrs. Sells tried to comfort him, whispering back, "I don't blame you. It is a funny feeling to dress and undress in front of strangers."

When the children explained their pictures about sad experiences, most of them were about death. Miriam expressed the general feeling. Miriam said it made her very unhappy to see her mother cry. Several children agreed, and described experiences similar to Miriam's.

David has a great love for animals and showed much emotion when he talked about his picture.

David: This shows the saddest thing that ever happened to me. It was when my dog got a porcupine needle up his nose and had to be taken to the gas chamber. The needle could not be taken out, and it hurt so much that two men had to take him away. Our whole family cried. My dad got me a new dog, but it's not the same.

Marion: They had to take our dog too, on account of our neighbors. We always kept our dog in the yard, but our neighbors kept on saying, "Why don't you let your dog out for a run? Why don't you let your dog out for a run?" Finally we did let him out. He wasn't used to other people and other dogs, so he ran across the street and bit the neighbor's dog. He tried to bite the neighbors too. Those same neighbors who told us to let our dog out for a run were the ones who called the police on our dog. The police came and took him away. We never saw him again. My dad said we could never have another dog until the dog across the street dies. This isn't very nice to say, but I wish that dog would die or run away, and then me and my sisters could have a dog.

The use of pictures to provide the setting for the expression of emotions seemed to be satisfying to the children. They looked forward to the special sessions and wanted to talk about themselves and listen to others, often discovering that they were not so alone in experiencing the fun and joy, as well as the frustration and pain, of everyday living.

Discussion

Mrs. Sells discovered that when children are permitted to be themselves, creative expression can result. Play is not always wild, confused, and noisy. The children learned in this classroom that quiet, personal exploration in drawing, painting, dramatic activity, and games is satisfying. The exchange of ideas and feelings among the children aided them in being themselves, exploring some of their feelings toward each other and others, and telling of their happy experiences, as well as unhappy ones.

Mrs. Sells learned that when she did not interfere, but permitted children to resolve their own problems, solutions were reached in the children's own way.

Should she have allowed the critical comments directed to Billy to continue? What the children were saying to Billy he had felt for a long time in his relations with them. Hard as it was for Billy to hear these feelings verbalized, they provided a basis for the development of a more accepting and genuine relationship with others. Apparently Mrs. Sells felt comfortable in allowing the discussion to continue. She trusted that, in spite of the painful experience, Billy would emerge with a feeling that others cared enough about him to be openly honest with him. In a temporary situation this kind of personal interaction perhaps would be destructive, but in the stability of Mrs. Sells's group Billy freed himself from the suspicion and doubt of his self-inadequacy. Once the superficial presence of accepting Billy was removed and children expressed their hostility, the potential humanness began to express itself, and true acceptance developed.

In this case the teacher's trust, Billy's willingness to listen and hear and yet continue to assert himself, the group's basically good feelings for Billy and actual desire to see him happier, provided the basis for a changing relationship between Billy and other children, as well as between Billy and his teacher.

Mrs. Haynes and Her Second-graders

All the twenty-five children in Mrs. Haynes's class came from lower-middle-class families. The group included both Negro and white children.

The experiment was conducted in an activity room, with music, drawing, stories, games, language, and free play making up most of the program. The room itself was pleasant and well lighted. It contained movable tables and chairs, an artificial fireplace that could be lighted by the children on cold, dark days, and a sand table which was in almost constant use. Other equipment included a piano, a homemade puppet show, and a large assortment of toys. Free discussion was always encouraged. No set amount of schoolwork had to be covered. Rules were few and simple and were worked out by children and teacher together. Reading, writing, and spelling were taught by a different teacher at another time.

The experimental sessions took place every day, usually during the early part of the afternoon, and lasted about forty-five minutes. The children were asked to make a total of nine drawings. A discussion followed each drawing. The teacher felt the discussions were much more important than the drawings themselves.

On the first day of the experiment, as the children and teacher sat in a group, the following discussion took place:

Mrs. Haynes: Children, would you like to make a special picture this afternoon?
Several: Yes. What about? I'd like to.
Mrs. Haynes: Let's pretend that you came to school today and no grown people were here—no helpers to clean, no men to take care of the furnaces, no nurse, no teachers, no principal, no one but children. Since there was no one here to tell you

what to do, you could do anything you wanted to. Think carefully of what you would do if you could do exactly as you pleased. When you have decided what you would do, take some paper and make a picture of yourself doing it.

Children: You mean we could do anything we wanted to? There was no one here?

Mrs. Haynes: Yes, anything you wish.

The children giggled and looked knowingly at each other, and gradually started to draw. Some worked quietly; others talked about their pictures to their neighbors. No child was forced to draw or talk about his drawings. He could do what he wanted during this special time. Many children were eager to tell about their pictures. A series of discussions lasting several days over a three-month period was necessary to talk about all the drawings. During these discussions the children expressed many feelings about themselves and others. These feelings were not always related to the drawings. Most of the children at first expressed positive attitudes. As they realized that they could express negative feelings without fear of criticism, they made the following comments.

Milton: When no grown person was here we could each take what we wanted.

Mary Jane: But if we took out a brick, the school would fall to pieces.

Allen: I'm going to chop the school.

Andy: I'll chop the piano.

Barbara: I'd chop up the chairs. Knock everything down. I'm scared.

Sharon: I'd chop up the teacher's desk.

Sheila: I'd break up everything in the room and you'd give me a spanking.

Allen: I'll chop off your head.

John: He ain't going to chop anyone's head. If he does, he'll go to jail.

Allen: If she comes and no one else is here, I'll chop her head and take her to her house.

Donald: I'm goin' to chop my brother's head. He's a baby!

Mrs. Haynes: Sometimes you feel like chopping his head off.

Allen: He's nuts! And here's my ax. I'm chopping down your head. And here's a bloody spot, and the day after tomorrow is your funeral.

Mrs. Haynes: So I'm going to be buried. You feel like burying me.

Allen: Yes, the day after tomorrow. There's bound to be trouble. The police are here.

A number of children shouted to Allen to keep quiet, but he went on saying over and over, "There's bound to be trouble. You'd better watch out. Red murder. See how she bleeds."

Allen: I done chop your body off. See the blood splashing on the floor.

Mrs. Haynes: I guess you feel like smashing it all up.

Allen: I threw her body into the garage. I have on boots. I can walk in the blood. Blood, blood on everything.

This was the first time that Mrs. Haynes understood how strongly Allen felt against her and all adults. She decided to take the time to find ways of strengthening her relationship with him and help him to be happier in the classroom. Mrs. Haynes learned that Allen had been reared without a father. He had lived in poverty and under severely punishing conditions all his life. In school he seemed full of worries and fears, and often wildly attacked other children. As the experiment progressed and the teacher's relationship with Allen improved, he became more confident in himself, more acceptable socially, and more successful in his schoolwork.

All the children continued to pretend they came to school day after day, in spite of the fact that they could have been elsewhere in their imagination. Aggressions increased in intensity during the third and fourth weeks of the experiment. Though some children brought out violent reactions, these were accepted by the others. The more timid children felt freer to express anger when supported by other children. Although many of their actions were directed against the school and the teachers, there was no actual destruction in the room or carry-over of hostile feelings in other school activities.

Fourteen of the twenty-five children seemed to have resolved their aggressions, as indicated in their drawings and their comments, and by the end of the semester seven appeared to have sublimated their aggressions, while four remained unchanged.

Aggression seemed to follow a pattern. At first there was considerable feeling expressed against the school and fantasies about destruction of equipment. Later these feelings were directed against other children in the classroom, and finally fighting in wars to preserve America was the common theme.

Children's feelings apparently were affected by what they heard and saw on radio and television, and in some cases the children identified themselves with the characters they had seen and heard.

At first individual remarks concerning the pictures of others tended to be projections of a child's own ideas and attitudes. Later the children showed greater insight into one another's feelings.

As the experiment proceeded, the class felt and acted more as a unit. Just being in a group over a period of time where common feelings and attitudes were expressed brought the children closer together. "We" was heard more frequently than "I." John remarked, "We don't have gangs any more." Mary Jane told a new child who started to quarrel, "We don't fight in this class." School became an important place to these children. One little boy said to his friend, "I just can't wait to get to school, can you?"

The children appeared to learn, to think, and to plan while expressing their feelings. One day they started out for recess. At the door Mrs. Haynes discovered that it had started to rain, so she told the children to go back to the room. She remained in the hall for a few minutes to chat with another teacher. When she entered the room, she found that all the children were seated together in a circle on the floor, playing a game they had organized.

Other teachers commented on the unity of the group. Special teachers to whom they went once a week remarked on their good behavior and their interest in learning.

The important conclusion drawn from this experiment is that

when children are permitted to express their negative feelings, these do not continue indefinitely to increase in severity. Actually they eventually become less intense, and positive feelings begin to emerge. Perhaps some of these changes take place anyway with the passage of time, or it may be that the change is not in the children but in the teacher—that her sympathy and understanding increase as she earnestly attempts to know and to understand children's loves and hates, worries and fears.

The Individual Child-Teacher Relationship

In addition to these group experiences, twenty-eight teachers in early elementary grades attempted to establish important personal relationships with individual children. The teachers were encouraged after the first month of the school year to select children who were of particular concern to them. Each teacher kept a record of his interactions with the children. It was possible for the teacher to examine the nature of his contact with the child several months after the special relationship had begun. At the end of the school year twenty teachers indicated that the special relationship had helped considerably in increasing the child's feelings of self-confidence and adequacy. Four teachers indicated that the child's behavior had not improved or had become worse. Four teachers were uncertain about the value of the special relationship. All the teachers felt that the relationship provided a basis for better understanding of the child.

Four of the successful special relationships have been selected for presentation. In the final chapter some relationships that were of questionable value, some definite failures, and a follow-up report of a successful case are discussed.

Mrs. Wilson and Jimmy

Mrs. Wilson started the year with the impression that her second-grade children were a boisterous group. Jimmy alone was quiet. He appeared nervous and uncomfortable and refused to participate in group activities. He seemed to be withdrawn, not only in the classroom but also on the playground. He was reluctant to be friendly with Mrs. Wilson or with other children and seemed suspicious of every overture of sympathy.

On the first day of school several children told Mrs. Wilson, "Jimmy did the same thing in first grade, he wouldn't talk." She decided she would attempt to create a special relationship with him. She soon discovered that Jimmy had attended six different schools in two years. Perhaps he was afraid to come too close to anyone, feeling any close contacts might be suddenly broken off.

During the first three days of school Jimmy refused to read aloud for Mrs. Wilson. She thought perhaps he was unable to read, but from his record she learned that his intelligence was superior.

His difficulties seemed to grow, but in spite of constant rebuff, Mrs. Wilson continued to make special comments intended to show him that she felt him worthy of her interest and respect. During this time Jimmy's parents came to see Mrs. Wilson and indicated a willingness to help out in any way. They engaged a tutor for Jimmy to help him improve in reading and spelling. His tutor asked Mrs. Wilson, "What do you think of Jimmy? I have never seen a boy like him." She went on to say that one day she deliberately had him work for an hour without a break. He did not ask to stop. The tutor thought this was wonderful, but Mrs. Wilson felt it only showed Jimmy's inability to question or dispute another person's wishes. It was particularly this extreme obedience to adult standards that troubled Mrs. Wilson. Shortly after the tutoring began, Jimmy would read in class in a low, unexpressive voice, but never voluntarily.

Only after Mrs. Wilson had made several hundred comments to Jimmy did he finally speak to her. One day he said, "I like to write better than print. Why can't I write all the time?" The teacher found it difficult to explain. She was expected to teach printing in the second grade, not writing. Finally she said, "Jimmy, I realize you would prefer to write all the time, but you are expected to learn how to print in this grade. There will be plenty of free time, and if you wish, you may write during that time." Jimmy agreed and followed the printing instructions when they were given.

In the classroom Jimmy's behavior became more spontaneous.

He began talking to the boys around him at times when Mrs. Wilson would have enjoyed a moment of silence, but she never corrected him, for she was delighted that he was beginning to interact socially with others. On the playground he started to join the boys in activities, but if anyone was aggressive or rough, he would give him a poke or a dirty look and walk away. Mrs. Wilson thought that Jimmy interpreted the playful aggression as a rejection of himself. He needed time to discover that other children really liked him. She did not interfere, but felt Jimmy and the other children would work it out in their own way. As Halloween approached, Mrs. Wilson put pictures and decorations on the board. One day during free time, Jimmy, instead of writing, drew a series of pictures. One of the children remarked, "Look what Jimmy has made. Isn't it good?" Mrs. Wilson said to Jimmy, "I didn't know you could draw. Those are wonderful Halloween pictures. May I put them on the bulletin board?" After this incident Jimmy became the class artist, and hardly a day went by that children failed to ask him to draw for them. Jimmy's self-confidence was growing and other children were beginning to notice his merit.

Early in November Mrs. Wilson saw Jimmy in a drugstore during the noon hour. Jimmy greeted her and said, "My mom works at the grocery there, and I eat at the drugstore. I can't go home because my dad is sleeping. After school I wait for my mom at the store or go home and keep very quiet, because my dad says I must not make any noise while he is sleeping." Apparently from an early age Jimmy had had to curb his natural exuberance to protect his father's sleep.

Jimmy's mother came in one morning and angrily said, "Jimmy is late because we were looking for his hat. He left it at his aunt's, deliberately I know, so he wouldn't have to wear it today. Well, I showed him he was not going to wear his good hat to school. We went and got the old one." She went on to tell how they had to "clamp down" on Jimmy, for when they relaxed their vigilance at home, he took advantage of them. Jimmy said nothing. Later, when she had the time, Mrs. Wilson said to him, "Jimmy, I think you were upset to have your mother come this morning, but I want you to know it doesn't matter to me. The important thing here is for you to be happy and do what is important to you." Mrs. Wilson realized more clearly than before the value of being lenient with Jimmy at school.

One day the class was making plans for a Christmas tree that was to be in the auditorium. Jimmy was the first to say he would ask his mother if he could bring a string of lights. That noon he came to school with the lights. He participated in all the activities and contributed ideas for decorations.

Jimmy's schoolwork continued to show improvement. He volunteered more often to recite or read or play games in the room. At recess or after school he would wait till Robert, his new friend, was ready before he would go. If Robert stayed after school for some reason, Jimmy would wait for him. A strong friendship developed between the two boys. One day Jimmy offered to stay after school and wash the boards. The first day he cleaned the boards he said, "Is there anything else I can do for you?" Mrs. Wilson responded, "No, Jimmy, not tonight, but maybe you could do some art work with me sometime soon. We can put together some new things for the bulletin board." Jimmy remarked enthusiastically, "OK. That would be fun."

The next week the group was planning a mural for the Christmas bulletin board. Anyone who wished could make a part of the picture. As the plans were made one of the children said, "Why not have Jimmy make the big church?" Other children said, "Yes, that's a good idea." The church was to be the important feature of the picture. Jimmy set to work.

One morning the class was preparing a Christmas program in which each child was to take part. Jimmy did not come to school that afternoon. The following morning when the children practiced on the stage, Jimmy stood back from the group. Mrs. Wilson remarked to him, "If you would rather watch today, you may, Jimmy." He watched for a while then joined in. Several days later his mother came to school and said, "You know Jimmy didn't want to have any part of this program at first. And then when he saw the fun the children were having, he decided he wanted to be in it. He talks about it all the time at home." Jimmy gained more by making his own decision to participate than he might have if the teacher had pressured him.

Frequently after the Christmas holidays Jimmy remained a few minutes after school to talk with Mrs. Wilson. He commented on recent experiences at home and indicated that he was glad that his mother was going to quit her job. A short time later Mrs. Wilson was surprised when Jimmy's mother came into the room and said, "I want to see the church Jimmy has been talking so much about." Jimmy smiled as she looked at it. He said, "Here it is, Mom, and look at the rest of the picture too." Jimmy's mother seemed quite pleased, and, turning to Jimmy, said, "That's a beautiful picture, Jimmy."

When the semester came to a close, Jimmy was doing superior work in all his school subjects. His interests had expanded. He had made several friendships. He responded cooperatively to suggestions. He participated in group activities. And, most important he had grown in self-confidence. There was still some hesitancy and fear but his schoolwork and social relations had improved.

Discussion

How did Mrs. Wilson contribute to Jimmy's growth? First, she sought to establish a meaningful relationship with him. In spite of his apparent indifference, she continued to respond to him. She gave him time to trust her. While encouraging Jimmy's participation in class activities, she did not pressure him or hurry him along. For the most part she permitted Jimmy to decide for himself whether or not he would join in activities. Second, Mrs. Wilson overlooked trivial misdemeanors, knowing that the pressures on Jimmy at home were severe. She tried to make Jimmy feel that his welfare and personal growth were more important to her than his occasional violations of school rules. When he began to change from a passive, withdrawn child to an aggressive one, Mrs. Wilson did not become disturbed. Nor did she interfere with his battles and conflicts on the playground. She gave Jimmy and the other children time to work out the difficulties on their own. And third, Mrs. Wilson encouraged Jimmy's expression in areas where he felt confident, and thus helped him to gain status in the group.

Mrs. Vinson and Tom

Tom, seven years old, is in the second grade. He lives with his mother and a ten-year-old sister. Tom is a small, pale child with average intelligence. He appears immature for his age. He makes some of his numbers backwards, his reading is below average, and his printing shows lack of coordination. He attempts to do all assigned schoolwork, but does it poorly and without much interest. Tom rarely volunteers information or makes comments. In games or songs, if he thinks he is being observed, he will go through the motions with minimum effort. Usually he will hide behind a larger child and not take any part in the activity.

Until a month before, Tom rarely talked or played with other children. He is always immaculate in appearance, neat in his personal habits, and never without a handkerchief and a comb. Since Mrs. Vinson had no difficulty with Tom, it never occurred to her that there was anything to be concerned about. Until just before Thanksgiving Tom was one of the forgotten children in a room of forty. Little personal interaction took place between Tom and his teacher. Only a few comments had been exchanged between them. For the most part Mrs. Vinson took Tom for granted and was rarely even conscious of his presence. Tom never took part in the telling and showing periods or volunteered information about himself.

A week before Thanksgiving the group was making booklets about "things to be thankful for." The rhyme for the day to copy and illustrate began "I'm thankful for Mother so kind and Father so strong, etc." Mrs. Vinson was standing a few feet from Tom when she heard him say to himself, "I'm not going to write that. My father is dead. I'm going to write 'I'm thankful my father is dead.' I didn't like him. He always hollered at me, and he was going to hurt my mother and my sister and me bad." This incident shocked Mrs. Vinson. She remembered all the experiences and stories at school in which Father was described as a wonderful person. She realized how they must have affected Tom. She wondered why she had always insisted that children write nice things about their parents. It had never occurred to her that a child could actually hate his father. Tom appeared extremely upset. He put his head part way down and was crying. Mrs. Vinson knelt next to him and said, "It's all right to cry, Tom. No need to feel ashamed here. And you don't need to copy the rhyme if you don't want to." This was her first personal approach to Tom. After this experience Mrs. Vinson made it a point to know Tom better, and she tried to convey to him that she cared about him and how he felt. He gradually seemed to lose some of his shyness toward her and occasionally talked with her spontaneously.

In December Mrs. Vinson told the children a story—"Pinky, the White Mouse." The next day Tom brought a white mouse to school. But instead of rushing in with it, as most children would have done, he put it in his desk and did not bring it out until late in the day, when Mrs. Vinson discovered him sitting on the floor playing with it. She asked Tom if he would like to show the mouse to the children. He was reluctant but brought it to the front of the room. He readily answered the children's numerous questions. It was the first time he had known more about something than anyone else in the room. Later in the afternoon, when the group was composing a story about a mouse, he twice corrected or objected to statements the children wanted to put in the story. He insisted that Bob, not his mother, had given him the mouse. When asked about Bob he replied, "Bob is my mother's boy friend. I like him. He gives me lots of things."

A few weeks before Christmas, after the materials had been distributed for Fathers' gifts, Tom asked Mrs. Vinson if he could make a calendar for Bob. The teacher nodded and remarked, "You like Bob, don't you?" Tom answered, "Yes, he never hollers at me and he took me to the football game at Ann Arbor, the one where the band had a big boat that the steam came out of." Mrs. Vinson commented that it was nice of Bob to take him to the game, and that she was sure he would like the gift Tom was making. Tom said, "I wish my mother would marry Bob, so he would come and live with me. But I guess he won't, because they had a fight." The teacher responded, "I guess you're worried that Bob won't come back again, is that it?" Tom nodded sadly and returned to his seat.

As the children were going out for recess this same day, Tom hung back until the room was empty, then said, "If my mother is mad at Bob, maybe I won't see him and I can't give him the gift I made." Mrs. Vinson attempted to reassure Tom, saying, "Well, it is quite awhile before Christmas. Let's wait and see. Maybe we can mail it to him," Tom's face lit up and he said, "I know, I can get his address and bring it to you and then you could mail it. OK?" The teacher responded, "All right, if that's the way you want to do it." Tom seemed relieved and happy.

A few days before Christmas vacation the children wrote letters to Santa Claus and then read them to the group. Tom asked for a live snake. Several of the youngsters groaned. One child said, "I wouldn't want a snake. They aren't any good to play with." Tom replied, "Snakes are *too* good. They can kill people. When someone is mean, you can let the snake out of its cage and it will go after that man and kill him." Another child answered, "They just do that on TV. The snakes you get in a pet store have had their rattlers taken off." Tommy was getting upset. Mrs. Vinson said to him, "Sometimes when people have been mean to you, you feel so angry you want to kill them." Several of the children talked about experiences that made them angry. As Tom saw that other children became angry too, sometimes very angry, his own feelings seemed to lessen and he did not feel so alone.

One day toward the end of the semester Tom was alone in the room with Mrs. Vinson. After a while he said, "Mrs. Vinson, do I talk funny?" His teacher responded, "Why, Tom, do you think you do?" He answered, "No." Since he did not continue, Mrs. Vinson said, "Why do you ask?" Tom replied, "At Christmas, when all my aunts and uncles were at our house, they were always trying to get me to talk, because they said I talked cute. Every time I said something they would laugh at me and try to get me to say something else. When they did that, I didn't talk any more, and I sneaked up to my room and stayed there." Mrs. Vinson remarked sympathetically, "Oh, you must have been hurt to have them laugh at you, though I think they were trying to show they like you." Tom continued, "When my mother's friends come to visit, they laugh when I talk, too. Why do they?" Mrs. Vinson said sympathetically, "Sometimes big people like to joke with children without realizing that some children don't like it." Then Mrs. Vinson added that no one at school ever laughed at the way he talked. She told Tom she thought he had a pleasant voice and everyone in school enjoyed having him tell stories. Tom thought a minute, then remarked, "Yes, I guess they just aren't used to hearing little boys talk."

Through these various experiences Mrs. Vinson got to know and understand Tom better. He came to feel more secure with her and the children. He is still shy and retiring, but he seems to be finding a place in the group and is taking a more active part in group activities. His schoolwork shows some improvement. Mrs. Vinson had two conferences with Tom's mother, who talked for over an hour, and told in detail of the stormy and unhappy family life previous to her husband's death. She said that the children, particularly Tom, had been very much afraid of their father, and that the father abused Tom and was always "screaming" at him. She also went into detail about her boy friends, and about how much Tom wanted her to marry Bob. Mrs. Vinson got the impression that she loved her children, and wanted to provide a normal family life for them, but was extremely frightened about marrying again.

Discussion

In a real sense Mrs. Vinson's relationship with Tom did not begin until after he had been in her group for eight weeks. From her own statements it is evident that she was hardly aware of his existence. Tom must have wanted his teacher to know about some of his real feelings, for he expressed them loud enough for her to hear. From this point Mrs. Vinson made a special effort to respond to him. She began by asking for his help with certain school functions. She took time to talk with him and encouraged him to feel free to talk with her. The children must have noticed this attention given to Tom and must have become more aware of his presence too. Mrs. Vinson used every opportunity to give

Tom recognition and to encourage his interaction with other children. When Tom's anger mounted and he expressed a desire to kill, Mrs. Vinson did not become frightened, nor did she deny the intensity of his feelings or try to change the subject. She accepted his feelings and permitted other children to discuss incidents that had made them angry, thus giving Tom an opportunity to see that he was not entirely different from other children.

Mrs. Vinson gave Tom emotional support when he needed it. When Tom told her about people laughing when he talked, she explored the problem with him and helped him to conclude, "I guess they just aren't used to hearing little boys talk." Most important, Mrs. Vinson took notice of Tom, responded to him as a person, and showed him she really cared how he felt.

Mrs. Weatherton and Bill

The first few days of school Mrs. Weatherton saw her group as an average class but this point of view soon changed. Bill, who had been quietly engrossed with materials brought from home, suddenly, on the third day of school, began jumping up and down on his desk, making loud noises and weird sounds. He chattered continuously in incomprehensible language. He frequently twisted his hair and made other nervous gestures.

At this point Mrs. Weatherton remembered Bill as the child who had come to her one morning, asking if she were "G-e-o-r-g-e." Mrs. Weatherton walked over to Bill and whispered that she could not permit him to jump up and down and scream in class. Bill responded with a shriek and continued his strange behavior.

After the first week Bill frequently ran around the room, laughing and saying, "Funny, funny work; funny, funny school," and other strange things. Mrs. Weatherton tried not to have the children become upset. She would go to Bill, take his hand, and say "We do not jump and scream in here." Bill ignored his teacher. Often Mrs. Weatherton ignored Bill too, but the episodes of disorganized activity, screaming, and running were becoming greater and were interfering more and more with the class program.

During this period of confusion Mrs. Weatherton discovered

that Bill could spell. One day she asked the children to draw a picture of their favorite breakfast. Bill drew a bowl of cereal and wrote "c-e-r-e-a-l" below his picture. Mrs. Weatherton was surprised, but did not comment on the spelling, thinking that if she did so, Bill would burst out in hysterical laughter.

That afternoon Mrs. Weatherton noticed Bill had put the word "printing" on his paper. She said quietly to him, "I see you can spell." Bill replied, "Yes, and I can spell your name too, W-e-a-t-h-e-r-t-o-n." Just then the principal came into the room. Bill said, "There is Mr. L-a-k-e-l-a-n-d," spelling the name. The next day Bill went to the blackboard and printed the name of every month and the days of the week, all spelled correctly. The group reaction was "Oh, Bill is smart. He can spell anything." One child said, "He can spell better than my sister in the fourth grade." "Where did he learn to spell?" Mark asked. Bill quickly replied, "Oh, I could always spell. I have spelled for years."

One little girl spoke up quickly and said, "Maybe he can spell, but he certainly does not know how to act." Several children made similar comments. Bill seemed hurt. The teacher permitted the children to discuss these feelings. Bill began to jump up and down and scream, something he had not done during the past week. Mrs. Weatherton wondered if Bill's bizarre behavior was not in some way related to his feeling of rejection. She decided to do what she could to strengthen his feelings of self-adequacy.

Three days before Halloween Bill was absent. He returned in the afternoon for the Halloween party. Mrs. Weatherton said to him "We missed you while you were absent, and we are all glad you could be with us for our party." Bill said, "I didn't have any fun at home. May I stay in the schoolhouse all night?" Before Mrs. Weatherton could answer, Bill asked, "Or would it be dark?" Mrs. Weatherton asked, "And are you afraid of the dark, Bill?" Bill looked sad and said, "Yes, I am. Where does the dark go when you turn on these lights?"

One day at lunchtime, when he was going home, Mrs. Weatherton called to Bill, "Have a good lunch." He replied, "I will have i-n-s-u-l-a-t-i-o-n. That is all I ever get at home." Though not certain, Mrs. Weatherton thought that perhaps Bill meant he would have isolation.

Mrs. Weatherton organized reading into several groups. Bill rarely remained in any group for long. His reading was advanced, and Mrs. Weatherton permitted him to decide for himself what he wanted to do. After reading aloud he frequently said "funny, funny work," and returned to his desk. Gradually the children learned to accept Bill's peculiar comments and not to laugh at him. Sometimes Bill moved from one reading group to another. Mrs. Weatherton let Bill's interest and motivation guide his choices.

One day Mrs. Weatherton asked the group to draw pictures of their families. All the children but Bill responded enthusiastically. He put his hands over his ears to shut out the children's happy comments. Instead, he drew ice-cream cones and a cat. Mrs. Weatherton asked him how many people were in his family. Bill replied, "I could tell you, but I would rather count my cats." Mrs. Weatherton accepted his decision to count cats rather than family members.

Bill's ability in numbers is amazing. During arithmetic Bill made up his own problems, most of which were beyond the third-grade level. When he adds, he never puts down numbers to be carried, but carries them mentally. Discovering this ability, Mrs. Weatherton gave Bill every opportunity to develop it. Sometimes Bill worked on arithmetic problems while other children were reading or spelling. Bill began taking attendance for Mrs. Weatherton. If four were absent he would say, "We have four absent. We should have twenty-seven present, because four from thirty-one are twenty-seven." From a brief glance he can indicate the number present and absent. One morning while he was out in the hall a second-grade teacher passed by with her group. Bill said, "How many children have you?" The teacher said, "I have twenty-eight but eight are ill." Bill said, "You should have twenty in line. I see that you do. Twelve girls and eight boys.

One morning on entering the schoolroom Mrs. Weatherton found a small piece of paper on each child's desk, with their first and last names spelled correctly. Mrs. Weatherton realized increasingly that Bill was a most unusual child and needed freedom to think and plan for himself. Bill's social relationships were beginning to show some improvement.

During the third month of school Bill sat with two different children for an hour or so and worked quietly with them. He did not take any of their belongings or act in a bizarre manner. When he returned to his own desk, Mrs Weatherton said, "Bill, I am glad you enjoyed sitting with your friends. We are all friends in this room. Any time you want to work with one of the children you may change your seat." Bill seemed pleased.

When any stranger comes to visit the room, Bill runs up, asks his name, and if he has children. Then Bill runs around the room and is very noisy.

Near the end of the semester Bill continued to write in his own personal notebooks. These were made at home and brought to school every morning in a box. One book contained drawings of elevators and pictures of high buildings. Another had several pages on the alphabet, with little stories written about each letter. Most stories were about elevators, fires, and ice cream.

One morning Mrs. Weatherton asked Bill if he would do a page in his *Think and Do Book*. He quickly completed the page without errors. The children praised him and he was pleased. The next day he did another page, but after it was completed, he took his purple crayon and scribbled through the page. This practice continued for three days. After the pages were colored completely, he ran up and down the aisles and showed them to the whole room. The children reacted negatively. Bill felt the rejection and laughed hysterically and shrilly. He began screaming and saying "Funny, funny work." Bill was upset but his teacher was not. She approached him and told him she understood why he felt like yelling and scribbling in his workbook. She pointed to a blackboard and told him he could scribble there as much as he wished. Bill went to the board, picked up the chalk, and made forceful strokes. The scribbling continued for two weeks. Then Bill returned to his workbook and completed several pages neatly and correctly.

One day Bill asked Mrs. Weatherton to punch holes in his notebook. Mrs. Weatherton had no punch and suggested that perhaps his father could do it. An angry expression appeared on Bill's face. He jumped up and down and screamed, shaking all over and clenching his fists. He said, "Don't mention it. That will never do. That will never do."

Mrs. Weatherton had a brief interview with Bill's mother and told her several favorable facts concerning Bill's adjustment. She added that she was working especially to improve his social relationships and to help him be happier with other children. Mrs. Weatherton wondered whether it would be possible to encourage social activity at home. Bill's mother indicated that every time she attempted anything in this respect she had failed and had given up. Mrs. Weatherton indicated that in school he had already shown growth in this respect, and she encouraged Bill's mother to attempt occasionally to bring another child into the home when she could supervise the play. Three weeks later Bill's mother reported that, to her complete surprise, Bill was actually able to play without destroying things. She described several incidents in which Bill and another child had played for an hour at a time without serious mishaps.

One day the group was making leather bookmarks for their mothers as a surprise Christmas gift. Bill made his bookmark neatly, and with a fine attitude toward the experience. This was the first time he had tried to make something to take home. He had always said, "Oh no, that will never do. Do not even mention my home."

A few days later a mother with a baby came to visit the room and sat in the reading group. Bill came up to the group, kicked the school door, screamed, and laughed hysterically. He asked Mrs. Weatherton repeatedly where Hal was. When Mrs. Weatherton tried to explain, Bill continued calling loudly, over and over again, "Where is Hal? Where is Hal?" The visiting mother became upset and said, "A child like that should never be in a public school."

When Mrs. Weatherton had an opportunity, she approached the visitor and said warmly, "You are fortunate to have such happy, healthy children of your own. You see, Bill is not happy. He needs more love, understanding, and help. Someday this cloud will all pass away and Bill will be wonderful too."

The day of the Christmas party Bill redeemed himself. The

mothers gave Mrs. Weatherton a Christmas present and chose Bill to present it. He did this in a gracious, childlike manner. All the parents were pleased with the change in his behavior. They had never seen him remain calm for so long a time. Bill took part in the Christmas program for the mothers. He sat with the rest of the children until time to go on the stage. While on the stage he did not sing, but beat time with the music. This showed further progress toward a group spirit.

Dr. Bennet was the next parent to visit the class. Bill sat in his seat, not asking questions, not attempting to annoy. The doctor praised all the boys and girls for being such good workers. Bill said, "Me too?" Dr. Bennet replied, "You are my friend and neighbor." This recognition pleased Bill, who beamed the rest of the day.

Early in January a new girl joined the group. She had no crayons or supplies and Bill immediately stepped up and shared his materials with her. A few months ago he had been breaking or taking other children's belongings, but not any more. He had learned to respond socially.

One day Bill took a piece of paper and drew a map of the United States. Each state was printed, spelled correctly, and placed properly according to size and location. On the bottom of the map Bill wrote; "My! Texas is a large state!" He also printed under Florida, "Florida is in the S.E. part of the U.S."

Bill still regressed occasionally. One afternoon at dismissal time the children went to the hall for their wraps. Bill had gone to the toilet before dismissal and put thirty-two pairs of galoshes in a pile in the hall. He carried three pairs of galoshes to the third floor. One pair could not be found. Every day for a week Bill said to Mrs. Weatherton, "Have you found Robbie's galoshes yet?" Mrs. Weatherton replied that she had not. Finally Bill himself brought the galoshes back. No one ever discovered where they had been hidden. Bill asked, "Are all these boys and girls my friends when I am bad?" Mrs. Weatherton thought for a moment, then replied, "We do not have any bad boys or girls here, but sometimes boys and girls do things that I do not like. I like you, Bill, but occasionally your behavior annoys me."

At this time Bill was participating in all the various school subjects. His work was accurate and completed in about one-tenth of the time it took other children to finish.

The first week after spring vacation Bill suddenly started masturbating, not so much in the classroom as in the lavatory. One of the teachers in the building became upset when Bill exposed himself before her. Mrs. Weatherton talked with Bill alone about this behavior. She tried to explain to Bill that it was perfectly natural for him to be interested in his body and to want to show it, but that school was not the proper place. After this talk with Mrs. Weatherton Bill's masturbation disappeared. However, a short time later Bill began to chew his pencils. This behavior continued for a period of two weeks. Then Mrs. Weatherton decided to bring snacks for forenoon and afternoon. These consisted of graham crackers, animal cookies, or a tiny candy bar. When Bill had the opportunity to chew crackers when he was hungry, he stopped biting pencils.

Bill made great progress during playtime. He learned to want to remain in the playground area, play with other children, and use the play equipment. During the arithmetic period Bill continually amazed the group. Before Mrs. Weatherton could put all the addition and subtraction problems on the board, Bill not only had the answers but had also computed the multiplication of the various combinations. One day a little girl had her seventh birthday. Mrs. Weatherton asked the children to write what they knew about the number seven. Bill put down the seven tables, all with correct answers.

Bill's art work continued to be unusual, detailed, and complex. He drew a map of the city, beginning with the community house, putting in the main civic buildings, and naming all the streets in a one-mile radius. The art teacher remarked that none of her sixth-grade pupils could draw buildings and streets with such perspective and detail.

One day Bill's sister came to see Mrs. Weatherton. She wanted to tell her how much Bill had improved at home. Both Bill's art teacher and Mrs. Weatherton noted a change, too, in Bill's attitude toward his mother. One day he made a unique design on a handkerchief for her and put it in an envelope with a note: "Dear Mother: I love you. Bill."

An important change occurred in Bill's speech. At the beginning of the year his speech was garbled and incomprehensible. Then he used only single words or brief phrases. Toward the end of the year he was speaking clearly and in complete sentences.

Mrs. Weatherton found inward peace with Bill. She no longer feared he would become so disturbed that she would have to remove him. Bill did not ask odd questions any more when strangers came to the room, but was relaxed and comfortable.

He no longer ran wildly around the room but learned to set limits for himself. At the beginning of the year he had become upset over even mild frustrations. He was learning to control his strong impulses and to carry out his projects without interfering with others.

Bill made friends, first with one child and gradually with others. The hair-twisting stopped and he sucked his first finger only when there was prolonged frustration. Bill's mother reported that the bed-wetting had ceased to be a problem.

Discussion

Mrs. Weatherton indicates that Bill was a seriously disturbed child at the beginning of the school year. He was constantly disruptive and noisy. It is amazing that it was possible for her to cope with his behavior at all in such a large first grade group. In her thirty years of teaching Mrs. Weatherton had not had an experience with a child like Bill, but she believed that every effort should be made to help him live fully in the classroom. She was willing to keep Bill in her group in spite of his bizarre, disruptive behavior. Her first approaches to him failed. She attempted to respond to him in a matter-of-fact manner, stating limits objectively but firmly, a method that had always been successful. But Bill was unlike any previous child in her experience. Mrs. Weatherton decided to extend the limits of the classroom to permit Bill to have more freedom. Given this opportunity, Bill began to show real ability in reading, spelling, and arithmetic, completing assignments at a third- and fourth-grade level.

Instead of condemning Bill's scribbling in the workbook, Mrs. Weatherton gave him a section of the blackboard and told him he could scribble whenever he wished. He soon discovered that other experiences were more rewarding. Her acceptance of Bill and his odd behavior was conveyed to the children. Soon they stopped laughing at him and began to make friendly overtures.

Mrs. Weatherton made no comments about Bill's language. She believed that when the interest and motivation were there, Bill would talk. It was not a matter of teaching him to speak but of helping him to want to talk.

Mrs. Weatherton accepted Bill's feelings and encouraged him to express them. She tried to show him that his strange expressions were understandable and took time to let him know she wanted to understand him. Perhaps most important of all, Bill, who could not bear to hear the name of any member of his family mentioned, was able to express his affection for his mother in a unique design he himself created.

Bill still had several problems at the end of the school year, but they interfered less frequently with school activities. He began having psychiatric treatment at this time too. The family had previously been strongly opposed to any kind of psychotherapy. Mrs. Weatherton talked to his new teacher and paved the way for continued understanding and acceptance of him in the classroom.

MRS. BARKER AND CHERYL

One day during the lunch hour, two weeks after school had started, Mrs. Barker, seeing a woman and a child looking into her room, walked over to them, and nodded when the mother inquired if it was a third-grade room. The girl said, "I am starting school for the first time here. I have been very sick. In fact, they didn't think I would live." Then she quietly pulled off the scarf on her head and showed Mrs. Barker a completely bald head. There was a large, ugly scar from the top of her head to her neck. The mother said her daughter Cheryl had become very ill with severe headaches, and that doctors, after several examinations, had found a serious brain condition. A section of the brain had failed to develop and an immediate operation was necessary. Cheryl remained seven weeks in the hospital, only to be told that the operation had been unsuccessful. She had to remain in the hospital for seven more weeks before being permitted to go home. These were anxious weeks for Cheryl and her family. Several times she was close to death, and when she was finally released from the hospital, the doctors were doubtful that she would ever be mentally normal.

While Cheryl stood in the doorway with her scarf off, the children all noticed this strange-looking child with no hair, and stared and whispered. "So you see what has happened to me," said Cheryl. "Yes, Cheryl, I do," Mrs. Barker replied warmly. Then the bell rang and Cheryl and her mother went to the office. When the whispers and questions had stopped, Mrs. Barker explained the importance of being kind and understanding with Cheryl. After a short discussion, the class agreed that whatever group Cheryl was placed in, they would do what they could to be friends with her.

Sometime later the door opened and Cheryl announced she was to be in that room. The children accepted her completely, and chose a desk for her from which they could look at her face and not see the back of her head. Cheryl smiled and was pleased with their friendly attitude.

The next day, while the group practiced writing, Cheryl raised her hand and asked if she could write her last name, since it began with the letter being practiced. Mrs. Barker gave her a piece of chalk and let Cheryl write on the board. Cheryl looked like a different child after recess that day. She smiled warmly and said she liked her new class. When the whole class wrote her name, she felt immediately a part of the group.

Mrs. Barker learned from Cheryl's mother that Cheryl would be able to attend school only for the afternoon session, as she was still in danger. Coming in from recess the second day of school, she took Mrs. Barker's hand and held it tightly. "I prayed very hard that I could come to school," she said. "I shall pray twice as hard tonight, because I want to come tomorrow too. I have some friends here now. I haven't had any friends for a long time." Mrs. Barker said warmly, "We are your friends, Cheryl, and we want you to come as often as you can. We hope it will be every day."

As the weeks went on Cheryl seemed happy in her new situation, but she was nervous about her work and became quieter with the group. She always seemed relaxed when she talked with Mrs. Barker. Since she was in school only for half-day sessions, she was permitted to read with whatever group she chose. Within two weeks she decided on the group she wanted to stay with. She is a superior reader, but when asked to read aloud, she speaks so quietly that the rest of the group can barely hear her. One morning during gym class, when Cheryl was alone in the room with Mrs. Barker, she asked if she could read one of the books on the desk. "If you would like to," Mrs. Barker said. "I would like to read to you," she said. She chose *Paddle to the Sea*, took it to the library table, and read so distinctly she could be heard in any part of the room. "You read very well, Cheryl," Mrs. Barker said. "I like to read to you," she said. "You can read to me in reading group," Mrs. Barker suggested. "'Yes, but I might make some mistakes," Cheryl replied. "We all make mistakes. I'd like you to try to read to me just as you did just now," Mrs. Barker said. "All right, I'll try," Cheryl replied. From this point she showed definite improvement in oral reading. However, there was still some tension in her voice when she read before the group.

One morning she came into the room very excited and shouted happily, "I've got a dog, a dog of my own, and she's just beautiful." Then she proceeded to tell the class about her new dog. She had spoken so spontaneously she was unaware that she was talking to the entire group.

Cheryl has various moods, brought about by the constant pressure and fear of further illness. One day on the way out to recess a child ran into her and bumped her head. Such incidents are a source of anxiety because of the possible seriousness of any blow, and Mrs. Barker was therefore constantly on the lookout for Cheryl. This bump caused her to become very dizzy. She cried, "Oh, thank God he didn't hit the back of my head. If he had, I might die, because there isn't any bone there." "You're all right, Cheryl," Mrs. Barker said, equally grateful. "I couldn't see a thing, everything went dark. I am frightened. Please, may I stay with you during recess?" Cheryl asked tearfully. "Yes, you may," Mrs. Barker replied, attempting to keep the worry from her tone of voice. Coming back into the room that afternoon, Cheryl took Mrs. Barker's hand and told her she felt wonderful when she was with her. "You're so good to me," she said, "and you don't worry about me the way Mommy does. Mommy is so worried that she's afraid to let me have fun, but you're not afraid, are you?" Mrs. Barker said calmly, "No, Cheryl, I think there are many ways in which you can have fun."

One day Cheryl brought a box of special shells to class and put one on each child's desk while the children were out of the room. She asked Mrs. Barker not to tell the class who put them there. Then Cheryl added, "Please don't tell them, because I want it to be a surprise. When I was in the hospital, I got so many surprises that I want my friends here to have some too. Do you think the boys and girls will like these shells?" she asked. "If you like them, Cheryl, I'm sure the class will like them," Mrs. Barker replied.

During her sad moods Cheryl often talks of death. Mrs. Barker never discourages her. Sometimes she talks of her young aunt. "I'll never have any cousins because my aunt took very sick and died only one month after she was married. She was so nice. I loved her very much." At other times Cheryl mentions fears of her own death. Mrs. Barker listens at these times but says little to Cheryl, except to encourage her to explore these fears further. Cheryl often jokes about her hair, which is just beginning to grow. The pictures she draws always have girls with long hair. One day she said, "You know, Mrs. Barker, before I took sick I had pretty curly hair, a lot like yours. Mine will soon be as long as yours."

When Mrs. Barker returned to school after being absent for two days, Cheryl was happy to see her and exclaimed, "Oh, you're back! I'm so glad. I was afraid we would have that other teacher again. She was always telling me not to do things, and she looked at me real funnylike, not the way you do. I hope you don't get sick again."

Mrs. Barker felt that Cheryl, more than anyone else in the group, needed special time and attention, so she looked for opportunities to be with her and tried to help her feel comfortable with her handicap. Mrs. Barker had hoped that this relationship would facilitate Cheryl's sense of freedom and value in the classroom, and enable her to feel that her struggle to live was worthwhile. It was difficult at times not to be over-sympathetic and protective, not to be fearful, and not to show favoritism.

Discussion

The first moment of a meeting is sometimes crucial; this proved to be true of Mrs. Barker's initial encounter with Cheryl. Meeting Cheryl as she did, gave Mrs. Barker an opportunity to prepare herself as well as the children. She took time to try to discover how Cheryl felt about herself and the school, tried not to be anxious over Cheryl's handicap, and attempted to minimize Cheryl's fear and worry. On the other hand, she did not deny the validity of Cheryl's feelings when she expressed her insecurity and anxiety and when she talked about death. Mrs. Barker used her relationship with Cheryl to encourage her to attempt tasks that were difficult and challenging. Her approach was to let Cheryl talk about her doubts and feelings of inferiority, but at the same time to help her face her fears. Mrs. Barker did not permit the girl's fears of death to stifle her; she continued to develop a relationship with Cheryl based on vitality and life rather than decay and death. Mrs. Barker supported Cheryl when she felt this was needed, but encouraged her to move forward on her own. Many of this teacher's decisions came from a belief that, as far as possible, Cheryl could participate in the same activities as other children. Cheryl found strength in attempting new tasks, knowing that her teacher had confidence in her and a genuine regard for her.

CHAPTER 6

Interpersonal Relationships
in the Later Elementary Grades

By the time children have reached the later elementary grades they have become habituated to classroom routines. They are more reluctant to talk about their feelings and significant experiences. They tend to be more suspicious. Too often they are motivated by extrinsic rewards rather than by growth strivings. Satisfaction comes from effective competition, achievement, and status, rather than from fulfilling unrealized potentials and from imaginative, original endeavors. In the light of these difficulties, thirty-four teachers in four school systems attempted to create a special classroom atmosphere conducive to growth of the self and intimate teacher-child relationship.* All agreed that considerable time was needed to create an atmosphere of warm permissiveness in the classroom, to convey to children that there would be no retaliation, and to show them that the teacher was sincerely interested in them as individuals.

The spontaneous use of interpersonal conflict in the school is illustrated by an incident that occurred on the playground involving a group of sixth-grade children. Several boys were in a huddle, laughing loudly. The teacher became incensed when he found them looking at photographs of nude women. He yanked the boy from the group who was displaying the pictures and reprimanded him in a loud, angry voice so that the entire group heard his rebuke. The class became extremely upset over the incident.

* The material in this chapter is based partly on anecdotal and verbatim records kept by these teachers. The illustrations were selected from their reports.

Back in school, the tension mounted. The entire group supported the boy and was angered by the teacher's attitude. When the teacher returned to class late that morning, he could sense the hostility in the group. He apologized for having lost his temper, adding that he knew a number of children felt strongly about what he had done. He wondered whether they would care to talk about it. The reaction of the class was immediate. Nearly everyone had a great deal to say, mostly negative, about the teacher's behavior. The children spent almost an hour attacking the teacher, at first only in reaction to the playground episode but later mentioning other experiences with the teacher in which injustices had been committed. Some of it was difficult for the teacher to listen to. He never dreamed so much hostile feeling had accumulated toward him. The teacher decided to stop the discussion after forty-five minutes had elapsed. During the next month, however, he gave the children numerous opportunities to express their feelings about school and teachers. The intense criticism continued for several weeks, the attack spreading to other teachers in the school system. When the teacher had almost decided that the amount of hostility the group felt was limitless, many of the children began to relate positive school experiences. Throughout this period the teacher recognized a positive relationship developing between him and the group. The children were freer not only in raising problems and offering contrary opinions, but also in making constructive suggestions for improving classroom procedures.

In one crowded school system a group of fifth- and sixth-graders were put together, a departure from the regular school practice. The sixth-graders resented it and formed a club, as a way of segregating themselves and attaining privileges entitled to senior students. The younger group resented being rejected, called names, and mistreated in other ways. For some time the teacher attempted to battle the clique, expressing a critical attitude toward its members. She spent considerable energy in combating the growing hostility between the two groups. One day she decided upon a new approach, accepted the idea of a special club for sixth-graders, and gave all the children an opportunity to express their feelings about being put in the same group. The reaction was tremendous. The two groups spent an hour each week for eight weeks revealing strong feelings against one another. The teacher attempted to accept all expressions without giving her ideas or evaluations. Just being a part of a regular group discussion and freely expressing feelings seemed to give the two groups a better understanding of one another.

Personal Interaction with the Group. Here the children have an opportunity to express their feelings and reactions to the teacher, school, and other experiences. The teacher listens and accepts these feelings, showing each child his perception is valid for him and worth while.

For the most part the hostile reactions disappeared, the relationships between the two groups improved, and the club was opened to fifth-graders. The teacher, in retrospect, decided that the more intensely she fought the factions, the stronger the cleavages grew. When she accepted the right of the groups to segregate themselves, and gave them an opportunity to express their feelings toward one another, these feelings changed and friendships among members of the two groups developed.

MISS LYONS AND HER FOURTH-GRADERS

Miss Lyons attempted different types of activities in which every child in the group could participate. These activities were continued over a period of three months.

In the first approach Miss Lyons asked each child to draw anything he wished about home or school. There was considerable discussion among the children before they started to work. When the drawings were completed, any child who wished to tell about his drawing could do so. One drawing was a picture of what a child saw on a recent trip to a television studio. Another showed a picture of the child's home. Other themes included skating at Grandma's farm; helping Mother; a dog chasing a cat up a tree; sister imitating how a child stands on his head in gym; a broken window; getting pushed into a pond; an old lady telling a child to put a wagon back; and a trip to Niagara Falls. None of these seemed to have particular significance to the children. One child, however, made a drawing about an unpleasant experience that had occurred earlier in the day. On the morning of the drawing session Miss Lyons had given a spelling test. Lucy had copied the words from the girl who sat in front of her. Miss Lyons asked Lucy to close her book and told her she could take the test later. As Lucy was drawing her picture in the afternoon, Miss Lyons asked if she would like to tell about it. Lucy hesitated a moment, then said, "This isn't this classroom, but the teacher is saying, 'Take out your spelling books,' and she's sticking her tongue out at the teacher." Miss Lyons said, "She must not like the teacher." Lucy agreed heartily and continued to put more detail into the picture. Later, during the group discussion of the picture, Lucy explained, "I just drew a picture of a plain old classroom. The teacher is saying, 'Get out your spelling book.' This girl is putting out her tongue. She doesn't like the rules. There are too many." Then Lucy added, "I can't take that picture home 'cause I might get thrown out of my house. It's such an awful picture and it's about something awful."

Before the end of the day Miss Lyons had an opportunity to

talk with Lucy alone. She explained that she realized how up-setting it must have been to be seen copying spelling words from another child. Lucy nodded but said nothing. Miss Lyons continued, "It's quite understandable that sometimes children don't like the ways teachers handle things, and they have a per-fect right to feel that way." This experience gave Lucy an op-portunity to tell about feelings which otherwise might have been repressed. Her feelings of resentment may have accumu-lated toward Miss Lyons and other teachers. Every child reacts in some way to being caught at cheating, but rarely is given an opportunity to express these reactions. Miss Lyons permitted and encouraged Lucy to talk about the experience, accepted Lucy's point of view and feelings, and thus enabled the relation-ship to continue on a healthy basis.

A week later the second activity was presented to the group. Miss Lyons asked the children to relax by putting their heads down on their desks and listening to a record. She selected one that conveyed a variety of moods. During the first listening ses-sion children started free actions, moved up and down in their seats, portraying riding a horse, leading an orchestra, etc. When the record was finished, the children began spontaneously to dis-cuss it. They talked about how different kinds of music made them feel. Almost every child indicated some feeling in response to the different moods portrayed in the record. Then Miss Lyons handed out paper and asked them to draw their feelings as she played the record a second time. During the replaying there was much verbal and physical expression. After the pictures were completed, Miss Lyons gave each child an opportunity to discuss his drawing individually. For the most part the children indi-cated only the theme. Several meticulous, neat children had scribbled all over several sheets of paper, even after the record had stopped. They had nothing to say about the scribbling, but indicated that they enjoyed the experience. They seemed more relaxed to Miss Lyons. Afterwards, whenever she felt tension in the group, she permitted the children to draw or scribble as a way of releasing pent-up feelings.

Two pictures that deviated from the sleeping, dancing, and

riding themes were those of Sharon and Arden, who drew similar love scenes involving the same boy. These girls have continuously competed for this boy's interest and attention. Miss Lyons felt that this experience was beneficial in the general release it provided of physical and emotional tension.

The next activity, involving the use of finger puppets, continued over a period of six weeks. The class was divided into five groups. In each group Miss Lyons placed one child who had been having difficulty in school. The children were free to create and dramatize any home or school situation, anything about the teacher, the class, individual children, or the family.

In one of the plays Bob spent his time telling the other players what to do. He had a tendency to domineer. As the plays continued, however, he realized more and more that he could achieve more satisfying results by cooperating. Kenny particularly resisted the domination and conveyed to Bob the idea that he would get further by being less demanding. Bob's orders decreased.

A particularly interesting play helped bring about a modification in Miss Lyons' teaching. Highlights from this play portrayed the children's perceptions of their principal and two teachers.

Sally (*In the role of the principal, speaking to Miss Lyons.*): The children threw rocks at someone and it's because you are too hard on them. (*All agree.*) You should quit bossing the children. The children get terrible when you treat them that way.

Carol (*As Miss W, another teacher*): I don't think she's too hard.

Bob (*A pupil*): I do. She's always making us do something, and we get mad and do things we're sorry for.

John (*A pupil*): I agree with you. I think Miss L is marking children too bad in studies. And Miss W too. One wrong and you get a D. She's too hard.

Carol (*Forgetting her role as Miss W.*): I think so too. I worry about my grades. My parents keep telling me I've got to do better. My sister always gets good grades. But I don't.

Sally (*Forgetting her role too*): Some of the teachers in the school are good, but how Miss W treats children is terrible. (*Becomes principal again.*) Miss W, you're fired. You shouldn't have become a teacher anyway.

Bob: All right, we got rid of her.

Children: Hooray! Hooray!

Sally: That's entirely too hard arithmetic. It's always too hard when it should be fun. (*All the children clap.*)

Discussion

These children were reacting strongly to the demands of schoolwork and the lack of meaning and interest in it. School subjects were something to be endured rather than experienced as enjoyable. Several children mentioned their worry about schoolwork, the fact that it was difficult, and the feeling that parents constantly put pressure on them. The majority of the children mentioned the domineering approaches of teachers; most teachers were perceived as authoritarian and disciplinarian. Miss Lyons became aware of her own phony role playing. She wanted something more than that from teaching. She wanted to help make real growth possible for children, to give them courage and strength, not to force them to submit to her will. Yet these children were saying "We work in school because we are forced to work, not because it suits our desires and purposes, not because it brings us personal satisfaction." The children were achieving for their teachers and parents but there was no genuine value in it for them. Miss Lyons was beginning to realize that something was entirely wrong with education that was so boring and meaningless, something was wrong with teaching that aroused fear and distrust in children rather than interest, self-esteem and self-confidence. Miss Lyons decided to use her new awareness to offer resources and opportunities that had personal value, and to help children become involved in their own learning.

An opportunity for sensitive listening occurred when the class presented a play on the trials of family life. Some excerpts follow:

Barb (*Mother*): Babs wants a hairdo.

Fred (*Father*): No!

Barb (*Mother*): Let's have the children decide.

Junior (*Son*): I think Babs should decide.

Fred (*Father*): Do you want to go up to your room? (*Then to Babs.*) What kind of hairdo do you want?

Babs (*Daughter*): Shorter and curlier.

The "Free" Activity Period. These children are seriously engaged in a variety of activities. The boy in the upper left is working on arithmetic problems; the two boys next to him using a bulletin board are beginning a new art project; two boys in the center are playing a game while another child looks on; the two boys in the front are engrossed in individual interests of reading and drawing. The teacher insists that children respect each other's choices at this time and not interfere or disturb others.

Fred (*Father*): I'll think about it and give you my opinion tomorrow. (*Fred asks a friend.*) Do you think my daughter should have a long hairdo?

Marie (*Neighbor*): Yes, I think so. But it's your family.

Fred (*Father*): Barb, Marie says she should have a long one. I don't want short and curly hair.

Jill (*Neighbor*): I got my haircut.

Fred (*Father*): What kind? Very long and curly. That's OK.
    Guess I'll get a haircut too. (*Goes and comes back.*) How
    does it look?
All: Terrible.

Individual Exploration and Group Interaction. Here is an illustration of the
individual and the group in close proximity. Two varied projects are developing in the children's own way and time.

Fred (*Father*): Junior, you'd better get your hair cut too. Get
    it brush.
Junior (*Son*): I don't want a brush. I want it long.
Fred (*Father*): And I said you'll have it brush.
Junior (*Son*): I want it long and you say get a brush. Babs wants

hers short and you say leave it long. You never agree with us.

Bill (*Neighbor*): My wife has gone to get her face changed.

Fred (*Father*): That'd be good for my son. Maybe they'd take off his mouth. He's getting into everyone's business.

Bill (*Neighbor*): You should see my wife. She has a terrible dress on. She gabs all the time.

Fred (*Father*): I'll go out and get myself a new topcoat.

Bill (*Neighbor*): My wife bought a terrible hat with a bird on it that has a feather in its mouth.

Essentially these children seem to be acting out their feelings that parents are sometimes uncertain and inconsistent in their behavior. Occasionally parents have two sets of standards, one for themselves and one for their children. This creates confusion in children and makes identification with parent values and standards extremely difficult. Several of the children in Miss Lyons' group showed an inability to decide what to do when the freedom of choice was made available to them. Uncertainty and vacillation characterized much of their work in school. It was a struggle for Miss Lyons to help them use their potential for creative thought and wise decision.

Another play described how the principal handled a "bad boy."

Darlene (*Mrs. K, another fourth-grade teacher*): Quit shooting those peas. (*Kenny, bad boy, continues making sound of shooting peas throughout the play.*) If you shoot any more peas, I'm going to tell Mr. R. (*principal*).

Joyce (*Miss Lyons*): What's going on here? Stop shooting peas at Mrs. K.

Darlene (*Mrs. K.*): Go into the office and quit shooting peas.

Paulette (*Pupil*): Balloons, balloons!

Kenny (*Bad boy*): I'll take the balloons.

Darlene (*Mrs. K.*): Give back those balloons. You're always in trouble.

Joyce (*Miss Lyons*): Give back those balloons, Kenny.

Darlene (*Mrs. K.*): You get out of here and don't come back again.

Kenny (*Bad boy*): OK, I'll go home.

Joyce (*Miss Lyons*): Oh, don't you think we'd better go after him? What am I going to tell that boy, Mrs. K! He never listens to anything.

Darlene (*Mrs. K.*): Don't let him get away with it. If you do, Mr. R will fire you.

Kenny (*Bad boy*): Good! You should be fired.

Jim (*Mr. R, principal*): You get out of here and don't come back again.

Kenny (*Bad boy*): Good! I don't like this school anyway.

Joyce (*Miss Lyons*): He never does anything I tell him. That boy seems to have that peashooter glued to his mouth.

Jim (*Mr. R, principal*): Well, I'll fix him. Go out in the hall and stay there the rest of the day.

Kenny (*Bad boy*): I never can have any fun at this school.

Other plays developed feelings around the tasteless food served in the school lunchroom, trouble on the playground, and difficulties with parents. Miss Lyons felt that the plays helped her to understand children's attitudes, to be more honest as a teacher, and to permit children greater involvement and choice in school studies.

Mr. Bell and His Fourth-Graders

Mr. Bell, principal of the Lincoln School, arranged to meet with a group of thirty-six fourth-graders, a number of whom were having serious difficulties in school. The group was selected particularly because numerous problems had occurred in the school and some of these children were being ostracized by their group. Twelve weekly meetings were scheduled.

In the first meeting Mr. Bell explained the purpose of the discussions. The children were invited to voice their opinions and feelings freely. Certain limitations were established before the discussions began. Mr. Bell mentioned the importance of taking turns, not laughing at what was said, and not carrying the discussion outside the class. These were accepted by the group without complaint or discussion. Mr. Bell's objective was to encourage the expression of feelings, attitudes, and conflicts among the children and to accept every response, expecting that in this way the group would resolve tensions and difficulties and achieve a more unified feeling.

The sessions were tape-recorded. Some of the excerpts are presented below.

Excerpt 1

Bob: Today I was picked on by the teacher. I didn't have my assignment done and she knew it but called on me anyway. I don't think that's fair.

Mr. Bell: You think Miss Norris called on you purposely to make you feel bad.

Bob: Yes. (*A pause.*)

Bill: Bob had plenty of time to do his work. He was just showing off.

Mr. Bell: You think he just wanted to show off?

Bill: He's usually wasting time. He could have done it.

Mr. Bell: Uh-huh.

Clan: Bob is picked on by the kids too. He gets blamed for everything.

Ken: The other day in gym the team on which Bob was playing was acting smart. They were called show-offs by the other team, especially Bob. Our team was doing the same thing but we weren't called show-offs.

Mr. Bell: It looks to you as though Bob is being treated unfairly.

Garth: Sometimes Buster shows off just to make us laugh.

Mr. Bell: He doesn't mean to cause harm.

Jane: But sometimes he teases to make us mad.

Cooper: Sometimes the boys call the girls "dumb dames." We don't like to be called "dumb dames."

Warren: In our gym class Mr. G asks us all to be quiet but the girls keep fussing after the boys have shut up. So we call them "dumb dames."

Mr. Bell: That's your way of getting even. Is that right?

Warren: Yes. (*A pause.*)

Bennet: Buster pushes me around in the gym. I wish he'd leave me alone.

Mr. Bell: It irritates you to have him bother you like that.

Bennet: I just don't like to be pushed around.

Weston: Buster is unfair in the gym class. He makes up his own rules and will not follow the rules which we have.

Mr. Bell: He takes the fun out of the game, is that it?

Bob: Weston teases Warren all the time. He hides his papers and punches him in the back.

In this first session the children expressed their feelings of resentment against their teacher and awareness of the preferential treatment she gives some children in the group, and the conflicts in boy-girl relationships. Mr. Bell listened to all these expressions and encouraged further exploration of the feelings.

Excerpt 2

Warren: I like somebody. All the kids tease me about it. I don't like it. I wouldn't mind a little teasing but they yell it out to the whole room.

Mr. Bell: You feel disgusted when they act that way.

Warren: They don't use good sense.

Garth: I don't see why we should be teased about liking people. We have a right to like someone. Ted always spreads it. He says, "Hey, look at the lovers."

Mr. Bell: You don't want it spread around?

Bill: Because you like a girl or have a date it doesn't need to go down in headlines.

Van: Ted told on Bob the other day. He was sitting in Lena's seat so Ted teased Bob by saying, "That's Nancy's seat. Why don't you kiss her when she comes back?" (*A pause.*)

Bob: I can't see why everybody talks about Lena. I don't like people saying you might get cooties. I like Lena but I don't love her. I like everybody.

Molly: I don't think the children ought to tease Lena. She's good to everyone. If somebody wants paper, Lena says, "Here, I'll give you paper." She always gives everybody something and keeps nothing for herself.

Mr. Bell: You don't like to see Lena treated unfairly when she is so generous to everyone.

Clan: When Lena comes back after being absent, the boys say, "Oh no! She's back again." Everybody has faults. She shouldn't be picked on.

Garth: Lena is very generous.

Cal: Lena is nice and the teacher always talks about her and never takes her part. Everybody seems not to like her. I don't see why we don't all like her. She's nice to everyone.

Mr. Bell: You like Lena very much and can't understand why others don't.

Garth: Lena is better than many others in this class. She gives candy to everyone and she's very generous to everyone. I don't think people should mind teasing sometimes but they tease Lena all the time.

Mr. Bell: You think everyone should accept teasing a little but with Lena they go too far.

Buster: Kids like myself who are always being bad, the teacher takes away our recess. After school when we leave the building, the kids tease us and yell at us.

Mr. Bell: You don't like to be teased.

Bard: I don't think teasing is fair at any time. Marilyn often teases me. She comes and says, "Oh, did you see Bard kiss Nancy?"

Warren: Marilyn says, "I'm going to spread it." (*Several children make negative comments about Marilyn at this point.*)

Weston: Last week we talked about telling the girls "Be quiet, you dames." I don't think boys should say this. Sometimes the boys get mad. This is not nice. Someday you'll be dating and girls won't like you.

Ken: You're just saying what Miss Norris says. You're always repeating her words.

Bob: The girls teased the boys about their shorts. Mr. Sans, in gym, had the boys wear shorts for gym practice. There's nothing wrong with shorts. I told Judy not to tease like that.

Lee: If we were going to wear shorts, you can bet the boys would be around teasing.

Buster: Our teacher doesn't pay much attention to girls and boys teasing. I think it's OK for boys to tease girls and the other way around. (*A number of children shout "I do, too!"*)

The session was particularly valuable for Lena. At one point earlier she had told Mr. Bell that none of the children liked her. Though Lena did not contribute verbally to the discussion, Mr. Bell noticed that she participated actively with facial and body gestures. She seemed pleased that so many of her classmates came to her defense, realizing for the first time that she had the support of a number of children, boys as well as girls.

In addition to the discussion about Lena, the problem of teasing was explored. Though no solution seems evident from the discussion itself, the group was apparently influenced by it. Several teachers in the school reported a decrease in teasing in the group.

Excerpt 3

Cooper: When Caron was doing ballet in our program Buster put his head down and twirled his eyes. I don't think that was very nice.

Mr. Bell: You think Buster was showing off?

Bob: Buster was just showing off. He's always showing off. (*A pause.*)

Garth: It's all right to tease for a joke. My brother starts teasing me, but it usually ends up in a fight. He can't stand it when I tease him.

Ken: Bob doesn't like to be laughed at but he laughs at Sam a lot. No one likes to be laughed at.

Garth: Some kids are always taking hats and throwing them around. The other night my hat was torn. I don't mind so much the teasing, but kids shouldn't be so rough and tear clothes.

Cooper: Someone tore my hat. I won't mention names. I was so darn mad.

Bill: This is about Bob. It's not so bad to be laughed at. I laugh too when everyone else is laughing at me. He can laugh along with everybody else.

Bob: One time Warren and Sam were doing geography. Once I leaned back and fell off from the back of my seat. Everybody laughed. I didn't like that.

Mr. Bell: You don't like people making fun of you when you've done something foolish.

Ken: When we laughed at Bob, we didn't mean any harm. Everybody laughs.

Bob: At home no one ever laughs at me. I guess I never learned to take it.

Several problems were discussed in this session, including further exploration of feelings and reactions to teasing. The group approached the problem of poking fun at others, indicating when this type of behavior was acceptable and when it was not.

Excerpt 4

Garth: Sam needs help in arithmetic and that's when he shouldn't be laughed at.

Bard: I don't see why Sam didn't learn his tables too. I think he should know his tables. He has as much time as anyone. He's free to ask or look it up in his book. He could learn it if he wanted to.

Hal: Same as Bard.

Clan: The teacher's punishment wasn't fair. She made Sam write his tables ten times apiece. I don't think it was fair. When you have to stay after school it might be unfair, because you might have things to do after school. (*A pause.*) At home my brother throws his football around and hits the lamp or something and I have to go to bed, and it's his fault. Sometimes I wish I didn't have a brother.

Mr. Bell: Your brother gets you into trouble and you almost wish he weren't around.

Warren: My little brother keeps picking on me too. I tell him to stop fooling around. I hit him, or something, and Mom comes in the door just in time to see me hit him. She jumps to conclusions and I get in trouble.

Mr. Bell: Parents often don't see the whole thing.

Van: I get punished. Sometimes at home my brother starts hitting and bumping me. I hit my brother back. Then I get a bloody nose from my older brother who is always picking on me. He's six years older. I wish he'd leave me alone.

Sam: My little brother climbs on me, pounds me, and when I protect myself, he goes to my mother bawling.

At this point younger brothers and sisters show they do not always get preferred treatment.

Lee: It isn't always the smallest who gets the best of it. My sister, who's fourteen, gets to stay up until eleven. She comes into my room and asks me where her things are, but I can't go into her room. She wakes me up and Mom says, "What are you doing up so late?" She gives me the dickens for being awake.

Molly: When Mom's away, Janet slaps and pinches me. She blames me for everything.

Weston: I'm youngest in our family. My brothers punch me and even their friends pick on me and I get heck for it.

Nord: I'm littlest one at our house. When I'm asleep, my sister bangs the door and wakes me up and I get blamed for it. She tattles on me. In the morning she says, "Get dressed or I'll tell Mother."

Bob: Well, I'm littlest. My sister's a bully. She comes in my room and fights. I sock and hit and kick her. Sunday after church Mom left a note to finish homework and not go out. Barbie kept after me and hit me and whipped me with a belt. I threw a coat hanger at her. She hit me with the buckle on my noggin. My mom blamed me and punished me. I couldn't go outside all day and thirteen new houses were being built. Boy, was I mad.

Grace: My sister wakes me up at five in the morning. I say, "Go away." She calls "Mom, Grace won't let me in her bed." Mom gets mad at me for waking her up. I think she should stay in her own bed.

In this session the group broached the problem of sibling conflicts and parental handling of disagreements. It is interesting that Sam first mentioned unfairness in a teacher's punishment of a classmate, and, after a pause, began to express some stronger feelings about unfairness at home. Several children felt they were unfairly held responsible for the behavior of younger brothers and sisters and were often punished unjustly. A few in the group showed that older siblings got preferred treatment in their homes.

Excerpt 5

Mr. Bell: Last time you talked about unfair punishment at home. Is there anyone who wants to continue this discussion?

Van: My sister stays up till nine. I have to go to bed at eight.

Mr. Bell: You feel she should go to bed the same time as you do?

Warren: When I do something to my little brother, my big brother massacres me. He helps my little brother and then they both pick on me.

Mr. Bell: They gang up on you, huh?

Buster: My big brother's friends go in my room and play with my airplanes. I tell them to leave them alone but they just push me out.

Mr. Bell: You think they should respect your property?

Bob: Sunday, when I was playing with Mac, I lost my gloves. Mother was mad and wouldn't let me go out. If I had wanted to stay in, she would have made me go out. Dad got tired of me arguing and made me go to bed.

Buster: I'm tired when I get home from school. My brother Ed and his Indian friends run through the house. My big brother also bothers me. When I get after them, my mother punishes me and gives me no dinner.

Mr. Bell: It would be nice to have peace and quiet after you got home from school.

Bennet: My little sister is the loud mouth in our family. She got up early and broke some china. Mother came upstairs and bawled me out for not stopping her. Why should I be blamed?

Clan: I'm supposed to play with my brat of a brother. I would rather do anything than that.

Mr. Bell: Its hard to have him always tagging after you.

Clan: He's supposed to stay with me all the time.

Winks: Bill and I get into a fight or are playing. Dad tells me to stop. But when Bill is getting the best of it, he looks the other way. He never yells at Bill.

Bill: My little sister waits until we stand on a rug. Then she jerks it. All my parents do is laugh.

Mr. Bell: Maybe you'd like to pull a few tricks on her.

Bill: I sure would but they wouldn't let me.

Molly: When my big sister wants her shoes, she wakes me up to find them.

Mr. Bell: She ought to be expected to do things for herself.

Warren: When I want to use something of my brother's, he comes home and won't let me have it. He takes my things without asking. Father always says, "Let him use it." But never when I want something.

Mr. Bell: You think your father unfairly takes his part.

The problems involved in sibling relationships were further explored. The strongest feelings were expressed toward parents who permitted one child in the family to behave in a certain way and punished another child for the same behavior.

Excerpt 6

Bard: Every time we play "English Bull," Buster stiff-arms me in the nose. He does not follow rules.

Ken: I stiff-armed Doug and he didn't complain.

Weston: I don't think it's fair to stiff-arm other people in the face.

Van: You don't mind when it's an accident, but Buster does it on purpose.

Bill: Yes, Buster does it on purpose.

Bob: Bill jumps on my back and tickles me. Ted hurt me too. Doug plays too rough. He sticks his elbow in my ear and I get mad. He really smeared me one day.

This type of criticism continued for the remainder of the period but lessened in intensity. The actual attacks of the children upon one another during the school day have subsided considerably.

Excerpt 7

Nord: We were playing "English Bull" and Ward kicked me. Miss Norris saw me crying and the kids called me a "brat." That made me mad.

Mr. Bell: Made you angry to be called a brat.

Nord: I couldn't help crying, it hurt.

Hardy: Not to mention any names, but people start fights when they know they are tougher.

Clan: Bob pushed me into a mud puddle and I was covered with mud. I hid behind a tree and watched. Didn't want to be seen. Then the teacher called the kids in. I wasn't mad, only cold. I don't mind a joke, even when its on me.

Mr. Bell: You were pretty uncomfortable, but not mad.

Clan: They were calling me names. They yelled, "Larry wet his pants."

Buster: Playing football, Clan took a flying tackle for King. That was a dive bomb that went out of control. King could have been hurt.

Cooper: I have two brothers. They are brats at times. They throw Lincoln logs and I get mad and call Mother. They keep throwing logs. Then I give them a couple of taps and Dad gets real mad and says, "Ellen Cooper, go to bed." Wish I was the youngest one in the family.

Mr. Bell: You think if you were the youngest things would be different.

Tom: Some of the fifth-graders came over to fight. They kept throwing snowballs at us. One of Miss Norris' pets hit Grace in the eye. Miss Norris looked the other way. I got mad.

Ken: Buster is the one who makes me so mad. He's always doing things.

Van: Doug tells all the guys to judo me. That really stings.

Feelings of being hurt in play and fair play were the major topics of discussion. The session gave all the children an opportunity to hear others talk about their experiences and realize that it is not cowardly to cry, feel ashamed, or angry when hurt in play. The group recognized that being hurt fairly is more acceptable to the person than being hurt when rules are violated and deceptions used.

Excerpt 8

Buster: I have to be in the middle in my family. I wanted to sleep in the other morning. I was snoring away when my little brother hits me in the stomach. I throws the pillow at him and Mom walks in and it hits her. My little brother tells Bill I hit him in the nose. I take off and he takes after me. Dad blows up. Bill tells Dad I'm too spoiled. Then I gotta get up. Get my bed made. I try to take a nap before breakfast. My brothers rip up my bed and take up the pillows. Mother blames me for messing up the bed. On the way to school I pound Ed. He gets all his little friends after me. I jump off the swings on the playground to run away, but along comes my big brother Bill and his friends and they pound up on me. Everyone picks on me. Maybe that's why I get mad and want to hurt kids at school.

Wally: At six-thirty this morning my little brother wakes me to say that today is Mommy's birthday. Then he wanted me to get him some comics. He made me so doggone mad.

Mr. Bell: Sometimes you wish he weren't around at all.

Winks: My big brother teases me. I get burned up like everything.

Mr. Bell: Your big brother picks on you, does he?

Buster: My big brother shows off to his friends. When I'm watching TV, he comes along and turns to another station. I wait until his friends leave, then ask why he changed the station. He says he has a right to change the station.

Mr. Bell: You feel your brother is given more rights than you.

Ken: My big brother changes the TV to the program he wants. I say that I was here first. He says I was here second, so what about it? I push him and run but I always get the worst of it.

Mr. Bell: You usually get the worst of it anyway.

Bob: I was walking home and the big seventh-graders came along. I was walking through the churchyard. They pushed me into the ice and water and shoved me around. They broke the ice with a rock. I got all soaked and got sick and couldn't go to a party.

Mr. Bell: You must have felt pretty miserable.

Molly: When we were at City Park this winter, I was wearing Janet's old gloves. Janet came along and took them because she had forgotten hers. I told Mom and she didn't say anything. I really didn't care because they were full of holes.

Hal: My big brother's girl friend is Rhea. When they were on their Washington trip, they broke up. I was real mad because I liked her very much. Now they're going together again so I'm happy again.

Mr. Bell: You were quite pleased when they made up.

Warren: My big brother and I sleep in the same room. In the morning he shakes up my covers and says, "Rise and shine." So cheerful and everything. I get real mad. If I don't pay any attention, he'll stop. Once when the folks were away, he stayed up late. When he came to bed, he shook my covers and I threw a screwdriver at his legs. He banged me one and cut my lip. I cut his eye. He thinks he is a big shot. I get so mad when he wakes me up in the morning. Sometimes I wish he would sleep late. Then he'd know how it felt if I woke him up.

This final excerpt shows a further exploration of the problem of sibling rivalry and unfairness in parental discipline.

Discussion

Early in these sessions the children expressed resentment against their teacher. Later they focused their feelings on themselves and their relationships with each other. The children began to think for themselves concerning fairness and fair treatment. The teacher, in consultations with the principal, appraised the expressions of the children and looked for ways of improving her relationships with them. Previous to this time the classroom teacher would not accept their behavior unless it coincided with predetermined expectancies of her own. There was a tendency too for the teacher to encourage group rejection of a child who irritated her or interfered with her program.

More opportunity was given the group to work on various school problems. Their ways of handling difficulty were respected. The relationships in the group showed improvement. There were fewer complaints from other teachers on the group's behavior. Most obvious improvement was in the relationship between teacher and children. Earlier the teacher's attitude was, "Why don't you use better sense? Anyone with an ounce of brains could do that assignment." Now her attitude is, "That is difficult to understand. Let me try to give a clearer explanation." In this case the children's greater acceptance of the teacher enabled her to show more acceptance of them.

Mr. Bell accepted the classroom teacher. He discussed with her the children's expressions but encouraged her to reach her own conclusions. He recognized that her group was an extremely hostile one to begin with, and he empathized with the teacher's frustrations in coping with the many classroom problems.

Mr. Bell helped the children to explore feelings and attitudes concerning themselves, their teacher, and others, particularly brothers and sisters. There was also considerable discussion of parental discipline. Mr. Bell's remarks helped the group to look more fully at themselves. He tried to show warmth and acceptance of each child. His relationship with the group helped several individual children to modify their attitudes toward other children and to reach understandings of their own behavior.

MRS. PERRY AND HER FIFTH-GRADERS

Early in February Mrs. Perry started a new project whereby one period each week was set aside for each member of the class to work on anything he wished. Limits were set up by the children themselves before the beginning of the activity. Some regulations which they imposed upon themselves were as follows: each child should have something to work on (games excluded), each would be free to move around as he pleased, so long as he did not interfere with the work of another, and talking would be permissible as long as it was not too loud and did not disturb others. The class as a whole thoroughly enjoyed this period of free choice of activity. The activities children selected were varied, including the making of models (cars, airplanes, etc.), knitting, designing hats for dolls, sewing, embroidering, needle point, jewelry designing, oil painting and water coloring, drawing, dramatic play, and small group discussions.

Control of the group was a group responsibility. If someone was reported for violating school regulations, or if someone was

The Cooperative Nature of Individual and Group Interests. These children are pursuing individual interests. This kind of individual creative expression has resulted in social interaction. Though apparently a group project, actually each of these children is exploring something of his own. There is no group plan or organizing here. Social relations result from the structure inherent in the individual project.

criticized for his behavior any time during the school day, time was provided for group discussion and, wherever necessary, decision for action.

One day several boys were throwing a ball in the room, against regulations, and knocked over a vase of water. Immediately the group came to Mrs. Perry saying, "We know we were not doing the right thing. While you weren't around we played with the ball. First it hit the window and then it hit the vase and knocked it over and spilled water all over everything. We cleaned up the mess." Mrs. Perry listened and accepted these comments. Nothing more was said. That was the end of the ball playing in the room.

Speaking freely, openly facing conflicts, and engaging in self-selected activities brought about more meaningful experiences.

Mrs. Perry felt that the group talks were also important. Sometimes the discussion was initiated by Mrs. Perry but often it was started by a student who was experiencing conflict over an incident or situation.

One day the school secretary called Mrs. Perry out of the room. When she returned, the class had formed small groups and were discussing some of their recent school experiences. Earlier in the day a serious battle had erupted on the playground. One group was discussing ways of solving the problem. Another group talked about unfair treatment of others. A third group explored the problem of self-discipline. Mrs. Perry permitted the discussions to continue. She joined each group for approximately twenty minutes, offering suggestions for further exploration of problems but always accepting opposite feelings and ideas. On the morning of April 1 the group was particularly excited. The following discussion occurred.

Fred: You know what my maid did this morning? She played a good joke on us. She tied the chairs to the table so we couldn't pull them out. She put rubber snakes in the coffee too. My dad put a rubber snake in the paper. I can't wait until my mother gets up and finds the snake in the paper. The maid put towels in the bottom of our cereal. My mother never wakes up until everyone is gone.

Pete: I'm going to put rocks in my little sister's bed. I'm going to put pins in her pillow, then when she sits down, she'll get up again. It's great playing tricks on her.

Cynthia B: I told my father he had a hole in his pants then said "April fool."

Susie: Yesterday we had to take a bath and then go to bed. We had to take Judy home. When we got back and went to bed, our sheets were folded over and we couldn't get in bed. I was teased by everyone and everything.

Beverly: Last night my grandmother had sauerkraut for dinner and I hate sauerkraut. She said I had sauerkraut in my milk. I picked up my milk and threw it across the room. When I get mad, I throw things and am sorry afterward.

John: We had buzzers all over the house. When we'd go to answer the door and one buzzer would ring, then another.

Gail: I told my mother I was going to get even by putting books in my sister's pillowcase. When I went upstairs, there were books in my pillowcase. Mother wasn't upstairs. I got so mad. I went downstairs and asked Mother if she had put them there. She said no but maybe Daddy had.

Mrs. Perry: When you try to get even with your sister, it seems you always get the worst of it.

Pete: I went downstairs and found an empty Canada Dry bottle and poured out soda into the Canada Dry bottle. I asked my sister if she wanted some and gave it to her. I made her drink it. There was waxed paper in our sandwiches today and there were books in my pillowcase.

Fred: I went to pick up a spoon and the spoons were tied together. There was a paper towel under our cereal. I saw it but kept it secret from my sister. When I went home from school, there was something cuckoo. My pajamas were tied together and the sheets were tied together. I put a board in my sister's pillow. She went to lay down and oh, her poor head. My maid put two snakes in my father's bed and one in my mother's bed.

This discussion helped the group to relax before the academic program was started. The following is a list of additional topics chosen for discussion. Stories were written concerning each and the discussions followed.

1. Good times with family or friends.

2. Things that make me angry and what I do about it.

3. What I do when I am alone. The things I think about, the games I play, things I imagine, or my dreams.

4. What I would do if I came to school and there was no one here.

5. Three wishes.

6. How my parents annoy me. What I wish for my parents.

7. How I feel about my brothers and sisters.

8. How I feel about school. The things I don't like about it and the things I do like about it.

9. What I would do if I were the principal or the teacher.

In each of these discussions children more and more talked about their real feelings. A strong sense of unity developed in the group, and this was recognized by other teachers in the school. It was Mrs. Perry's feeling that the discussions enabled children to talk through some of the problems connected with school as well as experiences outside the school. In some instances specific ways of handling school problems were worked out by the group.

Mr. Kramer and His Sixth-Graders

Mr. Kramer, a sixth-grade teacher, facilitated personal interactions in the classroom by requesting of each child that he keep a journal in which he would explore feelings which were aroused at school or at home. The journal was used by Mr. Kramer or by the child to initiate conversations between them or to begin discussions in the group. Each child had a code number to identify his journal which was submitted to Mr. Kramer once a week. The teacher then chose common feelings and attitudes of the group as a focus for discussion. An opportunity was provided for anyone who wished to do so to have excerpts from his journal read and discussed in the class. The children were free to express themselves about any feelings that were important to them. In addition, the children decided to set aside a certain amount of time on specified days to write in the journals. From the anecdotes and reports Mr. Kramer developed a heightened sense of awareness of individual children and of the group as a whole.

One day Mrs. Zeno, the language teacher, rebuked the entire

Photo by Merrill-Palmer

Personal Interaction Within A Small Group. The teacher is authentically present as a member of the group. The children are making plans for playground activity during recess. They develop their own ideas and make their own decisions. The teacher listens with interest and is an important resource person when needed.

group, calling them lazy and indifferent. The group felt that Mrs. Zeno's criticisms were unfair. The children were given an opportunity to discuss this experience. Brief excerpts from the discussion are presented below.

Mr. Kramer: Some of you seem to be feeling quite disgusted about what happened this morning. You mentioned in your journals that Mrs. Zeno unfairly criticized you. Would anyone care to discuss this at greater length?

C. M.: Mrs. Zeno is unfair. She blames us for things we don't do. She doesn't explain things too clearly and then tells us we're stupid when we don't understand.

Mr. Kramer: You don't feel it's entirely your fault when you don't understand Mrs. Zeno's teaching.

C. M.: Mrs. Zeno is a dope, nutty, and unfair about everything. She is the only one of all the teachers in the school that I really hate. The only thing I hate is language. I wish we didn't have to take it.

Mr. Kramer: It's the one thing you resent about school.

C. M.: Last year the sixth grade had language in here. Why can't we?

At this point, the teacher explained that something different in the school program was being tried out, and there was very little that could be done about changing it.

M. B.: I wish we didn't have to go into Mrs. Zeno's room for language either. I hate her. She isn't fair at all. She hits kids on the back with a yardstick when they talk. And she's always picking on me. I wish she would just send me out in the hall and talk to me later.

Mr. Kramer: You'd like it better if she would calm down before talking to you.

M. B.: Yes. Today I was in language. I had finished my work and I was just staring at the floor. Then she said, "Turn around, I like the back of your head better." I knew I was going to get in trouble because she was watching me every minute.

Mr. Kramer: Almost as if she were just waiting for you to do something wrong.

M. B.: Yes, when she yelled at me, I whispered to Sue, "I didn't do a darn thing." Then Mrs. Zeno said, "Sue and Marilyn, put your papers in the basket. We don't like cheaters here."

Mr. Kramer: You didn't feel you had that coming?

M. B.: I wish she'd go to blazes. When we checked papers, Sue and I checked them too, anyhow. We didn't throw them in the basket. I wish we could have language in here.

J. W:. Most people don't seem to like Mrs. Zeno, but I like her, and I think she's nice and she is fair.

L. K.: That's just 'cause you're her pet. She never gets mad at you.

J. W.: That's not so. I just like her, that's all. I think she's a fine teacher.

Mr. Kramer: You feel you get along fine with her, is that it, Jane?

J. W.: Yes. Except Friday in language. I was checking Larry's paper and he turned around to look at his paper, and Mrs. Zeno said, "Larry, my gosh, what is the matter with you?" And I don't think that was fair at all.

Several other children mentioned troubling experiences with Mrs. Zeno. Toward the end of the discussion the feelings were expressed in milder tones and more of the children came to Mrs. Zeno's defense. The more these children expressed negative feelings about their teachers, the more positive they came to feel toward them.

Shortly after Christmas vacation several middle children mentioned having difficulties at home. Mr. Kramer offered the group an opportunity to further discuss feelings about having both younger and older siblings.

Mr. Kramer: Your journals yesterday indicated that some of you had some problems at home during vacation. Would any of you care to discuss these problems with the group?

V. H.: I am glad that my grandmother is here, because my grandfather died in December. Every once in a while she starts to sort of cry. The trouble is it makes me feel uncomfortable.

Mr. Kramer: It makes you feel funny inside when you see your grandmother cry?

V. H.: Well, yes. I don't like to see people cry.

Mr. Kramer: I guess maybe your grandmother has been very nice to you.

V. H.: Yes, I don't like to see her unhappy. I don't like to be unhappy myself. (*A pause.*) I get mad sometimes, though. Right now I'm mad at my sister.

Mr. Kramer: You're kind of mad at your sister now, eh, Virginia?

V. H.: Yes, I'm mad at her because when my friends come over, she sits and talks with them. But when her boy friends come over, and I come in and start to talk, she calls my mother and I get into trouble.

Mr. Kramer: You think that's a pretty raw deal, don't you, Virginia?

V. H.: I sure do. I can't understand how she can get away with so much when I seem to get blamed for everything.

Mr. Kramer: Your parents always blame you and let her get away with everything.

V. H.: They sure do. If I'm not being blamed for something my sister does, I'm catching it for something my younger brother has done.

Mr. Kramer: You kind of get it from both ends, is that it?

V. H.: Yeah. Sometimes I believe my brother stays up nights thinking up ways he can get me in trouble.

Mr. Kramer: You think he really has it in for you some of the time?

V. H.: I know he just teases me and I should ignore him, but he eggs me on till I can't stand it any longer. Then I slap him and he screams and cries until I catch it from my mother. She says, "You must be nice to your little brother. He's younger than you, and you shouldn't push him around." Well, sometimes he hits me first and I don't like to be pushed around either.

Mr. Kramer: Your mother dosen't understand that you have feelings too.

R. E.: My brother gets me mad too. We get in lots of fights.

Mr. Kramer: You and your brother fight quite a bit, eh, Richard?

R. E.: Yes. You shouldn't feel too bad, Virginia. Most parents are that way. My folks pull the same stuff on me. They tell me I shouldn't hit Jim, 'cause he's smaller. Well, my bigger brother hits me. Why don't they tell him the same thing?

Mr. Kramer: You feel if it's OK for Bob to fight with you, it should be OK for you to fight with Jim.

R. E.: Well, I don't see much difference. I should be able to take it out on someone, but I get caught right in the middle of things.

Mr. Kramer: You feel like Virginia—getting it from both ends too, eh?

R. E.: Boy, I sure do!

Three others in the group mentioned like experiences at home. Mr. Kramer felt it helped children to hear others express similar feelings.

As the year went on several other discussions took place. Many of these revolved around problems at school and at home. The discussions became a regular part of the school program and proved worth while in releasing children's feelings both from temporarily frustrating and defeating experiences and from deeper feelings that had accumulated over the years in relationships at school and at home. As the children expressed more and more of their negative feelings, gradually more positive feelings toward teachers and family members appeared. They seemed to need the opportunity to talk about how they felt in order to feel better about their relationships.

The problems discussed by almost every group of later elementary children included unfair treatment in school, favoritism in school and at home, unjust punishment at home, difficulties in relationships with brothers and sisters, most often connected with parental favoritism, teasing at home and school, angry feelings resulting from rejection and disrespect by parents and teachers, and rejection by other children. Since these problems occurred so regularly in the discussions, it might be concluded that they are common to most children in the later elementary years and that children benefit from an opportunity to explore and discuss them.

In addition to the group experiences, the thirty-four teachers attempted to create special relationships with individual children who were of particular concern to them. Two of these relationships are presented in detail below.

Miss Leeds and Nan

Nan is nine and in the fourth grade. She is an attractive, dark-haired girl of average height. Miss Leeds's initial contact with Nan occurred in the first hour of school in September. The class was being assigned lockers. As the group walked down the hall Nan hit each locker, making a loud noise. Miss Leeds, feeling that a general announcement would handle this problem, said, "When we walk in the halls, we keep our arms at our sides." Nan stopped pounding but had a noticeable scowl on her face. During the remainder of the first week Nan frequently caught the teacher's attention. On the second day of school the class had gone outdoors to play. Miss Leeds noticed that Nan and Gale had remained indoors. They came straggling out to the playground. Miss Leeds stopped them and asked, "Why are you so late in getting out here?" Neither child answered for a moment, then Gale spoke up and said, "Nan has been holding me back. Look at my arm, Miss Leeds. She wouldn't let me go." Nan had a sneer on her face. Miss Leeds remarked sarcastically, "You seem delighted, Nan, that you have hurt Gale." Nan continued her attack on Gale, calling her names and irritating her in other ways. As the class was leaving the playground, Miss Leeds turned to Nan and said, "Nan, you're too nice a girl to behave like that." Nan replied, "I know I'm not nice and I don't care." Miss Leeds repeated, with some uncertainty in her voice, "Oh yes, Nan, I think you are nice." The class returned to the room and the children were to leave immediately for special music tests. Miss Leeds dismissed the rows. Gale's row was the last to leave. She burst out in tears. Miss Leeds stayed in the room with Gale while the rest of the class went on. Gale tearfully said that Nan had picked on her all last year when they were in class together. She had prayed that Nan wouldn't be in her class again. Miss Leeds listened for several minutes as Gale reported numerous incidents when Nan had picked on her. Nan eyed Gale for the rest of the morning. She boasted to other children that she had made Gale cry. Gale came up after lunch and reported that Nan had struck her when she was going home at noon. For about a week Miss

Leeds dismissed Gale's row first and Nan's last. That way Gale was well on her way home before Nan left. Gale's mother picked her up from school for a few days and also visited Nan's mother. After that Nan's conflict with Gale subsided. Apparently Nan listened to her mother.

The second week of school Nan attacked another girl in the class. She got one of her friends to torment this child until she was in tears. Then Nan proceeded to call her "crybaby."

The third week of school was climaxed by a love affair between Jay and Betsy. Evidently Nan became jealous. As the group went out to recess Nan started fighting with Betsy and continued the fight on the playground. However, Betsy, a much larger girl, pinned Nan to the ground. There were several other entanglements which Miss Leeds permitted to occur. When Nan seemed unable to cope with the situation any more, Miss Leeds told her to stay near her for the remainder of the recess. At this point Nan got her little brother beside her and persuaded him to hit Miss Leeds. Miss Leeds made no overt response. As the group came in from recess Nan suddenly slapped Betsy across the face so hard that tears came to her eyes. Again Nan was proud. She had made Betsy cry.

When the fourth week of school arrived, Nan was still misbehaving on the playground, calling children names, attacking them, and interfering with their play. A climax was reached one day when Nan was particularly insulting to Miss Leeds. The outside play period had just ended. Nan began making sarcastic comments to Miss Leeds, showing indifference to playground regulations. Some children came to Miss Leeds's defense. The class was so aroused no one moved to go indoors when Miss Leeds indicated it was time. Miss Leeds had the children go in one by one, leaving Nan until last. As she waited her turn, Nan became angry and hurt. She seemed on the verge of tears. When she got to the room, Nan stormed to her seat and sat down. Later in the day Nan pushed a girl hard, causing her to fall and cut her knees. Miss Leeds decided she needed outside help. She talked with the school principal, then called Nan's mother for a conference, believing this would help her to understand Nan's behavior better. The relationship between Nan and Miss Leeds had been a most unhappy one. Miss Leeds was beginning to feel inadequate in her attempts to create a positive relationship with Nan.

In considering Nan's experiences in the class, Miss Leeds began to see some common patterns. While in the classroom, she made little or no verbal comment and did not cause any type of disturbance. However, the minute she went outdoors she aroused a gang of boys to action, started fighting, and attacked children she wanted to torment. She usually fought with girls, selecting a different person each day for punishment.

The conference with Nan's mother, Mrs. Rayner, was enlightening. First, she reported that when Nan discovered that her mother was planning a school visit, she became immediately disturbed. She told her mother that her teacher was going to tell lies about her and she wanted to be present when these "lies" were told. Nan pleaded with her mother to be able to join her for the conference. Mrs. Rayner then described Nan as an exceedingly troublesome youngster at home. Nan constantly fought, tormented, and teased her two younger brothers and other boys in the neighborhood. The neighbor girls and families had excluded Nan from nearly all contact with them. Also, there was considerable friction between Nan and her maternal grandmother who lived with the family in the winter. Mrs. Rayner predicted that when Nan's grandmother came to live with them, Nan would become even more erratic and hostile in school. The grandmother favored the boys and had rejected Nan since the younger brothers' arrival.

Mrs. Rayner said Nan craved attention and was very anxious about school. She had always hated her teachers and had difficulties with them from her first year in school. Mrs. Rayner reported a history of negative school experiences and incidents in which Nan had created problems for herself and others. Before the interview ended, Miss Leeds asked if she might keep Nan after school at times in order to establish a better relationship with her. She explained that it was sometimes difficult to reach Nan during school hours. Mrs. Rayner agreed to this plan.

The next day Miss Leeds told Nan about the talk with her mother. Nan seemed pleased that Miss Leeds was willing to discuss the conference in such detail. Nan stayed after school twice that week and talked at length about some of her interests and her resentment toward her grandmother.

During the fifth week of school Nan came puffing in late one noon. She had gone to her grandmother's (quite a distance from her house) to get a piece of petrified wood for the science display. She had also picked some flowers. Nan said, "I just ate a marshmallow and a piece of bread for lunch. I wanted to bring you these." Nan had changed her hair style to approximately Miss Leeds's. Her behavior had improved markedly.

This change lasted for about three weeks. Then Nan proceeded to pick on Jon, who had come to school ill. Miss Leeds asked Nan to remain after school. Nan sat quietly for ten minutes, then got up and erased the board. She remained silent for another twenty minutes. Miss Leeds approached her. "I don't know what bothered you today, Nan, but I can't let you annoy other children that way." Nan did not respond. Miss Leeds continued, "Did you know that Jon was ill today?" Nan looked up and said, "No, I didn't," and, after a long pause, "I'm sorry." The next day, however, she concentrated her hostile feelings on another child.

For two weeks Nan had been critically watching Marie, who is a bit smaller than Nan and mentally retarded. During recess one day Nan attacked Marie. She was kept after school again. Nan sat quietly for about twenty minutes. Miss Leeds said, "You know Marie was hurt today." Nan remarked, "Oh, was she?" Miss Leeds said, "You like to hurt people, don't you?" Nan replied, "Yes. Sometimes I like to hurt people. There are thirteen guys in my neighborhood and they're all bigger than me and always picking on me. I never have girls to play with." Miss Leeds said, "Maybe that's why you pick on children who are weaker than you." Nan did not reply. Miss Leeds added, "You know Marie's parents are very poor. Have you ever noticed how worn her clothes are?" Nan began to cry. Miss Leeds continued, "Maybe you could help Marie. Today she wore a hair ribbon in her hair. Maybe if you would tell her how nice she looked, she might start caring a little more about herself." Nan remained silent the remainder of the time.

Following this session, Nan did not stay after school again.

Her behavior for the next six weeks was most acceptable. She gradually began to talk with Miss Leeds. The following conversations, arranged in chronological order, were initiated by Nan.

October 20

Nan: Miss Leeds, do you like school? I hate school. I hated the ugly teacher I had last year.

October 21

Nan: You know, Miss Leeds, my brother has the mumps.
Miss Leeds: Oh, he does, huh.
Nan: Yeah, he's swollen back here. (*Points to her throat.*) Both my brothers have them. I'm glad I don't.

October 22

The group was singing "Yankee Doodle" in class and Nan said, "I know another verse to 'Yankee Doodle' but it wouldn't be proper in school." (Earlier in the year there would have been no hesitation.)

October 24

Nan has been coming in early every morning to talk with Miss Leeds. She had no trouble during recess all this week. No reports were made by patrol boys.

October 27

Nan: I went out to Grandma's this weekend and haven't even been home yet.
Miss Leeds: That must be fun.
Nan: I fell out of a tree and sprained my little leg.
Miss Leeds: Oh dear, how does it feel now?
Nan: Oh, it hurts a lot, but that's OK.

October 28

While writing Halloween stories Nan said, "Kind of a silly word not to know, but it's black." (Nan never before admitted lack of knowledge.)

October 29

Marie's birthday was today and she told about getting a dog. Nan told about her dog as soon as Marie was through. She asked Marie to come over and see it sometime.

October 30

Nan: Grandma came home from the resort where she works. She's worked there fifteen years. Uncle Bob died.
Miss Leeds: Oh, that's too bad.
Nan: Yeah. I wish my grandma wouldn't come.

October 31

Nan brought suckers for every child for the Halloween party. About seven other children brought treats too. Some suckers were left over. As she started to go home that afternoon Nan told Miss Leeds that she had left a note for her. On the desk was the bag of suckers and a note, "For you—Nan." During this entire week Nan was cooperative and friendly.

November 3–7

This week Nan did not say much to Miss Leeds but began to interact with several children. On the playground she began playing with girls for the first time this year. On Friday she brought a treat for everyone.

November 10–14

During this week Nan was absent all but one day. Mrs. Rayner came to school for Nan's report card. She said, "Nan has been just beautiful at home lately. She takes care of her little brother so nicely. Her father and I can't get over the change. She is like a different child. We make a big fuss over it and tell her we think it's wonderful." When Nan came back to school, Miss Leeds greeted her, "Hi, Nan, sure good to have you back. Everyone is glad to see you again."

November 18

When the class had returned from art, Nan said, "The art

teacher put my picture on the board." Miss Leeds replied, "You seem to be doing much better in all your work."

November 19

Nan was absent in the morning, but at school in the afternoon.

Miss Leeds: Who will show us how to draw a duck's foot?

Nan: (*Raising her hand and showing her drawing, which several children praise.*) Yes, that's the way a duck's foot looks. If you spread out your fingers and imagine skin connecting them, that would look like a webbed foot like a duck has.

Nan: (*During lunch period, pointing to desk blotter.*) Isn't that new?

Miss Leeds: Yes.

Nan: It's pretty.

Nan: (*As dismissal time approaches.*) "Hurry up everybody, I've got to go to Brownies."

November 20

Nan: Miss Leeds, wow, I ran all the way home to get this (*radio program the children were to bring to school*). I got all the way to school, then saw Gale's and had to run home to get mine. Mom just tore the whole thing out of the paper. Is that all right?

Miss Leeds: Yes, that's fine. (*More and more Nan has shown interest and responsibility in class projects.*)

November 21

Nan: I cleaned out my desk this morning and all this stuff in the wastepaper basket is what I took out of it. Gol, now everything is out, except some comic books, I guess I'd better take them home. (*This is the first time Nan has shown any interest in orderliness.*)

Nan: When are our dictionaries going to come?

Miss Leeds: I don't know.

Nan: I wish they'd hurry up 'cause I paid for mine.

At recess Nan became hostile again. She stayed near Miss Leeds. She constantly shoved other girls or jumped on them.

When the girls ran to Miss Leeds, Nan promptly called them "chicken" or "sissy." She also pushed children into Miss Leeds. This behavior continued for the entire recess period. Since Nan has not been destructive in over a month, Miss Leeds hoped it was only temporary and decided to ignore it.

November 24

Nan: I went out to Grandma's Saturday and Grandpa had a horse there. I rode all the way down to Black Lake all by myself. Gol, my brothers had to stay on the property and had to have someone go with them. But I went on my own.

Miss Leeds: It's nice to have special privileges.

November 25

The group was in the art room. Mary said, "Sue did the horse." Then another girl spoke up and said, "Nan did the skier. Isn't it beautiful?" Recently girls in the room had been making favorable comments about Nan.

Nan: Miss Leeds, I'm going over to Grandma's for Thanksgiving dinner. Then we're going to the parade. Then I get to stay at Grandma's for the rest of the week. Am I going to have fun! (*Nan speaks more positively of her grandmother.*) I've got something I want to show you. Look at my gloves. They're my grandma's. They're too small for me. Grandma's smaller than me. My mom's larger than Grandma too.

November 26

Nan: Coming up the hill this morning there was such a strong wind I couldn't even ride my bike uphill, gol.

Miss Leeds: You must have had to work hard.

Nan: My uncle told me that he heard over the radio yesterday that there was twenty-two inches of snow in Tennessee.

Miss Leeds: Twenty-two inches of snow in Tennessee, huh.

Nan: Yeah, and forty inches in Texas, or somethin' like that. (*A pause.*) Gol, is this dictionary neat! Last night my little brother tore a page just a little. (*A pause.*) Miss Leeds, my brother lost his gun.

Miss Leeds: He did, huh.

Nan: Yeah, so I had to go to his grade with him 'cause he was afraid a boy in his room would beat him up. Then I came up to the office to look for it. Luckily the office was near our room. We found it there. (*A pause.*) I didn't know how to spell rhinoceros so I looked it up in my dictionary.

Miss Leeds: Good for you! You really are using your dictionary.

Nan: I finished my story. Aren't you going to read it?

Miss Leeds: (*Reads the story.*) You didn't want Mr. Rhinoceros to share his turkey, huh.

Nan: No, I don't know why. Mr. Rhinoceros is sort of a funny name for him, isn't it? I sort of like it, though. Do you think my title is good?

Miss Leeds: If you think it's good, that's what counts.

Nan: I don't.

Miss Leeds: What would you like to call your story?

Nan: "The Forty-pound turkey." I started writing a story about a wild turkey but didn't spell my words right so I tore up my paper. (*Returns to her seat and changes the title of her story.*)

December 8

Nan: (*Some children have brought Christmas records.*) Miss Leeds, I got a whole lot of Christmas records. May I bring them?

Miss Leeds: Of course, if you want to.

December 9

Nan: (*Some children have brought ornamental snowmen to school to decorate the room. Nan notices them.*) Miss Leeds, we made snowmen like that in Brownies last year.

Miss Leeds: You make snowmen just like that, huh?

Nan: Yes, maybe I can bring mine in.

December 10

Nan: Miss Leeds, Marie was beating up my little brother and he's only seven years old. That's why I've been after her lately. If she'd leave him alone, I'd leave her alone.

Miss Leeds: I'll talk with Marie.

December 12

Nan worked continuously today. She brought in freshly popped corn to string for the tree, and also a cane for the Christmas play. Nan helped change the desks around to make room for the Christmas tree.

Miss Leeds felt encouraged in the general improvement Nan had shown. Her interest in the group increased, her sensitivity and responsiveness were now apparent, and her ability to fulfill responsibilities was obvious. Nan's relationship with Miss Leeds was positive. She discussed her feelings, interests, and experiences more freely with Miss Leeds. Nan's aggressive contacts on the playground decreased markedly. By February the outbursts with Marie disappeared. Early in March Nan got into a fight with Mark, who was her equal in every respect. After the battle, Miss Leeds gave them time to talk about their conflict. Nan admitted she had been at fault, constantly irritating Mark. She said she wished she could stop being a pest. This was the first time Nan had recognized her own responsibility in a conflict with another child. The last week of school, after recess, Margaret came to Miss Leeds and said, "Look, Miss Leeds, Marie and Nan are playing together." Miss Leeds replied, "It's wonderful to see," and Margaret added, "It sure is."

MISS PIERCE AND GERALD

This is the story of Gerald, and Miss Pierce's attempt to influence his growth through an interpersonal relationship. Gerald is in the 4B and is ten years old. He is a healthy, well-proportioned boy. In classroom situations he has spoken in a timid, babyish voice. He is forgetful, daydreams, jerks his head nervously while speaking, and responds to questions with extreme difficulty.

When Miss Pierce looks at him, he looks away. He wants to sit in the last seat, to be by himself. In a sense he wants to be forgotten. At the beginning of the semester he made no effort to start an assignment or to listen to one being presented.

More and more Miss Pierce went back to his seat and tried to show an interest in him. There seemed to be no response from

Gerald. In spite of his indifference, Miss Pierce continued this procedure three or four times daily. Then one day, during reading period, he seemed to be following the passages in the story. Miss Pierce asked him to read and was surprised at the easy manner in which he did so. But his interest vanished as quickly and strangely as it had appeared.

Gerald has no friends. He constantly withdraws from other children. He prefers to stay in at recess and lingers behind every night, putting his things away or straightening up the bookcase. He wants to be near Miss Pierce, yet does not seem to care about her.

For several weeks Gerald did not talk to Miss Pierce directly, but as he arranged the books he glanced at her shyly. He seemed to want to talk but became tense as he turned to face her. All Miss Pierce's encouragement had failed up to this point. After persistent responsiveness to Gerald for a month, he began to say good night to Miss Pierce and occasionally would ask questions about his schoolwork.

One day Miss Pierce had an opportunity to talk with Gerald's mother. Mrs. Young said, "My husband, you know, is a physician and well, uh, brilliant. He gets so upset with Gerald. He won't have his son fail. We can't understand why Gerald is that way. His little sister started reading when she was only four and she helps him now. My husband gets very angry. Why, the first year he went to school and had a big scene with the teacher. He even went to the principal. I think he made it worse because the teacher got upset and failed Gerald anyhow. I don't know. I don't understand Gerald. He makes me nervous. I just had another baby girl—I was so nervous this time. I try to help him but he's so slow that I throw up my hands. Why should he be so dumb? My husband was in high school when he was eleven and was one of the youngest M.D.'s out of Ann Arbor. Oh, I just don't know. What do you think? What can we do?"

Miss Pierce told Mrs. Young about Gerald's behavior in the classroom and her belief that the boy had considerable potentiality. Miss Pierce explained his slowness in terms of his fears and withdrawn behavior, which somehow interfered with his ability to achieve.

Mrs. Young agreed. "Yes, he is timid. He's afraid of every-thing—people, the dark, just everything. He won't play with children his own age. He plays only with three-year-olds. He's afraid of the dark. My husband forced him to sleep alone in a dark room, but he cried so much we had to let him sleep with his younger sister. I don't know." She paused for quite a while, then continued: "What about his reading? What about a tutor? I thought you might give me the name of one out here."

Miss Pierce said, "Yes, I can, if you want someone to tutor Gerald, though I'm not sure that's necessary."

During the following weeks much more interaction occurred between Gerald and Miss Pierce. One day they were walking together on the stairs. He had stayed behind, as he did many times, putting his things away. This had become Gerald's way of letting Miss Pierce know he wanted to talk. As they neared the bottom of the steps the following conversation took place.

Gerald: I'm going to jump.

Miss Pierce: You are going to jump four steps? That's quite a few. (*Miss Pierce is more anxious than Gerald.*)

Gerald: Yes. Here I go. I jumped and I wasn't afraid. I'm going to do it again. (*Repeats this behavior several times.*)

Miss Pierce: That's something you've wanted to do for a long time and now you know you can.

Gerald: Tomorrow I'm going to jump five steps and every day after that one more step.

Miss Pierce: Well, be careful you don't break the floor."

Gerald: (*Laughing.*) Good-by.

One afternoon Gerald told Miss Pierce he was surprised school was over. It seemed to him that it was only time for recess.

Miss Pierce: Yes. Some days seem to go very fast. Did you ever notice that when you are doing things you like, time seems to go faster?

Gerald: Yes. Like when my father makes me listen to the news. (*Wrinkles up his nose to show distaste.*) Then it seems forever.

Miss Pierce: You don't like to listen to the news.

Gerald: Ugh, no! I like "Twenty Questions." It seems like it is over before it begins.

Another time, Gerald mentioned his sister.

Gerald: I have a sister at home.
Miss Pierce: You do, huh?
Gerald: Yes.
Miss Pierce: You have one sister?
Gerald: No. We have another sister.
Miss Pierce: Oh, how old is she?
Gerald: I can't remember. She's little, though, like a baby. Everyone wanted a boy—my mother, father, and sister. I wanted a sister.
Miss Pierce. You got what you wanted. You must be happy.
Gerald: (*A pause.*) Oh, I guess so. They like her better than me.

Miss Pierce approached Gerald one day.

Miss Pierce: Does your mother help you with your schoolwork? You've improved tremendously, you know.
Gerald: (*Smiling.*) Have I? No—well yes, once in a while she does. I keep forgetting my place and she gets fed up with me.
Miss Pierce: She gets fed up and then you do your work by yourself.
Gerald: Yes. There's a lady who helps me with my reading. I go there twice a week. She's—oh, I guess she's all right but she keeps telling me things I know. I try to tell her, but she doesn't understand and keeps on explaining.

As Miss Pierce straightened up her desk after school she pulled a piece of wire from one of the drawers. Gerald approached her.

Gerald: What's that?
Miss Pierce: Wire.
Gerald: What's it for?
Miss Pierce: I used it to fix things with, like binding things together. Now I have no use for it. It keeps getting in my way. I feel like throwing it away.
Gerald: Could I have it? I like to fix things.

Miss Pierce: Yes, you may have it.

Gerald: Can I? Gee, thanks. I like to fix things and straighten up.

Miss Pierce: Like my books.

Gerald: I help my mother. I shovel the snow and I get a dollar. I was saving for a bike, but I got it for Christmas so now I'm saving for a basket for my bike so I can go to the supermarket for my mother. I like to help her.

One day the class was asked to write about a picture on the board. It was a laughing refugee boy holding a pair of new shoes. Gerald's story was about a Korean boy. He said, "The Communists came along. The mother and sister died. The father was shot in the stomach. Some nice people came along. They were nice to him. He is laughing because they gave him new clothes and they loved him."

Miss Pierce's persistence in approaching Gerald to know and understand him better helped to bring about several changes in Gerald's behavior. As he gained confidence in himself and his ability, his academic work improved. He was more spontaneous with other children and with Miss Pierce. He frequently participated in class discussions and came to feel himself an important member of the group.

CONCLUSION

In order to establish the personal relationship with a child, the teacher often had to maintain an attitude of unyielding patience. Sometimes the feeling of not being understood or not understanding was strongly experienced by the teacher. Sometimes the teacher's interest and concern for the child were rejected. There were times when the child's behavior became more destructive or withdrawn just when the teacher felt that important gains had been made. But when the teacher maintained faith throughout the relationship, the definite, though unpredictable, growth strivings within the child began to influence the child's behavior toward a more satisfying way of life in school.

CHAPTER 7

Self-exploration
among High School Students

In the upper school grades the ten teachers who attempted to establish special relationships with children found that regular time for free discussion was the most effective approach. It was only after several sessions that teachers were able to convince groups that every expression would be fully accepted and held in the strictest confidence. In addition to the group discussions, several students from time to time asked for individual conferences. For the most part these conferences were used by students to explore immediate problems they were facing, such as failure in school, wish to leave school, difficulty in love relationship, specific problems with parents, and desire to leave home and marry.

Miss Rosen had a group of thirty twelfth-grade students in her human-relationships class. Since there was no definitely prescribed curriculum, she was free to develop the program in her own way. The class met twice a week for one hour over a period of one semester. Miss Rosen suggested a series of resources the group might be interested in using, including a list of films, special speakers, and a bibliography. At the first meeting Miss Rosen explained that the class would be handled differently perhaps than any that they had taken. She explained that the group would be free to present any concepts, ideas, or problems for discussion. Miss Rosen pointed out that the group itself was perhaps the most important resource in understanding human relations, particularly their own interpersonal relations. She indicated that each student would be required to grade himself in the course, adding that her role would be to help clarify ideas and feelings rather than to provide answers. She repeated that the group was its own best authority, and that no single person in the group, including herself, was more an expert than anyone else. Miss Rosen wanted each person in the group to function in terms of his own unique self. She wanted the differences existing in individuality to be expressed and explored.

Miss Rosen asked the group to keep a journal of their reactions to the class sesssions, and hoped the class would feel free to explore their experiences in these journals when there was no opportunity in class for discussion. She indicated that the journals could be turned in to her or not. Suggestions for modifying class procedures could be made in the journals.

The group developed slowly. For several sessions there were long periods of silence. At times Miss Rosen found it necessary to suggest topics for discussion. She offered broad topics, making it possible for a wide variety of ideas and attitudes to be expressed within them. The group discussed a number of problems in human relationships, including dating, petting, early marriage, child rearing, parental authority, independence, dominance and submission, and fears and hostility. The largest number of discussions revolved around self-perception and understanding. During these meetings the individuals in the group explored significant experiences in their lives which they felt influenced their development.

One rather dramatic incident discussed in the journals involved two students who were planning to elope. These students had given their journals to Miss Rosen and requested special help. Though they had never talked about it to each other, each of them had fears regarding elopement and had recognized problems that might result from an early marriage. Their journal reports indicated that both families would be strongly opposed to the marriage. Each of the students used the individual conference. Miss Rosen read sections of their reports to each other in a joint conference, making no comments beyond those in the journal. The young couple was surprised to find that each had similar fears regarding parental attitudes, education, working, and earning an income. Though they were aware that several complex problems might result, they decided to go ahead with their plan. In the journals each continued to express more intense anxiety as the date for elopement drew closer. Two days before the elopement they decided to discuss the marriage with their parents. The parents, with some reluctance, honored their decision to marry but asked them to wait until after graduation. The two agreed and were married in early June. Both sets of parents helped them in finding a home and getting started.

Toward the end of the semester Miss Rosen asked the group to write a comprehensive paper exploring personal experience. She suggested that they read their journals as a first step, and indicated that in the process of seeking to understand, insights sometimes emerged. No one was required to do the self-study but every student decided to attempt it and turned it in to Miss Rosen. Only three in the group did not sign their names. Miss Rosen felt that the autobiographical essays showed real self-understanding on the part of many individuals in the group. Four of these self-explorations have been selected for presentation. The reports are in the youngsters' own words.

SEEKING MY REAL SELF—MARY

I must have been about ten years old when I first discovered the mystery of my own being. I still see myself standing in front of my mother's mirror and marveling myself into my eyes. But the more I asked the more those greenish eyes out of the mirror asked back; the more I tried to get into myself the more I closed my inner self. Finally my eyes began to flicker and glitter and I said to myself in the mirror: "I hate you!" and I really meant it. After that I was so frightened I ran out like I had done something very bad. Playing with other children I soon forgot these troubles.

This little scene stayed very long in my mind because I was a very calm child and never expressed my feelings out of myself. I remember that I was a real shy child. Every time my parents had company I tried to get out of the room and out of their sight. I didn't trust them and sometimes they could talk and talk and talk to me and I still did not get confidential. I didn't let anybody touch me and I didn't feel good as long as strangers were anywhere near me. I just didn't think to be able to be myself when people were watching me. But I never said anything about these feelings.

I had a very happy childhood. I had a good father and a good mother; I had one older brother and three younger ones. One of the highpoints of every year was Christmas. I got dolls, babies, girls and boys. They weren't just to look at. They were real to play with but I never did. I had clothes for them, beautiful little things. I washed them every once in a while and just put them back in the box but never played with them. When my big brother played with my little ones with the soldiers, I sat by and listened. I took part in all the fates of the soldiers as he told about them. I had and still have a very large imagination, a strength to give things life in my mind. So I lived all the lives of these soldiers and felt with them. Sometimes I was so sorry when one was killed that I almost wept, but I never did. I was afraid and ashamed of my tears. I still am. One Christmas I got a beautiful kitchen with little pans and pots and a hearth, with plates and cups and bowls and silverware, just like in a real kitchen. I was so glad about it I felt like kissing my mother when I thanked her for it, but I did not. There was something in myself I couldn't get over; but I said thanks with shining eyes trying to shout how much it meant but I could not kiss her. My brothers and I baked beautiful cakes and cooked wonderful dinners but as soon as someone else came and my mother asked us to do something for visitors, all my joy was gone and I just did it to please my mother.

Both my parents were very good to me and my brothers. They still are. I know nobody in the world I love more than my parents. These feelings get always fresh food and strength out of an inner source; but still I never could tell them that I love them, never could put it into words. I try to show it but somehow I can't say it. Last year I often disagreed with my mother. It was the beginning of my getting independent in my outer life. It was strange that we couldn't agree when I wanted to be independent outside. My interior life had always been completely free. I had bitter quarrels with my mother about small things. Usually I said only a few words but my inside boiled and also ached. I thought I hated my mother and I was very, very unhappy because something had come between us and I knew I loved her. I loved her more than ever before. It was this time also that I learned more clearly that love isn't something which is always sweet and pleasant; I learned that love sometimes is the most hurting thing, that love doesn't always please you, that it may cut the deepest wounds and give the greatest tasks, that it makes you struggle the most to be wanted and feel the worst. You really must have hated, before being able to love. And still it is the same with me.

I never was taught to be afraid. When I went to school I learned it there. Not the fear of dark rooms or frogs or mice but the fear of the mob. Though I always had good marks I sometimes felt less than all the others. I thought I was dumb, I couldn't behave as graceful as they and I couldn't laugh about things they laughed at. Many of these feelings every child gets once in a while, the feelings not to be worthwhile. I felt unhappy in this time but it was my own fault that I couldn't feel close in groups. Sometimes things come back even now and I see myself, standing in front of the mirror again, looking at my face, which is too broad, and saying, "I hate you!" Like when I was a child. I am frightened of myself when I have done it. But sometimes I just feel like I was worth nothing and I feel ashamed by expressing this terrible feeling against myself. Then I am always scared by my passion.

I never had a boy friend. I know of them only in my imagination and therefore I don't trust myself. I never trusted myself in this kind of feeling. More than one of my poems, a hobby which I started about five years ago, deals with lies. How do we know what is a lie? Maybe all I am telling you now is a lie. Yet I hate lies, and I am afraid of them. Every time I met somebody I really liked I went back into my little house and tried to be as cold as possible. That was because I didn't trust myself when I cared about the other person. There were some who wanted me as a friend but nobody with whom I got close. I have a stiff pride and I can't bend it. Sometimes it was good to have it, sometimes it erected a wall of ice around me. Still, I am not willing to give it up because it is a part of me. Only once did I really get at ease with a boy. He was older than I and he fell in love with another girl. We are friends now. When I look close to my feeling for him all is only fear and insecurity which is probably a lower stage of development but I don't care.

When I first came to America, I was frightened at the noise and I pushed myself all the time. I found it difficult always to smile, always to be forced to be nice, to make compliments, to be thanking and grateful. Finally I got the idea that you have to divide your personality and be one for yourself and another one for people. I tried this method. I found out it was a good one. So it happened that nobody knows who or what I am, even those who see me every day. I make a real serious or deep statement in class just to impress others but inside myself cries out "lie, lie, lie!" So that what you think?

Am I fair to say that? Has there been doubt in your mind when I talked in class? I feel insecure in myself yet try to make others secure! Is this only my imagination speaking out to me? I can't be absolutely honest with you. I don't even know myself well enough to be absolutely honest.

My idea of a real human being is a calm friendly character, inside and outside, secure and I've always tried to be that way but it is real hard.

Till last year I had long thick braids. All my friends at school looked like adults but not me. Finally I let them cut off my braids and I have been sorry to this very day, because I didn't decide for myself.

One of my favorite works is gardening and I had the opportunity of doing it whenever I wanted to. We have quite a large garden and I knew each plant in it. Many of them I have grown myself. When I went to the woods or into the fields I always brought with me a new plant I had found and put it into my personal corner of the garden. Nothing could make me more happy than to have it survive. I felt good when my mother asked me about the plants and last year I was the gardener of our whole garden all by myself. It is the one thing I'll greet the very first of every day. I also loved to go to the woods. And I often went on Sundays right after having done the lunch dishes with one or two of my little brothers. We watched together the wonderful life of nature. Our parents have taught us a heartily affection and love for nature and we got out of that the most and purest joy a man can have. They taught us to love the small things as well as the big and I remember my mother and me sitting together and watching a bee, gathering honey, or a fly, cleaning herself. When I saw my first mouse I first was frightened because she has been so quick and I couldn't even see her. The next day my father caught her and he showed her to me. Since that I think mice are nice little animals. The first frog I saw was sitting right before me and my father was standing beside me and led my attention to him. When the frog closed and opened his eyes I had to laugh because it looked so funny. With the curiosity of a little child I tried to touch him with my finger. He jumped and I was frightened because this moving was so sudden. But there was my father standing beside me and he laughed. He took my hand and he showed me where the frog had gone and that he had been frightened by my finger.

I started to be fond of reading when I was nine years old. Since then I have read an awful lot of books. I can't remember that my mother ever told me not to read a book. We have almost a little library because both of my parents are fond of reading too. We have all kinds of books from the classics to the tales but not twenty-five cent pocket books with those mysteries. I could go to the cupboards and pick out any book I wanted. I often got one which wasn't good for me but I decided that when I tried to read it and saw that I couldn't understand it and I had no pleasure in reading it. So I taught myself good judgment and was able to put a book back which wasn't for me.

I followed the dealings in a book so closely that after I read it I still lived in the world of the book. Sometimes I was the loved girl, sometimes the unhappy boy, but always the person who impressed me most. Out of that I started to write myself. I wrote short stories. This first one was pretty much like the books I admired. One day I heard a speech of the minister at church and he spoke about lies. I didn't touch my writing for a long time after that and when I read what I had written I saw that all was wonderful pink boloney. I was ashamed of it and I would have damaged it if I had not had the feeling that it would have been cowardly. I hated cowardliness in others and I hated it in myself because I have tried to live with courage. Since then I started to write more reality into my fiction. There always were outstanding good characters and outstanding good happenings. I try to make myself believe that there is nothing outstanding in the world. Once I had an outstanding imagination. (I still am not rid of all of it.) I thought if I could prove that nothing is outstanding then I also could prove that I was not outstanding. I did not succeed. I still think that I am not replaceable. I like myself for me and when I go there shall be a hole where I have been. There won't be any me. There will be others but no one can replace any person.

One important thing in life, probably the most important, is faith. My father hates the church. My mother has become a stranger to her. When I was nine years old I lived with my grandfather whom I was not very fond of because of his great opinion of himself. He was a very good man, clever and right till the last. He was for long years the mayor of our town. He was an honored figure in political life. He even has the sympathies of many American men. I didn't love him, even when I knew I should. He loved church and he brought me to love her too. Even though I did not love him I learned to love his religion. But when I grew older I saw that the church was built on sand. I always got ill at church and became a foreigner to her. I couldn't go and my feeling for it got colder and colder inside of me.

Then when I almost lost my church I started to lose my God. I struggled against this. Since I was not trained this struggle was awfully hard. It almost wore me out but then I felt there was something growing in me which helped me and I got calmer. There were times when I wanted to give up because I had fought for such a long time, but something in me wouldn't let me. One day it came quite suddenly that this feeling never will stop—the strength to believe and the urge to doubt. All my lifetime I have longed for the possession of my God and I know that I never will give up. This is the only thing I ever trusted in myself because this is the only point I know which is positively true. I haven't succeeded with the church yet. But I go to church, I go frequently, and I finally got rid of the thinking that so many go only to show their faith but not to live it. One time maybe I'll get rid of these prejudices and accept people as they are.

I have an older brother whom I understand perfectly and whom I love. He is quite open to me, more than to anybody else. He can say all that is in his heart without giving one sound to him but to listen. I never want to lose him.

I have three younger brothers, whom I love as much as the older one but in a different way. They trust me, they are confidential to me. I couldn't think of losing any of them.

One great mystery in my life is death. There were times where I was afraid of death, so much afraid that I wanted to die. Now I'm not afraid. I want to get into the big nothing; I want to find complete peace. I think that death is the greatest thing in life and the most beautiful thing. To go over to this land, where I can sleep, lie down my head and stop to think, stop to hate and stop to love, but to completely relax. When I speak of not wanting to lose anything I don't think of losing by death; I think of the living losing. Death is as divine as birth and not to be feared.

Now I have tried to give a picture of myself. I wonder how much is true. Maybe you can pick out what is true, I can't. Someday I'll come to the place where I can say this is the way I am, but this point probably is far away and I'll have to live many years before I find my real self.

Discussion

Mary has given a moving account of herself as she sees herself. How much of her exploration is imagination and how much is real? Mary asks this question herself in several places in the study and is unable to decide. The important thing is that she explores many significant feelings and attitudes. She gives the impression that in many respects she feels inferior and inadequate. She tells how difficult it is for her to allow herself to feel warmly toward another person. She mentions her fears of rejection and her protective defenses against rejection. She seems to be saying, "If I don't get too close to anyone, I cannot be hurt." In contrast to the cold surface reactions she gives to people outside her family, she expresses feelings of love for her mother, father, and brothers.

Mary is bothered by contradictions in the American culture and in religion and tells of her struggle to reach an independent existence. She seems to conclude that adjustment is a form of pretense and deception and that the healthy goal of every person should be to be his real self in all important situations. Being oneself eventually leads to more genuine and happy relationships.

Mary seemingly wants to know the person that she is but is still in the process of forming values, attitudes, and beliefs. She recognizes she is not a person in any final sense but is growing and becoming. She is unable to decide what in herself is real and what is not. In several ways Mary values her individuality, her refusal to compromise herself, her independence and her freedom to act on the basis of her own ideas and feelings. In addition to the many doubts, throughout this exploration Mary conveys a kind of strength of self, a feeling of self-acceptance, and the notion that with increasing maturity, self-expression in fantasy is lessening. Mary's search for her real self is more a movement toward realizing her potentials than a struggle to resolve personal conflict and the paradoxes in social living.

THIS IS ME—NANCY

When I was younger some of the kids didn't take to me right away. That used to hurt and it got so I didn't make friends so easily. The other person had to be friendly first. In lots of cases that's still so but sometimes I approach others. If someone snubs me, who cares? Nobody is too special. Besides there are plenty of kids who like me for myself, not for clothes, money, home, father's position, or whether

I've got a cute figure, or the right religion. I've never stuck with one church. I've been to a Jewish Synagogue, Catholic, Methodist, Presbyterian, Episcopalian, Baptist churches—I went to a Christian Science Church for two years—the longest I've ever gone to any church. The same way with nationalities. I'm a mixture of just about every country in the world. It used to hurt to have people say "Hi" and then ignore me but not any more. I'm too busy making new friends and having a wonderful time.

Boys never interested me much other than to play games and kick-the-can with them. I did that until I was about fourteen. My pet peeve is the kind of girl who is bound and determined she is not going to make a wrong move. In other words she sits in a corner with hands folded or goes out and makes a fool of herself acting, or should I say trying to act, sophisticated. I like to have fun! I love to talk about hotrods, gas motors for toy planes, football, track, swimming, all sorts of sports and hobbies. How can you get enjoyment out of life if you don't unbend a little and really whoop her up. By that I don't mean getting into trouble, but just rough housing around, having a good time. When I swim to me it is not worth it if you're going in for just a short while. We used to go for six, seven hours a day. We dived, played tag, raced all that time. How can anyone just lie around in the sun and not swim when water is so wonderful?

I never was a whiz at sports but I had fun and laughed at my mistakes. At the Pointe we all played field hocky and it was wonderful to go galloping down the field swinging the stick. So what if I didn't make many goals? The object was to have fun, not to fight to win.

We also had an aquatic club. I belonged to that—couldn't swim worth a darn. But there weren't many who could. I was very proud of my pop kick and dog paddle. We used to dive from the deep end and swim under water to the other end. I nearly split my tank suit with pride the first time I did it.

I belonged to the Pointe Players and worked the required thirty hours in the scene shop mixing paint, stirring glue, and pasting, painting, and stenciling flats. There were about thirty of us all working our apprenticeship. We nearly drove our manager crazy with singing and dashing about.

Every year there is a "Nite of Plays" and one year I had my first and last appearance on the stage. I played the part of a Chinese girl and dyed my hair blue black (with a green part) for the role. All the girls swore up and down that *everyone* was going to dye their hair, but I was the only one. It turned out swell though, when I bleached it out—bright copper red—my favorite color for hair. Monday I was a blond, Tuesday a brunette and Wednesday a redhead—more fun!

At the end of the apprenticeship you work for a semester and then you get elected into the Thespians. I was not elected. I was hurt—but so what? Nicer things have happened to me since.

We used to skate at the park but not in the baby pool where we were supposed to, but way out towards the middle of the river where the ice piled up to a height of ten feet. We used to climb the piles. Some of the smart guys drank river water and got good and sick. We had fun playing pom pom and there was always the chance of falling in which just added to the excitement.

When I was eleven and a half Johnny, or rather Frankenstein, was born. There are entirely too many years between us and also very little good feeling. Mom and Dad tell me regularly that I'm jealous of him. At first I denied it but why anymore? Sure, I'm jealous of him and with good reason. I was a spoiled brat until Frankenstein was born, then I wasn't spoiled any more. Uh uh! He likes chicken wings so he gets them, a plateful all for *himself* and no one else. Why should I worry though? In a couple of years I'll be on my own and I can both pity and laugh at them for the fun they're going to have when he starts to *really* demand things. He's got Mom and Dad wrapped around his little finger. If he bends it they bow and scrape. The heck with that. Here's one girl who won't bow to a brat one third her age.

He used to say, "If you don't stop touching my toys I'll tell Mom you've been kicking them and she'll fix you." So now when he starts that I say, "Okay, let's go so you can tell. After all why wait?" It works fine. He always does the opposite from what I ask him.

Mom always says if I ever lay a hand on the "dear" brat she would give me twice as many slaps as I gave him. I've never touched him and wouldn't be bothered. I remember when kids used to slap me around when I was small and I know that feeling of helplessness.

He's actually worse than a trained seal. I swear he'd lick your boots for a toy, either that or raise the roof until he got it. I have no use for him. He's such a jackass.

At times he has trouble with his bowels, but not all the time. When Mom and Dad went to Florida he was just fine. For two weeks he was an angel. He ate vegetables, went to the john, obeyed, dressed himself, didn't whine, didn't cry, shriek or have tantrums. He was just perfect! Mom and Dad came home and, Lord, it was awful—just the opposite. He has a very vivid imagination and swore up and down I hit him. If I *had* hit him that much and that hard he wouldn't be here to tell about it. Neither would I. So much for Frankenstein.

My other pet peeve was Dracula, my grandfather. I have names for everyone. Mom is the General for obvious reasons and Pop is the Private. Anyhow, back to Dracula. He was and is the only person I've ever really hated and pitied. Those are such funny emotions, together like that.

He died last October and quite frankly, I'm glad. He had been miserable all his life. Hateful, temperamental, bull-headed, stubborn, coarse, unmannerly, humorless. One thing you can say is he worked hard, saved his money and didn't drink (to excess) or gamble. Outside of that he was hateful.

In a way my Grandmother and he were alike. Both were stubborn. She transferred the love which should have gone to Dracula to my Uncle Joe. He was a mama's boy and just as ugly and nasty as Dracula.

There were Christmases when neither one of them would open their presents because some little thing had miffed them. They neither opened or sent presents until around February and March. There never has been a decent Christmas since Mom can remember. And there were times when I didn't open a gift from them until late Spring.

The last Christmas Grandma was alive that old goat didn't buy her a present and he knew she was dying of cancer. She died last May.

In November, a year ago, she had her arm removed. That didn't stop her. She cleaned house, ironed curtains, scrubbed floors, marketed, went downtown, and still was cheerful and sweet although the pain must have been horrible.

In January he had a stroke and had the gall to ask her to pull him up by taking the crook of his cane. She could barely drag herself but that big heavy hunk of stupidity would ask her to do that. She had her arm off and a breast removed and cancer of the lungs. He knew all that. We all hated him for his treatment of her.

The November when she had her arm amputated, he bought her a present—a mop you could use with one hand. Very sweet! Mom nearly hit him over the head with it. Too bad she didn't. She told him that was about as kind as someone giving him a pair of roller skates. So I saved my money and got him a pair.

He lived with us one summer and it was my job to take care of him, clean up the mess after he went to the john. And it wasn't an accident. It was done on purpose.

He used to take his pajamas off and lie on the floor intending to shock me. After the first time or so I just saw red, yanked him up, got him into his P.J.'s and told him to keep them on and stay in bed.

He'd slip out of bed, intentionally, and be there moaning on the floor like mad till I'd come. He'd ring that damn bell constantly til I hid it.

We had a three-day row in August and after that he went down fast. But it nearly wound up in my Dad moving out and me threatening to go away too. What was everyone upset about he asked as if he didn't understand and everyone was being so unreasonable. Mom had to go to the doctor and found she was on the verge of a nervous breakdown.

It wound up on Thursday with me calling the police coz he'd gone berzerk and was throwing things. I had to knock him down. He acted as if he couldn't breathe but he sure as heck wasn't out coz I dodged his fist none too soon. The police came just at the same moment my parents did and Dracula called us all "damn rogues," "stealing my money, my house, my bankbook." The police just smiled and left.

But the General was far from smiling. She fixed his clock, wound it up tight, and he was sweet after that.

He changed a bit but every day I hated him a little more. I hated him especially for every time I picked him up off the floor, 150 pounds of hulk to haul around. Once after Mom and I hauled him off the floor and into bed he laughed and said, "I really made you sweat that time didn't I. I could have gotten in by myself but you're being paid to take care of me." A mammoth sum, ten dollars a week.

I pitied him because he always wanted to belong to the crowd of wealthy men, but his lack of education, manners, and narrowmindedness hampered him. His way was to get angry, and outshout everyone. Consequently, people left him alone. No one called when he retired or when he was sick. No one liked his great boorishness. The only way you could win an argument with him was to put on a worldly, all-knowing air, throw in a few large words, and you had him stumped.

He was selfish to the nth degree. All summer long he watched the programs he wanted to watch on our TV while we sat around being bored.

Last October we had a nice temper tantrum. He took to banging everything. His banging just made me burn so I went to his room, took off his ring, took away the stool, slippers, shoes, and ashtrays and told him all he had left to bang was his head. He did.

When I was eleven I had one run in with my father. He took off his strap and gave me such a whipping I'll never forget it. I never made a sound but the tears rolled down my cheeks. He said he wished I was dead and that hurt worst of all. I nursed a bruised thigh for about three weeks. There are still the scars from the welts. I have never been able to forgive him for that. He isn't very demonstrative towards me but he sure goes overboard for Frankenstein. But no matter what Mom does or says she's always right in my opinion because I know she loves me. I'll always stick up for her even though we have some terrific battles. I'll listen to my Dad and do the opposite, but what my mother says counts. Perhaps it is because I have more feeling for her or perhaps I resent my dad's constant attention to Frankenstein.

They gave me art lessons, music and dancing and dramatic lessons. I stuck to art, the rest I didn't work hard at. I didn't enjoy it in the first place. I hate to have anyone behind me pushing, pushing to get me to do something. I like to do things when I want and then I usually do a god job. But when someone pushes me I can't and won't get started.

Mom has, and still is, going through the stage of trying to pick my friends. She isn't going to go around with them, I am. I've picked some doozies mainly because she didn't like them, but after a few weeks I always drop them if we don't have similar interests.

I've been accused of being snobbish but you have to be a little snobbish to keep from being walked on. I am still amazed with our town after a year and a half. Everyone is so friendly and interested.

This summer I saw "The Thing" and for a while I had nightmares, dreaming he was coming through the door. Real gay!

I used to blush easily and get nervous but not any more. Other people probably have had these same experiences.

Sometimes I get moods where people irritate me no end and then I go off and fiddle around with plants or find a stray dog and talk to and tell him how much people annoy me. I don't get mad easily at people I don't know well but I blow up at my parents often. I'll take a lot from some people before I call it quits but absolutely nothing from my parents.

Sometimes my parents try to shock me. For instance when a close friend of the family died, they were peeved at me and told me so when I didn't say a thing or change expression at his death. He never did like me so why should I care. I had to be honest. They have a gay time saying I can go to college, then its no, then yes until I finally say, "That's fine but when it's time to go I'll decide anyway."

They also lecture like mad and I nearly go wild from boredom at times. They back me into a corner. When they go too far, I explode and we're off to the races again.

As I said, my Dad has never shown his love for me. That may be one reason I never dated too much and turned down a lot of dates.

When we lived in the Pointe a whole gang of us liked to go out early in the evening and ring doorbells, play tag, hide and go seek. But that was tomcatting according to my dad; yet Frankenstein can stay out until late playing around and that's O.K. I guess I'm dumb but I just don't get it.

I guess that's about all I can think of to say about me.

Discussion

In this exploration Nancy shows an ability to see through the frailties of human nature. She seems to accept the weaknesses as well as the strengths in family living. She recognizes her position in the family, understands her relationship with her mother and father. Though she realizes that both her parents hold her brother as their favorite, she still finds security in her relationship with her mother. But her resentment toward her father is very great. As Nancy points out, the difference lies in her feeling that her mother has always loved her, whereas her father has not. She indicates that she can forgive her father for everything but his failure to love her. Nancy seems to understand how her relationship with her father has affected her attitude toward boys, her reluctance to date them, and her cautious feeling toward them. Perhaps originally she wanted to excel in boys' activities, games, and sports in order to convince her father of her adequacy. But failing to achieve outstanding success in these, Nancy accepted her status and decided that the satisfaction of participation itself was more important than achieving stardom. Her goal in activity became one of personal satisfaction rather than attempts to excel over others. Nancy's account of her relationship with her brother and grandfather again showed her ability to accept difficult and painful situations and see them in a humorous light. Throughout her experiences her greatest forte is perhaps her way of seeing the funny side of human conflict, disturbed behavior, and personal weaknesses. In spite of some severely frustrating and defeating family experiences, Nancy seems to have achieved a healthy approach to interpersonal relationships. She seems to feel satisfied with the person she is, the weaknesses as well as the strengths.

Why I Am What I Am—Earl

Well, to begin with, I am very backward and shy and I think I know the reason why I am like this. You have probably wondered why I do not talk up in class when I am given so many chances to do so. Well, it is because I am backward and afraid that if I should talk up in class, that my classmates might laugh at me and at what I say. I have always been like this since my first day in school, ever since I can remember. The reason for my being like I am, I think, is because I never got to meet many people when I was younger and therefore never got to talk to people. My parents never went out to visit friends unless it was absolutely necessary.

I remember once, when I was about ten or eleven years old, there was a girl I liked very much. At this time, I even got up enough courage to go to her house to ask her if she would go to the movies with me. But when I got to her house and was told that she had already gone to the movies with someone else, I was very disappointed and made up my mind then and there that I would never ask another girl to go out with me again. In fact, to this day, I have never asked another girl to go out with me for fear of being turned down or that someone else might have asked her to go out before I did. I truly wish I could overcome this problem of talking up and asking girls to go out with me because someday I hope to get married and raise a family. But as long as this problem stands in my way, I will never get anywhere.

I also remember, very clearly, the time my parents were thinking about getting divorced. They were always quarreling and fighting over some little thing that never was very important in the first place and I think they knew it wasn't important also. It seemed as though they were just looking for a chance to start a fight. This may sound crazy, but it is true. Once, my parents were even talking about who would take care of me after they were divorced. Neither of them seemed to want me. At this time I really thought they would get divorced and I was wondering which parent I would turn to. But to this day they are still married although even now they do not get along with each other. At one time I thought it would be best if they did get divorced but today I am glad that they did not. Although my parents do not know it, I think that this had a lot to do with my being shy and backward in life. I think their behavior made me ashamed of them and of myself.

The thing which affected my life most is the fact that I never got out enough. Even when I was little, I was told that I could not go out and play with the other children because I might get hurt or dirty. I was told that I must stay in the yard and keep clean. And, if I did not keep clean, my mother would nearly take a fit. When I first started school, I was told that I must come straight home from school instead of playing with other children. I was told the same thing if I ever went to the store. At one time I had thought of running away from home and never coming back, but I was too afraid of what my parents might do if I should come home again so I decided to stick it out and try to please my parents to the best of my ability. Just one or two years ago I thought of taking my own life. But at the end I could not do it because I realized that God would never forgive me if I should ever do such a thing as that. I decided my problems had to be decided in life, not in death. I am not ashamed of telling you about this for I think that everyone, at one time or another, probably has the feeling that life is not worth living. I think now that I have a good life ahead of me and there is a real chance that I can be happy in it.

But now to get back to my being backward. I have tried nearly everything that I can think of to overcome this obstacle, but they all seem to have failed. I know I would be much happier if I could only overcome this problem. So, in closing, I would like to ask you to read this to the class in the hope that I might receive some suggestions as to what I might do to help myself.

Discussion

Miss Rosen read Earl's exploration to the group. Several girls mentioned that they had wondered why Earl did not ask them to go out and assumed he just did not like girls. They made it clear that if Earl asked for a date, they would be happy to accept. Knowing that he would not be rejected, Earl gained enough courage to ask a classmate to a school dance. Miss Rosen saw Earl at several school functions, following the dance, with the same girl. Earl's inhibition in this respect seemed to be removed. By actually doing the thing he had been so afraid to attempt, he apparently gained confidence and a feeling that girls could see him as a desirable person.

Earl's strong feelings of inadequacy of self, however, did not change. He seems to understand why he feels inadequate but is unable to modify this attitude. He shows strong resentment toward both his parents, their arguments, conflicts, and restrictions. He indicates a feeling that his parents neither wanted nor loved him. He shows how he was different from other children and how his parents continually made him feel the difference. The lack of stability in his parents' relationship raised doubt and confusion in Earl's mind and make him feel unworthy. In his paper he recognized how his background had influenced his current attitudes. Awareness of this type is sometimes the first step toward change in feelings. His group helped Earl to move forward, but he was still finding it a struggle to come to believe in and value himself.

ME, MYSELF, AND I—TOM

In 1932 my father made one of the worst mistakes in his life, and nine months later I was born. Due to my early arrival I was born on a kitchen table. To add to the doctor's worries, I was born Caesarian. As time went on, I gained weight and my mother recovered completely. Due to my Mother's and Dad's teaching school, we had long summer vacations, in which we spent most of the summer months traveling.

I don't remember much of my early childhood, but I do remember my first day in kindergarten which I detested very much. There was nothing they had in kindergarten that I didn't have at home except kids and a teacher who would have passed for the Goodyear blimp. During the summer after kindergarten, we moved to Detroit where we lived for one year while our house was being built. In Detroit, I attended a school which was more like a university than a grade school. Again, I formed a bad impression of school and the city of Detroit. While I was attending this school, the race riots took place in Detroit and I guess that is when my bad impressions were formed.

From **Detroit** we moved to a subdivision called St. Johns Woods where there was not a house within miles. It was here I entered the third grade. Due to my shyness and the long distance to my schoolmates' houses, I had few playmates. As I advanced in school, I made more friends. But during the summer I would lose contact with them, having spent all my vacation with adults at our new cottage or farm.

When I entered the sixth grade I was still the shy little towhead, but was making friends slowly but surely. Then in the eighth grade my parents sent me to a catholic school to get a better education. This I detested more than ever as I had to start making friends all over again.

By taking the flight method, I spent more time home sick than I did in school. Much to my happiness, the school only went up to the eighth grade. After the graduation exercises, I again took my long summer vacation. This was the first summer that I hadn't spent all my vacation at the lake. In August, I went to California with six adults, none of whom had any interest in the things I did or would have liked to do. It seems all my life (long as it was) I had always spent with older people.

When I returned in September to go to school, I had to start making friends all over again. My schoolmates seemed to be all strangers to me and I found it hard making friends. But I was very interested in the girl who lived across the street from me because she attended a different school. Because of this I spent little time at my own school activities, but went to most of hers. This also hindered my relationships with my own schoolmates. As time went on, we had sexual relationships. I had always been shy about mentioning it to anyone and always denied ever having any sexual relationship with anyone, but I'm glad I have this chance to tell it to you. This went on for quite a while until the following summer when her father was transferred because of his work.

The following fall when school opened up I was lost. I had very few friends and was selfconscious. I began to realize that sports were very important in any boy's life. Due to my father's lack of interest in sports, and my long summer vacations, I knew absolutely nothing about football and basketball, and just a little about baseball. During the summer months, I always did a lot of riding, swimming, fishing, and playing tennis, but my father wasn't the athletic type. That was all there was to it. He took no interest whatsoever in any kind of sports, and never bought me any sports equipment. I have always resented that fact, although it really isn't his fault I suppose. I always used to wish I could play school sports and be good at it. Because of my lack of sports knowledge, I plunged into school activities. In the tenth grade we were offered a speech course in school. That has been the most beneficial thing I have ever taken in school. This class gave me selfconfidence in school and a gift of gab that won me many friends. In the same year I became class president which boosted my ego even more. I plunged even deeper into school activities. I wrote for the school paper, was in the operetta, and was in the Hi-Y. I also had taken a liking to dancing in the ninth and tenth grades. I read all the books I could on dancing and practiced with my sister every spare moment I had. I thought this would be one thing I could do as well as the rest of the kids at school. I went to every dance I could both in and out of school. This dancing knowledge helped me make more friends and I tried to teach them all I could. Dancing was my way to be noticed and to make friends. Noticed I was and friends I made, for in the eleventh grade I was picked as most popular boy in the class by the school paper and to blow up my ego even more, I was picked as assistant editor of the school annual. These had been my biggest ambitions and now I was accomplishing them, all except the one I wanted most of all, to be active in school sports. I was beginning to think of sports as a lost cause, but I still wished.

By now I was directing all my dating time to one girl again. The girl was very popular, a classmate of mine, and had always gone with older fellows. I found her the perfect date because she was a very good dancer and was lots of fun—*but very over-sexed*. I soon lost all respect for her and detested even being around her in school. But she was always the old stand-by for a quick date at the last minute.

It wasn't long until it was summer vacation again but I had been working in a drug store since the beginning of my Junior year and only had two weeks vacation, so I spent most of the summer at home.

In the Fall I was picked as best dancer of our class which boosted my ego up again. I was appointed editor of the annual and vice-president of the class. This was more than enough to keep me busy at school besides working at the store and my homework. I spent most of my time at school that Fall and I began to dislike everything at school except the kids. I didn't give a tickers damn about school-work because I had accomplished my goals that I had set except the one. This one will never be accomplished now. But I figure I·will always be able to look back on the school activities, the four dances I was chairman of, the head of the decoration committee for the Junior Prom, the operetta I was in, the parts I took in the Junior and

Senior plays, my dancing and year book accomplishments, and my editorials in the school paper. These give me some satisfaction that I was of some help or credit to the school.

Discussion

Tom's exploration focuses on his struggle to overcome early childhood shyness. His story in a sense is a success story. He shows how he overcomes his shy feelings, achieves success, and becomes the most popular person in his group. For the most part, Tom has realized his major goals, and by social standards he would be considered a happy and secure person. His one misgiving is his lack of success in sports. Tom's sense of satisfaction comes in social rewards and approval. He does not find satisfaction and joy in activity and in learning itself but rather his guiding lights are success and popularity. Thus Tom moves toward goals which bring material gains. Basically he is motivated by the expectations and approval of others, and though he recognizes that something imperative is missing he does not seem to know that it is his own real self.

CONCLUSION

Miss Rosen was surprised that so many of these young people responded to the opportunity to explore their personal experiences of tension and conflict. The deep, meaningful expressions of self in the journals, discussions, and essays paved the way for open, direct, honest contacts between student and teacher. From these initial dialogues, Miss Rosen invited her students to join her for individual conferences; sometimes the student himself requested an interview. With some individuals the conferences were extended to three or four meetings, until the issue or problem was clarified and a solution was reached. Miss Rosen came to know each of her students; she came to know their important interests, fears, problems, and aspirations. This was not solely an academic class but rather a community of individuals each struggling to find himself during periods of confusion and each seeking to relate on a more genuine basis.

In the many procedures she employed, Miss Rosen found that every person in her group had at some time faced painful experiences of varying duration and intensity. Frustrations in interpersonal relations, failure, defeat, and conflict were a common pattern rather than the exception.

Most of Miss Rosen's students were grateful for the opportunity to talk over experiences of fear, anger, resentment, and shame. Many of them explored an experience for the first time. The use of discussion, the individual conferences, the journals, and the self-explorations encouraged understanding of individual problems, helped in the solution of some minor but important difficulties, and developed a sense of individual freedom, group acceptance, and unity.

Some of the self-explorations showed severe, intense emotional backgrounds. It appeared that some individuals had resolved the problems which came from severe rejection in the family while others had not. Why some persons achieved self-satisfying, healthy orientations, in spite of early experiences of defeat and failure, while other persons did not is difficult to account for. However, from the experiences of these youngsters, it cannot be concluded that rejection in early childhood inevitably destroys a sense of self and forever dooms the individual to a diminished life. A common experience of those individuals rejected in the early years but realizing values of love and self-fulfillment later was a significant relationship with at least one person. These youngsters mentioned at least one special person in their backgrounds with whom they had a deep, warm relationship. In spite of painful, early experiences, in each of these lives, there was one loving, supporting, and encouraging person. Apparently one significant interpersonal relationship is enough to enable the individual to move toward personal identity, acceptance, and effective social living.

CHAPTER 8

Success and Failure
in Creating the Interpersonal
Relationship in the Classroom

Whether or not the interpersonal relationship created in the classroom has lasting values is a question which has not been fully answered. However, we know from adult reports in later life that many individuals have singled out the experience with a teacher as the turning point toward increased self-esteem, creative accomplishment, originality, and effective living. Few adequate follow-up studies of special relationships of any kind have been conducted. Conclusions have been indefinite and inconsistent. As yet we do not know how pervasive and lasting personality changes are even in long-term, intensive psychotherapy. However, it is reasonable to assume that a meaningful and significant relationship leaves permanent traces of value.

The relationships described in this book were considered successful when the teacher felt that important changes had taken place in the relationship, leading to greater acceptance, understanding, genuineness and involvement by the teacher and a more satisfactory school experience for the child. Success was based on the teacher's judgment. Not all the teachers who attempted to work out special relationships with individual children were successful. Some were uncertain about the results and others indicated definite failure. Of the ninety-two teachers who attempted the special relationships, sixty-seven considered them worth-while experiences, nine classed them as failures, and sixteen were uncertain. Some of these uncertain and unsuccessful relationships, as well as a follow-up report of a successful relationship, will be related in detail, and the various factors which influenced the success or failure of the relationships will be discussed.

1. DANNY AND MRS. HORTON—FIRST YEAR

Danny is a blond, blue-eyed, good-looking, and sturdily built boy. Mrs. Horton was introduced to Danny by his mother Mrs. Loren, who said that Danny was an only child. His parents were especially anxious that he should succeed in school. As Mrs. Loren talked, Danny wandered about the classroom, looking at the science books on the reading tables. He showed special interest in nature and conservation books. Mrs. Horton was impressed with Danny's intellectual curiosity but noticed his restlessness.

During the first month of school the children worked mainly as a total group. The daily program included oral discussions, blackboard work, easy reading, and reviewing second-grade materials. There were frequent play periods, singing, rhythms, exercises, walks around the neighborhood, and bringing and sharing things related to plant and animal life.

For the most part the emphasis was on familiarizing the group with classroom procedures. Little individual initiative, self-reliance, and independence were required. Danny did not misbehave for several days. Then he began to flap his seat up and down a great deal, sitting on the edge of it, and banging it down. Mrs. Horton explained the danger of slipping and hitting his face on the front edge of the desk, but Danny ignored these cautions. He looked through many books, talking incessantly all the while.

Mrs. Horton discussed the importance of sharing and taking turns in classroom activities, but Danny always liked to be first in everything, leaving the room, getting drinks, going out to play, on "special-purpose" walks or tours. He would shove others aside, and tease children sitting near him until they begged to be moved away from him. On the playground, he developed a habit of grabbing the ball, knocking down anyone who got in his way, demanding "another turn" and "another turn" in games. He would proclaim loudly "Jack wasn't fair" or "Mary cheats." Sometimes he knocked down children's hats and coats, saying someone "had moved" his things and he was getting even. Mrs. Horton tried to listen calmly to all his numerous complaints and attempted to explain the fairness of decisions which Danny questioned.

One of the playground activities was jumping rope. At first he thought this was only for "sissies." After he saw other boys learning, he was determined to jump too and wanted to beat everyone else. Arguments always ensued, with Danny saying the rope-turners made him miss. He was soon pleading to Mrs. Horton to help swing the rope so that others would not cheat him. When Mrs. Horton helped, Danny quieted down.

He rode his bicycle to and from school and was frequently in trouble with the patrol boys over infractions of the rules. He was also reported nearly every day by the Service Squad girls in the halls. Mrs. Horton excused Danny's behavior by saying that he was new to the school and would cooperate when he was more familiar with the reasons for school regulations.

One day the class received a new volleyball. When the group was ready to go out to recess with the new ball, Mrs. Horton suggested that the jump rope be left in the room. Danny leaped to his feet and complained loudly. Several others joined in. Mrs. Horton was quite upset and sat down weakly. Then she said, "All right, all of you sit down quietly. There are many things I can accept, and you have never seen me angry, but this is one thing that really makes me angry. I cannot permit booing at one another. You may have heard audiences booing an important person or a team or a boxer. In my opinion it is entirely unsportsmanlike, and un-American thing to do. You may object, you may discuss, you may vote on things, but in this room I will not allow you to make that noise. Those of you who wish to say anything may now have the floor."

Mrs. Horton felt a little ashamed for the outburst and several children muttered "It's all Danny's fault" and "Danny started it." Danny exploded. "Well, I don't care. I want to jump rope." Mrs. Horton replied, "I do understand, Danny, but I object to your way of telling me." Danny said, "OK, OK, I'll try to remember." Mrs. Horton was beginning to hope that Danny had seen the light and would be more cooperative. She decided to spend more time with him. She felt she had to be on more comfortable terms with him for her own peace of mind. It was difficult to talk with Danny alone. He came to school and went home on the bus. His mother told Mrs. Horton that Danny had an accident with his bicycle and could not use it any more. Mrs. Horton finally arranged for Danny to remain after school one day a week so that she could help him with his arithmetic and also get better acquainted with him.

A few of these special periods were spent in discussing trips, the summer camps he had gone to, hunting and fishing, and famous science institutions. Mrs. Horton permitted Danny to wander about during these times and work only when he wished. He did not discuss his personal feelings or background. Frequently Danny's mother came to pick him up before Mrs. Horton and Danny started to talk. He missed several sessions due to other commitments such as visiting his "den mother" and participation in extra choir practice.

One cold morning Mrs. Horton found Danny outside her door long before belltime. Danny explained that his mother had brought him because she had to get him "out of the way."

A few days later Danny's mother and father came to "Open House" early, looked around the room, and explained that they came to sign up, but could not stay because they had another appointment. They again expressed their desire for Danny to get good marks, indicating they wanted him to be a teacher like his father. The mother reported that Danny had enjoyed staying after school.

For several weeks following the special sessions Danny was very attentive, dashing to get Mrs. Horton's coat, holding it for her, asking to help her in many ways, walking in step with her up and downstairs, holding her hand, or getting a chair for her to sit down.

Mrs. Horton made special remarks to Danny in class that would improve his status, such as "Let's hear what Danny thinks about that," or "Danny can explain what the word 'carnivorous' means," or "Danny has read so many books, I'm sure he can tell us more about that subject."

Mrs. Horton was encouraged one day when Danny had been booing some children's suggestions. He stopped midway, saying, "Oh, that's not the right way to do it."

Danny was made a member of the class quartet, responsible for singing Christmas carols in the school.

In general, Danny's behavior in class had improved but Mrs. Horton still felt anxious with him, fearing that at any moment there would be a violent outburst. She invited Danny to remain after school shortly after Thanksgiving vacation. Before they could begin their talk, Danny's mother entered the room and started talking. She talked loudly enough so Danny could hear. The following conversation took place.

Mother: I've noticed Danny is not behaving very well at home lately. He is rude to me and his father, and won't settle down to do things I ask of him.

Mrs. Horton: To what kinds of things do you refer?

Mother: Well, all he wants to do is turn on the television and watch, and I don't want him to strain his eyes after being in school all day.

Mrs. Horton: I see.

Mother: Then he fools around when he should be practicing his piano lessons, playing any notes or chords instead of his required lessons.

Mrs. Horton: He takes regular piano lessons too.

Mother: I've been checking up on him and the children tell me two girls have asked to be moved away from him, since he bothers them so and makes them nervous with his constant fidgeting. The Sunday-school teacher tells me the same thing.

Mrs. Horton: Do you have any idea as to why he behaves in this way?

Mother: Well, I suppose part of it is my fault. (*Biting her nails.*) I am very nervous and I do scold him a lot, but he has been getting worse and I don't think it is all me.

Mrs. Horton: You feel he's becoming more of a problem to you.

Mother: Yes, and then his father gets very angry at him and really wallops him. I know he is fond of his father and tries hard to please him, so when his father punishes him, it takes quite awhile for him to get over being upset.

Mrs. Horton: He is fond of his father even though he is punished?

Mother: That hasn't been happening so much lately, but Danny isn't sleeping well. After all, I can put him to bed early, but I can't force him to sleep. I was just saying to my husband the other day that we'd better get him some sleeping tablets. (*Laughs and bites nails.*)

Mrs. Horton: Have you any idea why he can't go to sleep?

Mother: I just don't know. (*Silence for a while.*)

Mrs. Horton: I wanted him to be able to stay and work or visit quietly with me once a week but he's so busy with his cub scout meetings or choir or piano lessons. Perhaps he would have more time if he rode his bicycle to school.

Mother: Maybe he ought to ride his bicycle more, especially on nice days, but I will not have him staying away from home all day.

Mrs. Horton: Well, it is extra exercise for his large muscles.

Mother: I think he got into some trouble with his bicycle. I have questioned him but he won't tell me. I could tell him he can have his dimes for bus fare, and put them in his bank to save for charity. He saved up quite a bit that way earlier.

Mrs. Horton: That should please him, as I've noticed he is sensitive about such things.

Mother: He has plenty of time to eat his lunch and I can check up on him and tell him to be a good boy.

Mrs. Horton: Well, he's being a good boy now. Here he is, all finished. Hm-m. What are these? Bright red "fences" around the problems?

Danny: Well, I put those around each set I finished so I wouldn't get confused.

Mrs. Horton: Oh, that's why. Your work looks fine, and your mother is here ready to take you home.

Danny: Can I take my arithmetic book home tonight and do that other page I missed last week?

Mrs. Horton: You want to do more now that you have such a

good start? I'll be here on Thursday if you can stay, so you had better ask your mother about it tonight.

Mother: I don't want you to strain your eyes too much and you have other things to do.

Mrs. Horton: See you tomorrow, Danny, so good night now.

Mother: Good night. It's been good of you to talk to me. I'll see you soon again.

Mrs. Horton: I'll drive Danny home when he can stay again.

Danny: Oh yes, Mom, please let her.

Mother: Well, we'll see. Good night.

Danny had been unusually quiet during Mrs. Horton's talk with his mother. He glanced back often, and would call out "only eight more," "just six more," etc. He didn't flap up and down on his seat but sat quietly.

One day Danny brought a book of Christmas songs which he showed to the class. He asked Mrs. Horton if he could stay that night. Mrs. Horton said she would be glad to have him stay. That day Danny had a perfect paper on an arithmetic test. After school the following discussion occurred.

Mrs. Horton: This is the first Wednesday you have been able to stay after school in almost a month, isn't it?

Danny: Well, really I never knew it could be fun to stay.

Mrs. Horton: You didn't know it could be fun, so you just said you were busy.

Danny: That's partly so, but I ought to be shoveling snow right now, and I had a cub scout meeting last night.

Mrs. Horton: So the snow just has to wait.

Danny: Well, my father is always too tired when he gets home and my mother went downtown.

Mrs. Horton: And there wasn't time at noon.

Danny: After I ate, I had to practice my piano lessons, and I didn't get to go out until I came back on the bus.

Mrs. Horton: Didn't even get out in the snow with any pals?

Danny: I don't have much time. One of my pals is right in the next room but he eats in the cafeteria. I don't know why my mother won't let me. The kids on the bus are all in the kindergarten.

Mrs. Horton: Oh, all in the kindergarten.

Danny: Yes, and I don't play with little kids.

Mrs. Horton: (*After Danny finishes the arithmetic assignment.*) Good! Fine-looking work. I knew you could do it. No fences around these either.

Danny: Well, I can do better when there aren't a lot of kids around me to distract me.

Mrs. Horton: I know. It's hard to concentrate. You did such fast work, now I'll see how fast I can check it. And just look what you did on your first speed test. Every one right. A perfect paper.

Danny: Oh boy, will my mom be glad to hear that!

Mrs. Horton: You know she'll be pleased.

Danny: Yeah, my dad is a college teacher and they keep telling me I have the ability to do better work. They weren't pleased with my arithmetic mark.

Mrs. Horton: How do you feel about it?

Danny: I suppose I could do things better only I'm too itchy and wiggly.

Mrs. Horton: I know. When you're itchy and wiggly it's hard.

Danny: An ambulance went by. I saw those kind when I was up at the hospital.

Mrs. Horton: You were at the hospital?

Danny: Well, my mother was there last year. She was always having headaches and backaches so they took something out.

Mrs. Horton: What did you do when she was in the hospital?

Danny: My father took care of me. My grandmother came sometimes, and my father would call up the neighbors and I'd eat around with them.

Mrs. Horton: And was that fun?

Danny: Not much, and then my father would forget to fix my lunch and I'd eat lunch with the neighbors too.

Mrs. Horton: But that's all over now.

Danny: Yes, but my mother still has headaches.

Mrs. Horton: Many people do, you know. Well, we'd better get you home so you can shovel that snow.

Danny: But I want to do that poem. I have it started somewhere.

Mrs. Horton: Let's look. Well, you'll need some quick energy if

you're going to work some more. I have some "stones" for
you to eat.

Danny: Stones?

Mrs. Horton: Try one. (*She eats one and both laugh as it turns
out to be candy. She explains they were made out West
and she bought them at a science museum.*)

Danny: I'd like to fool my mother with some.

Mrs. Horton: Help yourself.

Danny: Oh boy! This is going to be fun. I'll have one in my
hand and pretend to pick up some stones and eat them
when I'm really eating this, and then I'll give her one.

Mrs. Horton: That will surprise her.

Danny: (*On the way home.*) Can I stay sometime and help you
with some of your work even if I get my work all done in
school?

Mrs. Horton: Sure thing, Danny. You do your work with my
help and then I'll do mine with your help.

The next morning Danny arrived early. After he greeted Mrs.
Horton, he straightened all the tables, bookshelves, and records.

Mrs. Horton did several other things that added to Danny's
prestige in the classroom. She chose him and another boy to
make a large central tree as children drew pictures of "What
Trees Give Us." She put Danny in charge of special reading materials. She continued to call on him in discussions.

At the end of January Mrs. Horton noted some change in behavior. Danny frequently supported Mrs. Horton's decisions,
sometimes saying, "Keep quiet, sometimes Mrs. Horton knows
best." Another time Mrs. Horton suggested that the children
use the paper tissues on the desk to cover coughs. Several children
began a little flurry of reechoing coughs. It was Danny who
shouted, "OK, OK, You don't need to overdo it."

Danny finished several class requirements on time and derived
great satisfaction, indicating "a good feeling that's done." He has
more time to participate in activities he has been missing, such as
reading and drawing. However, in general his relationships with
other children have not improved. He still has restless, destructive
days. Mrs. Horton was constantly anxious about Danny, con-

tinued to feel threatened in his presence, and worried that Danny's hostility would destroy her work as a teacher. This feeling remained unchanged at the end of the school year.

2. DANNY AND MRS. DANE—SECOND YEAR

Early in the Spring Mrs. Dane was requested to take Danny into her group for the following school year. She had heard quite a bit about him and did not look forward to having him in her room. Mrs. Dane found the following comments on the cumulative record, written by Mrs. Horton at the end of the previous school year.

His parents and I had a conference to discuss Danny's problem. They had a great deal to criticize the school for. I felt that if Danny were given a lot more love at home, he would be a much happier and better-adjusted child. They are too busy with their careers, and a new home which is being built, to give him the attention he needs.

Danny should work this summer to be ready to go into the fourth grade or there will be too much frustration with consequent danger to other children in the room. He is likely to seriously attack other children if his hostile feelings break loose.

The first few weeks of Mrs. Dane's contacts with Danny were smooth and calm. He apparently wanted to make a good impression. But this quiet behavior did not last long. He began chewing up bits of paper (torn from paper he was supposed to be working on) and pieces of his arithmetic book.

Whenever a paper was handed back to him, he argued about it. For example, in spelling he had missed the word "people."

Danny: What's wrong with this word?
Mrs. Dane: You have an *a* instead of an *o*.
Danny: There isn't any difference between an *o* and an *a*.

When given an assignment or when reminded to do certain things, his usual comment was, "Maybe I don't feel like it."

Danny asked to take his spelling book home so his mother could copy words for him to study. Mrs. Dane told him he could not take the book home but could copy the words himself. The next morning Mrs. Dane noticed Danny carrying his spelling

book. She asked him about it and he said his mother had gone
to the office, asked for the key to the room, and had taken the
book out of his desk.

Mrs. Dane checked with the clerk who told her Danny's
mother had not been there. Danny had come back after school
and asked for the key. He told the clerk he had left his glasses
in the room. Mrs. Dane decided to overlook the incident.

One day the class assignment was a written lesson in social
studies. There were ten questions. Danny answered two of them
and said he was too tired to do any more. He asked to be seated
in the front of the room. He had been sitting in the back,
constantly irritating children around him. Mrs. Dane changed his
seat to the front, hoping this would make it easier for other
children.

Danny was often in difficulty during gym period. He frequently called the gym teacher "chicken" and other names. He
was openly defiant. He regularly annoyed other children. The
gym teacher punished him but Danny's behavior did not change.

One morning Danny went into the cloakroom and began pushing a child. Mrs. Dane told him to sit in the clerk's office until
school started. Danny was cooperative for about an hour after
this episode. Then on the way to the lavatory he began making
loud noises. When he refused to stop, Mrs. Dane told him to get
out of line. He ignored his teacher, who finally took him by the
arm and drew him out. Later that day Mrs. Dane put Danny in
the back of the room again because he kept making disturbing
noises and distracting gestures. He refused to get out of his seat.
Mrs. Dane had to take his arm and pull him out. He remarked
angrily, "I'll sure drive her nuts if I have to sit back here."

Danny refused to stand up straight while singing "America"
and saluting the flag. He made distracting noises with his mouth.
He asked about changing his seat to the front again. Mrs. Dane
told him that when he had decided that he was grown-up enough
to stop making disturbing noises, he could move back to the
front.

Mrs. Dane let Danny paint on the mural most of one morning.
In the afternoon he refused to take a social studies test. He made
remarks to other children, such as "What's the use of getting a

low mark in social studies? If I don't take the test, I won't get a low mark."

Another time, before school started, Mrs. Dane saw Danny fighting in the hall. When she spoke to him about it, he said, "Maybe I feel like fighting." Mrs. Dane told him she wished he would talk sensibly. Danny raised the standard of his musical instrument to strike her. Mrs. Dane took Danny to the clerk's office by force. She left a note saying Danny could return when he was ready to change his conduct. Danny sent back his own note saying he was not ready. At 10:30 Danny was sent for to take his music lesson. Danny entered the room and jabbed Mrs. Dane in the side with his elbow. She took him back to the clerk's office again. Danny attempted to hit Mrs. Dane while she was forcing his return to the office. Mrs. Dane let him stay in the office for a while until he became a little more calm; then she let him go to his music class.

In the afternoon when the class was having a practice spelling test, Danny got five words wrong. He threw his spelling book across the room, saying, "I didn't know 'October' and 'Friday' began with capital letters." Before the test Mrs. Dane had particularly called attention to the capital letters.

In social studies the class started talking about the Plymouth Colony. Before the discussion got under way Mrs. Dane asked if anyone knew about the first Thanksgiving. Danny mimicked his teacher, saying, "First Thanksgiving," in a loud, high-pitched voice. He spent the rest of the afternoon in the clerk's office. When he was excused to go home, he said, "I'll do the boards for you in the morning Mrs. Dane." He really seemed repentant.

The next day started calmly and was a peaceful one until Danny went to gym. The teacher sent him to the clerk's office because he was running around in the balcony. He sat there the rest of the morning and part of the afternoon before returning to class.

Shortly after this episode Mrs. Dane asked the children to draw a picture about John Smith and the Jamestown Colony. Danny said he did not want to draw. He walked around the room, looked at the bulletin board, took the globe to his seat, and folded his drawing paper like a hat. He then kept folding and unfolding it. His stand for his music was on his desk. He kept taking it apart and putting it together again. He also kept putting it in the case and taking it out again, latching and unlatching the case.

During arithmetic he said he had no pencil. Mrs. Dane asked if some child could lend him one. He said he guessed he didn't need one. Mrs. Dane assumed Danny had a pencil but, on looking closer, discovered he was using a screw, scratching into the paper with it. When she insisted that he use a pencil, he said, "All right, if that will satisfy you."

For many weeks Danny's behavior vacillated from noncooperative to cooperative. His comments became increasingly sarcastic and derogatory during the negative phase. One afternoon he started making disgusting noises with his mouth and refused to do the class assignments. Questions for the social studies lesson were on the board. Danny was sent to the clerk's office. He not only had refused to do the work but had made obscene remarks to Mrs. Dane. He remained in the office about half an hour. Mrs. Dane told him he could go out for recess. For the first time during the year Danny played with the group. Usually he spent the recess period by himself or teased and chased girls. After recess Danny was cooperative except for occasional nasty remarks. During the art period in the afternoon he refused to put the scissors down when the teacher told him to do so. He was sent to the clerk's office again.

One day in November Danny was talking with a boy across the aisle from him before school started. Without apparent justification, he suddenly began to fight. Mrs. Dane told the boys to get out their reading books. Danny responded angrily, "Maybe I don't feel like it." He began kicking the case of his musical instrument. Mrs. Dane ignored this behavior. After awhile Danny started reading and completed the assignment. Mrs. Dane encouraged him to help another child. He agreed but the cooperative attitude did not last long. He soon began making caustic remarks in a loud voice.

That afternoon he continued making loud noises which irritated Mrs. Dane and disturbed the class. Mrs. Dane decided to remove him from the group. He had to be taken by force to the clerk's office. A short while later he returned. The class was correcting spelling papers. Immediately Danny began to argue about spelling the word "swimming." He had spelled it with a capital letter. He said his mother said it should start with a capital letter and she should know. Mrs. Dane accepted his explanation but insisted the word be marked wrong.

During the entire next morning Danny continued to maintain that "swimming" should begin with a capital letter. He insisted his mother had told him so. He did everything to irritate Mrs. Dane. For the most part Mrs. Dane listened and tried hard not to become angry.

At noon he brought macaroni and passed it around to the other children. They seemed to like this. In music class he started yelling because he was not chosen to pass and collect books. He refused to give his book to the child who was collecting them. When English papers were passed, he threw his paper on the floor. Danny immediately started making remarks about the paper which had been handed to him. He said, "Who the heck graded this paper?" He talked and made remarks constantly. Then he sent an obscene note to the child who had scored his paper.

Danny continued to refuse to do tests in social studies. Before report cards were given out he was heard to make the remark that if he got "a bad report card, someone is going to get a punch right in the nose." When he got his report card, Danny started screaming. He caused a scene, called Mrs. Dane a "dirty liar," and made several other remarks. As he left the building he called Mrs. Dane an obscene name. Mrs. Dane accepted all these attacks and told Danny he had a right to feel as he did but not to talk that way in school.

When he came to school the next morning, he seemed to have calmed down. He said his mother had told him to do the tests. He had been given an Incomplete on his report card in social studies. For a while he tried to do the assigned work.

One morning Danny refused to stand when the group sang "America." He draped himself over his seat. Mrs. Dane took hold of his arm. He then acted very belligerent and put out his fists to fight. He was sent to the clerk's office and told he could come back to the room in fifteen minutes.

In reading class he insisted he had read the assignment and

refused to work. He was unable to answer any of the questions. He then said, "All you want to do is argue." Mrs. Dane warned him that if he kept making remarks, he would have to leave the room. Danny ignored Mrs. Dane and was ordered to go the clerk's office. He hung on to his desk. Mrs. Dane had to pull him out of his seat and force him to go.

The next day Danny cooperated fairly well until the group got in line for lavatory period. Mrs. Dane said something to him about the way he was acting in line. Danny told her to "shut up." He was sent to the clerk's office. During art period he would not draw or work. Again he was sent to the office. When he returned, he was silent for over an hour. Then he kept making remarks and became unruly, knowing that since it was nearly dismissal time he could get away with it.

The fluctuating relationship with Danny continued into December. Mrs. Dane still felt uncertain in Danny's presence. She sensed a feeling of retaliation, and sarcasm creep into her voice as she talked with Danny.

During recess time Danny frequently chased girls. He got into a fight with another boy who protected a girl against Danny's attacks. "Why don't you send me to the office?" he asked. Mrs. Dane told him he could go if he wanted to. While Danny was in the clerk's office the children made Christmas cards. He seemed upset when he saw what the group had made while he was away.

Danny came in the cloakroom the next morning and hit a child with his music standard. Later he asked to go to the lavatory but went down to the cafeteria instead. Mrs. Dane heard him remark that he was going to "get" somebody. When a small girl came in, he asked her about a riddle book which he had had in his desk. She said she had just lent it to him but he insisted that she had given it to him.

Danny: You gave it to me.
Patsy: No I didn't, Danny. You asked if you could borrow it.
Danny: You're a liar.

The argument grew louder. Both children were sent to the principal, who tried to make Danny see that the riddle book belonged to Patsy. Soon both children returned. Danny was quiet the rest of the morning. During afternoon recess he played ball with the boys. Mrs. Dane noticed that three times during this period he ran after boys and hit them but remained in the game until recess was over. He voluntarily stayed after school that evening. He seemed somewhat calm, so Mrs. Dane thought she would talk to him about his work.

Mrs. Dane: Danny, why don't you take your social studies book home and have your mother read it to you or help you read it? I know you want to do better.

Danny: My mother doesn't like to have me bring work home.

Mrs. Dane: Wouldn't she help you with it?

Danny: No.

Tommy: (*Another boy staying after school.*) What about your father? Wouldn't he help you?

Danny: Neither one of them is very calm when they get home. When they are home I have to mind my p's and q's.

Tommy: What did your father say when he saw your report card?

Danny: He doesn't care what marks I get.

The principal asked to see Danny the first thing the next morning. He had been in trouble with the patrol boys. Danny sat in the office until after recess. During a spelldown later in the day he missed the word "Thanksgiving," failing to spell it with a capital letter. Mrs. Dane told him he would have to sit down. He refused and insisted he had spelled the word right. Again he was sent to the clerk's office. He came back in time to take his spelling test. When the arithmetic assignment was given, as usual he did not listen.

Danny: Is this multiply?

Mrs. Dane: Look at the top of the page and see what it says.

Danny: (*Very sarcastically.*) Thanks for the information.

Then he made some other remarks under his breath. He refused to tell Mrs. Dane what he had said, so he was sent to the clerk's office again.

In the afternoon he refused to draw a map. He was told he could study something else. He kept making noises, shoving his desk about 4 feet forward and then back again. He was sent from the room. When he went home, Mrs. Dane said, "Well, this has been rather a hard day for you, hasn't it, Danny?" Danny said, "Yes, and I caught my finger in my desk too. Good-by, Mrs. Dane, see you tomorrow."

Later that week Danny started another argument with Mrs. Dane.

Danny: What is the matter with November?
Mrs. Dane: You didn't have an *m* in it.
Danny: There isn't any *m* in November.
Mrs. Dane: Well, let's look back in the spelling book and find out.
Danny: Oh. (*This is the first time Danny has admitted an error.*)

At recess time Danny kissed some girls in spite of their objections. He spent from three o'clock to three-twenty-five in the clerk's office.

The next day during reading period the following conversation took place between Danny and Mrs. Dane.

Mrs. Dane: Danny, we're going to have reading now. Take out your reading book.
Danny: No, I'm going to work in my workbook and get caught up.
Mrs. Dane: No, you are going to read with the rest of the group.
Danny: I have to get caught up in my workbook.
Mrs. Dane: No, you are going to read with the group.

The argument continued for several minutes. Then Danny was given a choice of starting the reading assignment or going to the clerk's office. To Mrs. Dane's surprise, Danny took out his reading book and began to work.

After gym the children told Mrs. Dane that Danny had sworn at the gym teacher and the teacher put him in another room. Danny screamed out, "I'm not afraid to swear at you either." Mrs. Dane warned him, "Well, I wouldn't advise you to do it."

After lavatory period the gym teacher came in and asked for Danny. He hung on to his desk and refused to get out of his seat.

Mrs. Dane finally persuaded Danny that he would have to go with the gym teacher.

During recess, a few days later, Mrs. Dane was unable to go out with the group immediately. When she reached the playground, all the girls seemed indignant. Danny apparently, in frenzied rage, had thrown rocks at the girls, hit them with his fists, etc. One boy had taken it upon himself to take Danny to the office. Mrs. Dane told Danny he would have to miss recesses for a week. He shouted that he did not care.

Danny continued to battle with Mrs. Dane at every opportunity. He refused to do his arithmetic. Mrs. Dane had to ask him several times. He told Mrs. Dane that he didn't like arithmetic. Then he made a remark about a "crab-apple teacher." He was sent to the clerk's office.

Mrs. Dane tried to get him to finish an arithmetic test he had started. He finally did part of it. When his paper was handed back (his mark was 30), he threw the paper on the floor. Mrs. Dane insisted that he pick it up. He did not start an argument for a change but sullenly put the paper in his desk. He drew Patsy's name for the Christmas party. He said he was going to give her a punch in the nose as a Christmas gift.

On the final day of his loss of recess Danny refused to go to the office. He shouted over and over again that he had made up all his time. Mrs. Dane forced him from his desk. In doing so the desk was tipped over. He was sent to the clerk's office.

When the group went to gym to practice for the Christmas program, Danny took off his belt and put it through the chair so that when he stood up, the chair would come too. He was sent out. Soon the gym teacher saw that Danny was crying and looked hurt because he could not practice with the rest of the group. Mrs. Dane let him come back again. Danny said he was sorry. In the afternoon he refused to do his written work.

At recess time the next day Danny again chased and teased girls. Mrs. Dane told him to sit on the steps. He picked up a piece of ice and threw it at Mrs. Dane. He was taken to the clerk's office. After recess he was requested to come back to the room to take his arithmetic test. He refused and was sent to the principal's office. When dismissal time came, Danny barged through the girls' line. He then went through the cloakroom, pushing, shoving, and jabbing his elbows into everyone. Mrs. Dane made him take his seat until after the other children had gone. When he left, he said he was not coming back in the afternoon.

He came back. The group started to do an arithmetic test. When told it was a test, he put his paper in the desk and slammed the top down. He said he would not do it unless he could look up the answers.

A motion picture was scheduled for the afternoon. When it was time, the boy who runs the projector had not arrived. Mrs. Dane told the group they could tell riddles until he came. Someone gave a riddle. Danny said, "Is it a ———?" using an obscene word. He was sent to the clerk's office until school was out.

About a week and a half later Danny hit a girl in both eyes while in the gym class. The gym teacher took him to the principal. Since that time Danny has been excluded from the group. The principal put Danny's desk out in the hall. Danny had too many visitors while in the hall so he was moved to the principal's office.

He returns to his room for only short periods of time. He had told the principal that he did not like the other children anyway, so he did not care to be with them.

Mrs. Dane noted some improvement in Danny's behavior in spite of all the difficulties. He no longer tears up papers and parts of his books. He accepts correction occasionally. He does not say "Maybe I don't feel like it" so often. The children accept him more than might be expected. For a time he brought things from home—marshmallows, peanuts, etc., and shared them with the class. The children tried not to antagonize Danny and he could occasionally play with them for lengthy periods of time.

Discussion

Both Mrs. Horton and Mrs. Dane attempted to accept Danny and help him to have a satisfactory experience in the classroom. They permitted him to express considerable hostility, expecting that eventually these feelings would dissipate. They gave Danny responsibility in the classroom, encouraged other children to play with him, and gave him freedom to make decisions on his own.

Also, they were patient with him. To some extent Danny used these opportunities to explore the tensions and restrictions in his own family situation, but for the most part he remained antagonistic.

In the past, these teachers had been particularly skillful in effecting successful relations with problem children. In spite of their experience, they were unable to develop a healthy relationship with Danny. Why did these teachers become more irritated and disturbed in their experience with him?

Perhaps their most obvious frustration was their inability to remain with Danny during the destructive outbursts. Continual failure must have been a serious threat to the teachers' perceptions of themselves as effective teachers. As they failed, more and more Mrs. Horton and Mrs. Dane came to feel tension and threat, and accompanying this anxiety was a feeling of uncertainty, discomfort, and defeat. Having lost their confidence in themselves in their relationship with Danny, they found it more difficult to accept him and to continue to believe in his capacity for constructive activity. They came to see him as a wild, destructive child and thus lost touch with his positive strivings for growth and self-actualization. Danny's constant interference with class projects exhausted the group's mental and physical resources and energy. Eventually their relationship with Danny became a negative one, the kind of relationship he had always developed with people.

These teachers initially were interested in Danny and wanted to help him. They were challenged by the idea of reaching him and freeing him to use his capacities in constructive directions. In time these early aspirations changed and the teachers came to feel more and more helpless with Danny. He managed to destroy what they needed most in order to help him—a feeling of confidence in themselves as teachers. Thus Mrs. Horton and Mrs. Dane failed to help Danny resolve his emotional conflicts and discover a good life in school.

Perhaps Danny's difficulty too could be seen essentially as an impairment in his own belief in himself. Danny felt deeply inadequate and rejected by everyone in general and by his parents particularly. In his own mind no teacher, as a matter of fact, no person could ever feel positively toward him. Danny believed that no one could ever love him. Thus he attacked others at every opportunity. People in authority were primarily responsible for his inadequacies and fears, so they were most subject to his attacks.

It is amazing that his teachers, in spite of his harmful effect on their own self-confidence, were able to permit Danny to remain in their classrooms. Actually Danny had no place else to go, for his parents refused to cooperate in any way and rejected the notion that Danny needed intensive psychiatric aid and perhaps a special school. Therefore by keeping him and not insisting on expulsion, although no important break-through occurred in the relationship, perhaps a real tragedy was prevented.

Though no major changes occurred over these two years, Mrs. Horton and Mrs. Dane reached Danny in a number of situations and there were numerous good experiences and good days. There were occasional glimpses of the real child and times when he used his intelligence in constructive ways. In spite of the hard struggle against it, his achievement in reading, spelling, and arithmetic remained above grade level. In addition, the harmful effects of Danny's behavior on other children were lessened. Danny occasionally had days in school in which he was cooperative and responsive to others. During the first and second grade, Danny had several teachers who refused to let him remain in their groups. Two teachers threatened to resign unless he was removed from their classes. One of his teachers did resign. So Danny had to make several changes before he completed the full year with Mrs. Horton and Mrs. Dane. And, although in the end the relationship was uncertain and unpredictable, his teachers continued to work with him and continued to search for positive ways of being with him.

FAILURES

1. Dana and Miss Walton

The relationship between Dana and his teacher is described by Miss Walton herself.

When school started in September, from all appearances my class contained no so-called problem children. Within two weeks I realized just how wrong I was! On the day Dana's problem arose to the surface the class had been quite noisy, so I said I would give each person I saw talking three warnings before I asked him to go to the corner. Two children did not heed my warnings and consequently were sent to a corner until they decided they could be quiet. I warned Dana three times and then told him to go to the corner. He said, "I won't." I started toward him. He continued to remain in his seat. I kept insisting that he go to the corner. He kept saying "I won't." I explained that I had told all the children what would happen if they kept talking. I told him the others had accepted their punishment and that he should too. He said, "I bite." I said, "You are not any different from anyone else. You must accept yours. "I kick," he said. I asked him what his mother did when he misbehaved. He said, "Sometimes she spanks me. Last night I didn't come home when she told me to, but she didn't do anything."

By this time we were both standing in the corner. I realized he would not stand in the corner alone and that nothing was to be gained if I stood with him, so I told him he was to go to his seat and decide what I should do when he misbehaved. Later when we went to get our drinks and to get in line to go outside, Dana stayed in the room. I told him we were waiting for him to get in line. "I don't feel good." "Do you feel bad enough to go home?" "No." " You must either sit in the office or go outside." I picked him up and literally carried him out to the playground as he screamed and kicked. When we reached the playground another child said, "Come on, Dana, let's play," and with that, off he went and his tears vanished. And I could relax for the first time that day.

A few days later he began playing instead of doing his work. So I began saying, after I explained their work, "You must not talk to people who have not finished their work." Dana complained bitterly but did his work for a few days. Then he began singing in a loud voice, whinnying like a horse, whistling, or bothering other children who were also slow workers. Consequently, little work was accomplished by him.

I called his mother in for a conference and we discussed Dana's behavior. She said I was to do anything I thought should be done. We decided he was to do his work when others did or he was to stay in at recess and do it in the office. The next day Dana remained inside for recess. I half-carried him to the office and told him as soon as his work was done he could come out. Five minutes later Dana appeared on the playground. "No, I have not finished," he said. I carried him back inside and a tantrum developed in the office. His mother was called in. Dana quickly settled down and returned to the room. The principal said he was not to be forced to do his work, that his biggest problem was his immaturity. If his work was not where it should be in June, he would be held back.

A few weeks later he appeared with the rest of his reading group for the first time in ten days. He began hitting the children, talking out loud, and finally left the group. When Dana gets mad he says "Everyone hates me. They all try to fight me." Actually the children like him but become annoyed when he takes their things. He is the smallest child in the room, but every ounce is packed with dynamite. He is very quick to sock others. He and Billy are quite antagonistic toward each other. At every chance they take pokes at each other. Dana gets very mad and starts screaming.

For a period Dana whinnied like a horse or made a noise like a machine gun all day. He didn't come up with his reading group. He came up and asked me to help with his number work. Then he returned to his seat because I was busy with a reading group and couldn't help. He began teasing the children by erasing their work, by taking their money, pencils, paste, etc. If the children chased him, he would run madly around the room. If they ignored him, he gave their things back. That afternoon we played "Tappers." No one tapped him, so he came up to me and said, "No one ever taps me." "Maybe it is because you take their things." I asked whom he liked best in the room. "No one." He then returned to his seat and half played the game. Next we cleaned out our desks and he asked me to help him. When they left, I asked him to see just how quiet he could be and just how much work he could get done when he came to school the next day. "OK. If you will keep the other kids quiet." This was the second time he offered this as an excuse for not doing his work. This excuse, of course, is inconsistent with his own noisy behavior.

The next day he did his number work after I wrote out part of it for him. When I called up his reading group, he said, "Not me." He began poking people with a clothespin. The next day he again refused to do his work. He began fighting with another child. I told them to stop and go to their seats. The other child did, but Dana slapped him across the face as hard as he could.

The following Monday he was fairly quiet. He came up with his reading group and did a little work. We have music Monday afternoons. The music teacher asked him to put his things away. "No." He became extremely noisy. She sent him to the hall. He began rattling the door. The music teacher suggested I take him to the office. I went out and told Dana what she had said. "Let's fool her. You be so quiet and she won't even know you're out here." "OK," he remarked.

The next day the room was very quiet. He came up with his reading group and did a little of his work, but he started wandering around. "Dana, the room is quiet, why don't you do your work?" "They'll get noisy." He returned to his seat and did a little more. Later I began to erase the number work. "Don't do that, maybe I'll finish my work." "What are you doing that for?" he asked me when later in the afternoon I erased the board. "Now I'll never do my work. You always take it off before I finish."

A few days later Dana began knocking books on the floor. He quarreled with the children and as usual took their belongings and hit them. The class began to discuss why we should keep the room quiet. Dana said, "Make them stay in and do their work." Another child ask him if that meant him too. He thought a while and then said "No."

Dana never seems to accept punishment. When the rest of the room puts their heads down, Dana keeps his up and sings and colors. When he is punished, he rebels unless sent to the hall. Then he usually knocks on the door. When I tell him to be quiet, he gets louder. When the children tell him to be quiet, he hits them. He hits anyone who is within reach, except me. When I suggest he might want to hit me, he says "No." "Why do you hit people who don't even bother you if you won't hit me?" He shrugged his shoulders and didn't answer. Dana never rebels physically by kicking and biting me, although he has done this to other adults.

The first of November approached and found Dana still not working and still antagonizing others. When Billy approaches him, he yells for me. During his reading time we were working in our workbooks. Dana did one of his pages wrong. I explained how it should be done. "I know how to do this; I've done it before." He left the group and returned while I was checking someone else's work. "Check mine." "I can't until you do it the right way." For a change he was willing to wait.

Later that day he began waving a pair of scissors which had sharp points. "Please put your scissors away." He refused. "Whose are they?" "Yours," and he pushed them toward me. Every day he comes up to my desk and visits with me. One Monday he said, "You didn't notice my haircut." "Oh, yes I did. I noticed it as soon as you walked in. It looks nice."

Dana continued to take things and when the owners came up to me, I tell them to ignore him and he'll give it back. He takes money and quite often refuses to give it back. One day I asked him how I could trust him if he didn't trust me. "I don't trust anyone." "What have I ever done to make you not trust me?" "You called my mother." "I called your mother because I wanted to help you." He then returned the money. A few days later I called his home to get his parents' permission to call in a special teacher. They readily gave it. The father said he had told Dana that the next time I called and gave them a bad report, he would not get something he wanted, like a bicycle. I suggested that too much pressure at home would only make a bad situation worse.

The next day he took a child's ruler. I suggested that he use mine instead. He did. During his reading group, and while Dana was reading aloud, I turned to answer another child's question. Dana stopped and looked at me. "Now you know how other people feel when you talk while they are trying to read." He half nodded. Later when others were turning their work in, I asked him where his was. "I don't have to do that." He went to the cupboard and got his number workbook and did the work for the day before. Then he took a child's lunch money. I asked him to give it back. "No." I took him by the arms. He reached in his pocket and threw the money across the room and began hitting people with his number book. I asked him to stop. He didn't, so I picked up a number book and began to hit him. "That dosen't hurt." "I know that; why should I want to hurt you?" I took his book and led him back to his seat. "Why don't you clear off your desk and get ready for lunch?" "You help me."

One day I took a box of crayons to school for him to use and suggested he use them instead of other people's. He settled down and drew a picture for me. When he returned the crayons he said, "I broke one." We fixed it with scotch tape.

The next day he began annoying other children. I suggested that he do his work. He wandered around taking others' papers. I called him to my desk and told him report cards were coming out and that his wasn't going to be very good. I told him to get busy so his next one would be good. I told him to go to his seat and get busy or go out in the hall. He began to smear paste on desks. When he was ignored, he settled down and did his work.

The next day after he finished his work he took another child's colored pencil. I suggested that he use mine. "I don't have to," he yelled. I gave the other child my pencil.

Toward the end of the semester, after being absent for a day, Dana came in wearing a new shirt. Everyone told him how much they liked it. He became very excited and began running around the room, taking things and laughing hysterically. He and Billy had an argument, both talking loudly. I sent Dana on an errand. When his reading group came up he said, "I'm not coming because I have a bad cold." After much talk he came up coughing and sniffling.

Shortly after this Dana and his family moved and Dana went to a new school. Billy, who also was a problem, has straightened out. The whole room has a different atmosphere. The group is far calmer, quieter, and more cooperative.

Discussion

Miss Walton made an effort to understand Dana but there was no real feeling behind it. Basically she was concerned with two goals in her relationship with him. These goals she put into two questions to Dana: "How much work can you get done?" and "How quiet can you be?" It never occurred to Miss Walton to ask: "Who are you, Dana?" "What do you want from me?" "How can I help you to develop a genuine identity and self-esteem?"

Miss Walton insisted that Dana stick to the assignments and focused on reading and number work rather than on discovering resources that would help him locate, pursue, and develop his own interests. Thus the battles centered around conventional school work rather than the real issues and problems that existed in Dana and in his relations with others, including his teacher.

Another factor in the deteriorating relationship was Miss Walton's lack of a sense of direction. She sought direction both from Dana's mother and from the principal of the school (and the advice given by these two people was diametrically opposed). Instead, Miss Walton might have followed her own intuition and judgment, emerging out of conflicts with Dana in the real situations in which they met.

Furthermore, Miss Walton was unable to face Dana openly

and honestly in setting limits and adhering to them. Either she manipulated him by indirect and devious means, or she capitulated and was contradictory in her behavior, or she withdrew. Her attitude was not one of genuine openness and presence. Although she was concerned with Dana and wanted to reach him, her concern never got beyond academic incentives. Basically, she tolerated Dana and avoided him until he forced an issue between them. Thus she never confronted Dana on firm ground; she failed to meet him on an authentic basis. Dana needed freedom and love to find himself but he also needed strength from someone who could meet him in battle and remain firm until a constructive resolution of the issue could be reached. Miss Walton was unable to express her own real feelings in the relationship; she was unable to be herself. In his resistance Dana revealed his teacher's weakness, her inability to manage him, and her fear of challenging him.

Dana's early departure probably saved a more severe break in his relationship with Miss Walton. Both were relieved when the separation occurred. Miss Walton reported that with Dana gone she could progress without continual frustration to get her group ready for the next grade. Dana's new teacher indicated surprise that Dana had been a trouble maker. She expressed a genuine interest in him and a relationship emerged in which both teacher and child found meaning and value.

2. Carol and Miss Senter

Miss Senter described her relationship with Carol as follows:

About the end of the second week of school I noticed Carol and the fact that her personality was annoying. Carol comes from an average unbroken home and has only one brother, younger than herself. I met Carol's mother at "Open House" and she seemed very nice. I felt she monopolized the conversation, however. Carol's father is a kind of loud-speaking "Mr. Know-It-All" type. He is very strict with Carol. Carol's work in school is very good and her behavior as far as complying with rules is excellent.

I found Carol's tone of voice and facial expressions irritating. Carol's main problem is an overly sweet, adult manner of speaking. She seldom speaks to other children, but when she does, it is in an officious way. She doesn't seem to know how to talk children's language. When she sits at her desk, she gives the appearance of being very busy even while doing the most simple tasks. If a child says something to her while she is busy, Carol gives the child a mean look and goes on about her work. The children have little to do with Carol. However, when she is included, she enters into the activity with great enthusiasm, almost to the point of taking over. It is always at this point that the children crowd her out. An instance of this occurred one day when Carol and I came out on the playground just before Christmas and climbed on the merry-go-round where my girls were singing Christmas carols. Carol had stayed behind to help me with my coat and discuss one of the children I had to correct that day. After the song was finished Carol chose the next song and shouted out in a big voice, "Now, everyone get quiet and I'll start the next song." The children didn't stop talking right away so Carol looked at me and said in a very soft voice, "I'm just not going to start until they're quiet." She pursed her lips, held her head high, and appeared to be looking over their heads in an aloof and patient manner. When they were quiet Carol said, "All right now, begin—'Deck the halls with. . . .'" After this song she chose another and then another. After the third song I suggested she choose another person to pick the next song. She chose someone else and after the song was finished Carol left the merry-go-round and sat on a bench alone. I went over and discussed taking turns with her, and she said, "Oh really, I was quite tired of singing those songs anyway," missing completely the point I was trying to make.

Carol seems to be constantly trying to establish a different relationship with me, a sort of "we-understand-these-children" attitude. The other children do not like her. I have tried hard not to let my feelings show, in hopes that the other children would not pick them up from me. I have been told that the children did not like her last year either. I can only remember once that another child ever chose her for anything, and she was so pleased and polite in thanking the boy that his face turned many shades of red.

As I mentioned earlier, Carol's attitude toward me is one of sweetness and flattery. I don't believe a day goes by during which she doesn't flatter me in some way.

Two weeks ago Carol came up to say something to me. She excused herself several times and when she left, the assistant principal spoke of what a sweet and polite child she was. She said she had noticed Carol several times and it was a pleasure to see such a courteous child. I started thinking that perhaps this feeling I had built up in my mind about Carol was something I had let get out of hand. For the next two weeks I thought Carol didn't bother me as much as she did. I thought I had accepted her. Since then four different teachers and the principal of the school, who knew Carol from previous years, made such remarks to me as "How are you able to tolerate that child's personality?" They were quite strong in their feelings against her. I realized that they saw the same things in her that I did. I slumped right back into the same feeling I had had, and I knew then that I really never had changed my feelings about her. I am always aware of this feeling, though she does not bother me as much as she did. I am trying not to treat Carol differently than I do the other children, but I don't seem to be able to help myself. I have never been harsh or sarcastic, but that is only because I don't say what I think. Carol is mine for all day and it bothers me that I must tolerate her and also that I am not helping her any, and may, unconsciously perhaps, even harm her. I am certain that she is not a happy child and I am not happy about what has happened between us.

Discussion

This is the report of a teacher who recognized the issues and problems in her relationship with the child but who did not openly express her feelings. As a matter of fact, Miss Senter plays a game with Carol, pretending to be interested in her but actually carrying heavy feelings of irritation and rejection. She says, "I have tried not to let my feelings show." Yet when a teacher is "nauseated" by a child, the child gets the message but in hidden, devious ways. The child actually receives two messages, the outward interest and patience and the inward feeling of disgust and contempt. Carol too engages in the duplicity, pretending to be positively received and encouraged but knowing she has been denied and rejected. What is required, and missing, in both persons is a basic honesty and an openness, a willingness to meet in a genuine way and struggle with the conflict to a point of real involvement and caring.

Miss Senter was not honest with Carol and Carol was not honest with herself. Miss Senter had definite feelings of resentment toward Carol, as did all her previous teachers. She could not express these feelings. Thus, the more she inhibited the negative feelings, the more extreme they became.

Carol, on the other hand, wanted basically to find someone who could trust her and value her, help her to feel important as a person. Her dishonesty and insincerity had to be expressed and accepted, her right to be dishonest had to be recognized long enough and strongly enough before more acceptable patterns could emerge.

Miss Senter could not be herself as long as she distorted her experience with Carol. With each incident of distortion both teacher and child were extending their alienation. An open discussion with Carol might have stopped the negative feeling from growing, and a more satisfying relationship might have resulted. As long as she only pretended to accept Carol, she could not really accept her. Miss Senter resented Carol's insincerity and also her own insincerity in response to it. Carol longed for someone who would regard her as a worthy person. She felt this kind of relationship could be effected through praise, so she praised constantly. The more she used this approach, the more she irritated Miss Senter. Thus Carol and Miss Senter related dishonestly and superficially and in the process the potentially positive feelings were buried. Genuineness and respect were missing in this relationship.

FOLLOW-UP OF A SUCCESSFUL RELATIONSHIP:

Ned and Miss Martin

Miss Martin first met Ned when he was in kindergarten. He was sitting on the ground by his teacher's feet, playing in the gravel. Miss Martin recognized him as the child who had caused a great deal of trouble around the school. Ned impressed Miss Martin as a quiet and shy child. As she observed him she saw that he was unable to play with other children.

Miss Martin did not see Ned again until he entered the first grade as one of her pupils. She was surprised to find a more cooperative, social, and outgoing child. Miss Martin had several talks with Ned's previous teacher, Miss Morton, who had worked hard to establish a personal relationship with him. She learned that Ned slipped occasionally and needed special understanding at these times.

The first day of school Ned came into the room by himself. The majority of children had come with their mothers, who saw that they were seated and comfortable before they kissed them good-by. Ned came in alone and seemed lonely. Miss Martin greeted him with a hearty "Good morning, Ned." He was pleased and surprised that his teacher already knew his name. He was excited about school and talked incessantly that first morning.

The first few weeks of school Miss Martin let Ned do what he wanted to, but at points he became so noisy and rough with other children that Miss Martin decided to set some limits. He would occasionally hit and push others and bring them to tears. If a child was working with a puzzle, Ned was apt to grab the pieces and run around the room with them. He also took children's possessions. He pinched children, smeared clay on the tables, and hit people on the head. He was always out of his seat. When Miss Martin tried to explain a page to the group, Ned would shout out. Miss Martin had spoken to Ned many times but, more often than not, he ignored her.

On the playground Ned frequently pushed children off the merry-go-round and threw stones. One day he had a little girl down on the ground and was forcing gravel in her mouth. Miss Martin arrived on the scene in time to stop him before real damage was done. She had a long talk with him, explaining that he just would not be permitted to do things like that. She told him she knew he would feel terrible if he really hurt someone, and added that if he kept it up, no one would want to play with him. She told Ned she liked him but she could not permit some of his behavior.

For a few days Ned got along fairly well on the playground. One day a group of boys in the room ganged up on him for no apparent reason, except to pay Ned back for his many attacks of the past. Ned came to Miss Martin and complained he had not hurt anyone for a long time and that the boys had been picking on him. Miss Martin explained that some of the boys still remembered his attacks but that now maybe things were even.

Ned eats his lunch at school. During several noon hours he had been reprimanded for hurting others. One afternoon Miss Martin heard loud screams in the hall and found Ned hitting and kicking at a patrol boy who was bringing him in for pushing little girls down while waiting in the school lobby. This was the only temper tantrum that Ned has had in the first grade, compared to the several which occurred during his first months of school in kindergarten. The patrol boy thought that Ned should be taken to the principal for punishment. Ned was frightened about this. Miss Martin said that if he would promise not to attack girls again, it would not be necessary for him to report to the principal. Miss Martin explained she would not be able to help again. She knew how he might feel, but no matter how much he wanted to hit other children, she could not let him. She told Ned that sooner or later everyone feels like hitting or pushing someone else, but people have to control the way they express their feelings even though they have a right to feel that way.

Ned became very affectionate with Miss Martin and frequently kissed her during the day. He told Miss Martin how much he liked his kindergarten teacher too. Ned stayed after school a couple of times and Miss Martin had long talks with him. She went out to his locker with him one time while he was putting his coat on and told him to go straight home because his mother would be worrying about him. He said, "Oh, it doesn't matter when I go home 'cause my mom works and she never knows where I am anyway. I stay at Mrs. Carr's house and I only see mom when my dad comes and gets me and we go shopping at my mom's store."

One day Ned told Miss Martin that he had twelve brothers and sisters. Miss Martin knew that he was an only child, so she said, "Do you like to pretend that your friends in school are your brothers and sisters?" "No, I really do have twelve brothers and sisters and that's no lie either," he replied. He added, "They are all in the first grade and they all live at my house. We sure do have lots of fun playing together."

Ned loves to hide behind doors and jump out at people. When the group comes back from recess, he always hurries to the room and goes in the closet, so when Miss Martin hangs up her coat, he can jump out at her. He also hides under the teacher's desk and jumps up at her. He is pleased when he gets special attention.

While discussing "Open House" Miss Martin said that parents would be coming to school one evening to see the children's work. She told the class she would put their handwriting papers on the board for parents to see. Ned's work is usually fairly neat and he tries to do it well. The day the group talked about doing extra neat papers, however, Ned poked holes, drew airplanes on his, and made it extremely messy. When Miss Martin collected the papers Ned said, "It doesn't matter if my paper looks messy, my parents won't come to school anyway. My dad has never been in this school. My mom has only been here once. That was 'cause I was in trouble when I was in the other room."

The next morning Ned came in and said, "See, what'd I tell you! I knew my mom and dad wouldn't come." Ned had thought that "Open House" was the previous night. Miss Martin explained that it was still two weeks away.

Ned's mother did come to "Open House," to Miss Martin's surprise. Miss Martin told her how much she enjoyed Ned and how well he was doing in reading. She seemed pleased to hear such a good report. Miss Martin invited her to come to the school again.

Several children in the room brought treats to pass out during rest period. One morning Ned came running down the hall, all smiles. He was carrying a big paper bag. He rushed up to Miss Martin and said, "I'll bet you'll never guess what I have in here." Miss Martin made several guesses and Ned finally opened the bag and showed her. He had graham crackers to pass out for a treat. Every few minutes he asked if he could pass them. He was so excited he could hardly wait. When the time came, he served his crackers, which were filled with frosting. Miss Martin told him it was a nice treat and that his mother must have worked hard to make them. Ned said, "Yah, she's pretty nice sometimes. You know, she worked so hard fixing these that it took her all night."

The next day on the playground Ned approached a little girl and threw his arms around her so hard that he knocked her down. He had only wanted to show how much he liked her. Ned has become a good friend of this girl. They occasionally tell Miss Martin they are in love, and the feeling seems mutual.

Ned was the only child without a costume at the Halloween party. He was troublesome all morning. That afternoon when the other children came in all dressed up, Ned approached Miss Martin and said, "The kids sure look nice in their costumes, don't they?" Miss Martin asked if he would like to be "Bozo the Clown" and gave him a mask. After that Ned felt more a member of the group. There were no more disruptions from him.

As the children were leaving to go home Ned approached his teacher and asked if he could keep the mask. When Miss Martin told him he could, he threw his arms around her and said, "You know what? I really love you. I can't wait till I see my mom and tell her that I was 'Bozo' at our party. She'll be surprised."

At the beginning of the year Ned frequently entered the room early each morning. He ran around purposely bumping into other children and creating general havoc during the fifteen-minute period before the bell. One morning when Ned arrived early, Miss Martin asked him if he would like to play some records. She taught him how to operate the record player. He was thrilled to have this privilege. Up to this time only Miss Martin had worked it. Ned behaved well the first few days at this new task but soon he began to put a record on to play and then he would run around. He would also hit anyone who walked anywhere near the phonograph. He became bossy and shouted at the children in their seats to listen to the records.

One noon hour when Ned was acting up while playing the records, Miss Martin sent him to his seat. Not until he knew how to act would she let him play the records again. He felt badly and sat at his table with his head down and cried softly. He would tease every day to play the records. After a full week of good behavior Miss Martin gave him back his job. Since then he has behaved well when playing records and has followed suggestions of other children. The good behavior has continued for many weeks.

Ned has learned to work alone and play alone, as well as to participate in activities. He is finding that he can depend on his own inner resources for making decisions and carrying them out.

Socially, problems still exist, particularly when he thinks that he is being ignored.

Miss Martin feels that Ned trusts her. His feeling of being loved has given him a sense of importance and has enabled him to work with satisfaction in class.

Discussion

In the beginning Miss Martin did not meet Ned on firm and genuine ground. She was reluctant to set limits with him; she did not challenge him when he violated rules that were important to her. Ned's behavior became progressively destructive. Finally Miss Martin had a lengthy talk with him and openly expressed her dissatisfaction with some of his behavior. She explained that she was mistaken in permitting him to break limits, told him his behavior upset her at times, and emphasized that she wanted to have a completely friendly relationship with him. Miss Martin was determined to relate to him in a more open and personally significant way and help him develop his interests and grow in self-confidence.

By the end of his second year in school, Ned's academic work was above average. He was still having some difficulty in social relations but for the most part he was enjoying friendships and handling conflicts in a more constructive way. The important thing is that he continued to make progress in a classroom environment which was nonthreatening and conducive to growth.

Miss Martin was able to effect something common to all the successful interpersonal relationships in the classroom—a bond of trust, acceptance, and respect between the teacher and the child. All of these teachers were able to set limits firmly and consistently but in a warm, accepting manner. The children in these classes were given time to express feelings and attitudes. They were helped to feel that their feelings would be respected, however different or intense they were.

The interpersonal relationship was thus a relationship between a teacher and a child or a group of children where there was freedom of expression within the necessary limits of the classroom, where each person could state himself in terms of himself without fear of criticism or condemnation, where feelings were expressed and explored, where ideas and creative thinking were treasured, and where growth of self was the most important value. In such an atmosphere the emphasis is not on knowledge, in the sense of knowing about, from the point of view of an outside observer. There is no special attempt to explain and analyze attitudes and ideas or to discover "facts" in children's lives. These teachers wanted to experience an authentic life with the child in the fullest, deepest human sense. Genuine presence and love are not expressed solely in verbal comments. These values exist in the total experience in feeling and in attitude, in silence and in solitude.

Authentic interaction frees the teacher to function in terms of his own values, ethics, and convictions and frees the child to explore his uniqueness. In this kind of relationship growth occurs naturally and spontaneously. There is a feeling of being confirmed within, and a sense of movement that makes work personally satisfying and life in school a real experience. In spite of pressures, frustrations, and anxieties, when teachers and children can be themselves, that is, honest, authentic persons, there is always hope that difficulties will be resolved, blocks removed, and meaningful living experienced. Human creativity is then fostered, and reality is perceived fully and completely through the total being of the individual person.

What are the conditions which facilitate freedom, openness, choice and responsibility, the conditions which encourage authentic existence in the classroom? Rogers (2) has abstracted these conditions from the pioneering efforts of creative educators and from pertinent research in psychotherapy and in the classroom. It is necessary that the individual, at whatever level of education, be confronted by resources, issues, and problems which are meaningful and relevant to him. It is essential that the teacher hold an unyielding and deep trust in the child as a person of value with capacities and talents which when free to be expressed will eventuate in positive and constructive experiences. If we trust the capacity of the individual for developing his own potentiality, then we can permit him the opportunity to choose his own way in his learning. It is important that the teacher be a real person—enthusiastic, sad, angry, joyful, calm, excited, stand out in an honest way with the range of feelings that differentiate the living person from the mechanical role player. It is essential that the teacher prize the child as a person, be aware of and value his feelings and thoughts, convey genuine understanding based on the child's own perceptions, and accept his tempo and pace, his way of perceiving and relating to the life of the classroom. It is also important that the teacher provide resources.

In such a setting, initially the student may experience much frustration, struggle, and disturbance; but gradually he comes to be clearly present as a unique individual, as a genuine and integrated being, as someone who can relate, and grow in his life with others.

The moment for initiating an authentic life and departing from alienation and dehumanization is always present. No matter how entrenched a teacher is in the world of the other, in rationalizing, in analyzing, in intellectualizing, no matter how immersed in standards and values and goals of the system, he still can, in the next moment, decide to alter the course of his existence. He still can become the one he really is, creating meanings and values and actualizing potentialities that are consistent with his real self. No one can take this away. And for any particular person, no one can predict what the individual will do (1). Regardless of his past, in any situation the teacher can choose to activate genuine talents and resources, real directions of the self. It is true for every teacher that at any moment he can choose to become himself, which is the only way to authentic existence.

REFERENCES

1. Frankl, Viktor, E. *From Death Camp to Existentialism.* Boston: Beacon Press, 1960.
2. Rogers, Carl R. Learning to be Free. *Pastoral Psychol.*, Part I, Vol. 13, No. 128, 47–54. Part II, Vol. 13, No. 129, 43–51.

Index